CRISIS CINEMA

Crisis Cinema

The Apocalyptic Idea in Postmodern Narrative Film

edited by

Christopher Sharrett

PostModernPositions, Vol. 6

Maisonneuve Press
Washington, D.C. 1993

Christopher Sharrett, editor. *Crisis Cinema: The Apocalyptic Idea in Postmodern Narrative Film.*

PostModernPositions, Volume 6

© copyright 1993 Maisonneuve Press
    P. O. Box 2980, Washington, D.C. 20013-2980

Maisonneuve Press is a division of the Institute for Advanced Cultural Studies, a non-profit organization devoted to social change through cultural analysis.

Printed in the US by BookCrafters, Fredricksburg, VA.

Library of Congress Cataloging-in-Publication data.

Crisis cinema : the apocalyptic idea in postmodern narrative film / edited by Christopher Sharrett.
    p. cm. -- (PostModernPositions ; v. 6)
    Includes bibliographical references and index
    1. Motion pictures--Social aspects. 2. Postmodernism--Social aspects. 3. Apocalypse in motion pictures. I. Sharrett, Christopher. II. Series.
PN1995.9.S6C75 1993   92-38584
302.23'43'09048--dc20   CIP

ISBN 0-944624-18-9 cloth
ISBN 0-944624-19-7 paper

This book is dedicated to my wife, Joan Hubbard,

whose insight, encouragement, and affection

helped make the project happen.

41

Christopher Sharrett

Introduction: Crisis Cinema

It would not be quite accurate to say that this book on the cinema of postmodern culture has coextensive priorities in discussing this culture and its representation in the cinema. As has been suggested in numerous locations, postmodernism dispenses once and for all with issues of a world "out there" and its representation in art. While the question of the role of art in tired base/superstructure configurations is obsolete, cinema has, as Fredric Jameson notes, replaced the novel in art's traditional function of illustrating the characteristics of the society in which it is produced, even if the culture of the simulacra makes this relationship problematical. It is perhaps because cinema so clearly apprehends the conundrums of the present circumstances that it is able to convey the ground-tone of society as well as the novel ever did, especially since the discourse of cinema has in the seventies, eighties, and nineties been so heavily involved in a new yet familiar American apocalypticism based first in a crisis in meaning, second in the end of the social, two key elements which now seem essential to the thing called postmodernity.

Terms such as "crisis" and "catastrophe" seem to reappear in postmodern culture as discussion centers on postmodernism as an epistemological and historical break with all that has gone before. There is a fear among radical critics that much of the criticism (and cultural production) coming out of the historical moment called postmodernism smacks too much of old-fashioned American millennialism (with all the dangers of that reductionist and determinist tendency), and indeed a good deal of the current discourse shares something in common with "end-time" thought that saturates conservative *fin de siécle* society. At the *fin de millennium* this discourse may be especially pronounced, but distaste for apocalyptic rhetoric should not deter scholars from addressing the material circumstances that seem to construct postmodern society as a crisis scene.

Along with discussions of postmodernism as a moment of epistemological breaks—with, for example, a total discrediting of traditional narrative, scientific reason, all forms of representation—there is considerable discussion of the various "legitimation crises" of postmodern culture. The rending of the social fabric associated with late capitalism is a subject of concern for scholars liberal (*Habits of the Heart*) and conservative (*The Closing of the American Mind, The Cultural Contradictions of Capitalism*). The radical critic finds a more profound problem than the mainstream doomsayers of academe, who are unwilling to see the West's failure to come through on its promises rooted in assumptions of the West itself.

Oddly, the term "crisis" often seems comfortable both to radical and conservative critics of postmodernity since it contains a sense of renewal reassuring (and intellectually respectable) to Marxism and late capitalist theory alike. "Crisis" has always suggested a cyclical occurrence: the crisis signals to Marxism upheavals in capital that will set the stage for socialist developments; for capital it stands for an aberration that will, if properly represented (a key concern of the media age), focus the public only on the necessity of bolstering existing institutions. "Catastrophe" would seem to be a more or less anathema term to all camps, suggesting religious fatalism and pessimism or a caving-in to a pernicious, ahistorical Nietzschean worldview. Yet it is interesting that as Nietzsche, the original postmodernist (especially in his simultaneous deconstruction and valorization of the West), becomes increasingly predominant in the critical theory of postmodernity, many of his current progeny ultimately opt for a language that makes the political/cultural debate of this moment not out of step with the vagaries of postmodern culture and, for that matter, main currents of American apocalypticism. While "crisis" is invoked, the dead-end aspect of the debate produced is catastrophic. To wit: the legitimation crises of Habermas and Lyotard.

Habermas' rather dull, pedantic recycling of Frankfurt School theory, despite a dollop of Nietzsche inherited from Adorno and Horkheimer, wants to prop up Enlightenment reason against the brutishness of late capital. Lyotard, a proponent of "ludic" postmodernity through an emphasis on Nietzsche-the-subjectivist, sees possibility in the total collapse of political and historical truth into language games and perspectival appearances. While this very visible poststructuralist response to late capital would seem the healthiest antidote to the forces of reaction that now force "canons" of Western truth into a clearly panicked, cynical, and wary population, I would argue that this antidote is perfectly in keeping with the sensibility of contemporary consumerist pluralism, with its you-have-your-opinion-I'll-have-mine type of talk-show politic as the public sector is scrapped and all discourse moved into the realm of privatized (media) fantasy. The retreat into "aesthetic" liberation or fractal, atomized movements now appears the accepted, common-sense response to the death of totalization. The real catastrophe here would seem to be an utter disregard for the changing nature of power and its ability to co-opt and absorb challenges to its assumptions, even to totalizations such as patriarchy. With much postmodern theory, we find catastrophe in a steady, inexorable collusion of apparently critical, contentious thought with the dominant order.

As for catastrophe theory as such, that is, theory that refutes the remedial aspect of critical analysis (for which Jean Baudrillard is the example *par excellence*), its principal virtue may be its focus on the duplicity and intellectual dishonesty of "gaming" amid a tidal wave of reaction. At his best Baudrillard calls attention to theory's collusion with and replication of power; at his worst he does the same thing, with the perverse *jouissance* of nihilism. But Baudrillard represents the best updating of Nietzsche, particularly for this epoch, in his abrupt dismissal of ontology and epistemology, his long litany of demises (the death of the social, the death of the subject, the requiem for the media, etc.) with the triumph of the simulacrum. This temperament has special relevance for the postmodern cynicism replicated in media.

If Baudrillard represents a Nietzschean great (and terrible) awakening to the nullity of knowledge and being as Western triumphs open up its void, Fredric Jameson, with his faith in Marxism and historical materialism, reveals specific catastrophes associated with the dysfunction (probably the most common term of popular discourse) of late capital, postindustrialism, and media culture. Jameson's language wavers in its catastrophic aspect as he steadily yields more ground to poststructuralists and talks about the previous status of the signifier rather than previous historical/material circumstances, and also acknowledges that he is a rather interested consumer of postmodern culture. Yet if Baudrillard's contribution is an insistence on the failure of ways of knowing and of the critical enterprise, it is Jameson and remaining political analysis that informs us it is not the destruction of subjectivity that has transformed experience, but historical circumstances that have transformed the subject, making impossible the apprehension of the social moment and producing a stalemate (for Marxism) regarding the possibility of revolutionary change. Nietzsche and Marx now appear important antidotes for each other, a tag-team for the next millennium: In the age of media, Nietzsche can regularly provoke, at some level of consciousness, the most untutored of our citizens

with doubts about all terms, categories, dichotomies, about the worth
of intellectual exploration, while Marx, manifest not in Jameson but
in the evisceration of the public sector and the collapse of traditional
notions of the social, reminds us that the catastrophe is not the product
of our poststructuralist-trained imaginations but of our depoliticization
and irresponsibility. Contemporary theory aside, critics must pay
attention to the apocalypticism of the postmodern moment simply because
the horrific nihilism of cultural production indeed has a relationship
to measurable, material circumstances of society. We must also note—
and a little panic here would do us all good—how loudly the current
power structure has announced the apocalypse with its "end of history"
declarations as supranational corporatism "wins" the Cold War.

Given the flavor of the debate about postmodern civilization, theorists
have very obviously (disclaimers notwithstanding) returned old-fashioned
apocalyptic consciousness to us with a vengeance. By the same token,
cultural production of the last two decades has consistently represented
the catastrophic sites of the epoch, and the apocalypse of postmodernity
is almost always couched in that very popular misuse of apocalypse not
as revelation but doomsday, disaster, the end.

The essays of this volume are concerned with charting the ways by
which the apocalypticism of the postmodern ethos is reflected in cinema.
Although cinema studies is the discipline of most contributors to this
book, their concern is not primarily the developments in the medium
itself as the intricate relationship film/television culture has with
postmodernity, which in fact has synonyms like "media society" and
"the society of the spectacle." Indeed, as suggested, it is very difficult
anymore to talk about film's "reflection" of society according to the tired
rules of mimesis; the hegemony of the media (and the changing relationship of mediation to consciousness) is a significant component of
the apocalypticism producing panic discourses on all fronts. It is
interesting also that when the cinema is discoursing on certain
postmodern theorizations (the impact of media and cybernetics, etc.)
or merely playing out and exhausting tired genre conventions within
a postindustrial topography, it does so with unbridled negativity. The
most important "postmodern" movies of the last decade (*Blade Runner*,
the films of David Lynch and David Cronenberg, the Mad Max films,
Repo Man, Brazil, etc.), when not viewing material conditions at the
end of the century as catastrophic and unrecuperable, suggest that the
sensibility of the postmodern moment, even when placed in a humorous
context (*Something Wild, Insignificance*) advancing carnival with the
fading of totalizing systems and patriarchal authority, nevertheless
projects a profound nullity and bankruptcy.

Questions have already arisen about poststructuralism's role as cultural terrorism. In accepting the agenda of the contemporary culture's refusal of dialectics, its vague nostalgia impulses or anti-utopianism, have radical critics allowed a steady co-optation of adversarial discourse and admitted that history is closing down? David Lynch is a case in point. Lynch has been posed by many as a radical artist because of an acid and mannered vision of suburbia that he always ends up affirming with the perfect schizophrenia of neoconservatism. For some the "reflexivity" (read, forced irony) and presentationalism in postmodern art qualifies it as radical, even as this art is so unconcerned with political circumstances (contemporary issues of race and gender, social and economic justice) as to sneer at the sociological critique of art. Critics who focus on the reflexivity of postmodern cinema, with its constant toying with the apparatus and overturning rules about point-of-view, editing, and subject positioning, are very misled if they believe these changes significantly disturb the rules of bourgeois subjectivity. With many TV commercials as experimental as Brakhage or Frampton, we face not only the obsolescence of any notion of an avant garde, but also the foolishness of associating innovations in representation and technique with social progress and human liberation. Even the complex, cautionary remarks of Marcuse, Foucault, and Barthes on various strategies of repressive desublimation, inoculation, and cooptation seem to be regularly absorbed into the media spectacle. (Note the popularity of the Nickelodeon TV network, with it campy recycling of our "television heritage" of sixties sit-coms—contemporary culture is now at the stage of recognizing the bankruptcy of capitalism and patriarchy, but validates them anyway).

This book is not, finally, a response to postmodernism per se nor to poststructuralist critical practice (which it makes use of more than a little) for its apocalypticism. What most of these essays share in common, aside from attempts to study cinema's depiction of postmodernism's impact on notions of the subject, economy, technology, the social, and narrativity, is a concern for the ways by which the postmodern cinema either refutes or teases out the dialectic and the impulses behind these tendencies. These essays are very focused on the end-of-history ethos of a frequently conservative postmodern art that presents conditions, as Robin Wood has noted, as sealed-over and seamless, as unproblematical and uncontentious not because a return to a halcyon yesteryear has been achieved by the neoconservative reaction, but because conditions are portrayed as beyond transformation—the latter is the dystopia that seems to titillate the contemporary audience and resonates an older American teleology.

Arthur Kroker and Michael Dorland's "Panic Cinema: Sex in the Age of the Hyperreal" is a kind of preamble for this book, a piece whose "hyperpessimism" (Kroker's term) replaces dialectical criticism as a new radical gesture. While the tone of these remarks may suggest something of the apocalyptic character of poststructuralist theory, the piece reinvents Frankfurt School logic by dispensing with faith in dialectics, that is, with the typical response of much Marxist criticism that seeks sites of struggle in the consciousness industry when culture is everywhere (Baudrillard's idea) while politics vanishes. Kroker and Dorland invite the radical critic to chart a postmodern mediascape that can no longer be distinguished from the predatory culture from which it has developed.

James Combs' piece on the dystopian imagination in contemporary cinema is another sort of preamble, providing an overview of the ways millennialism and notions of disaster inform American political culture and have special relevance to the conservatism of the postmodern moment. While Combs keeps a perspective on the historical foundations of apocalypticism, he also insists on the specificity of postmodernity and the problems of the apocalyptic in bolstering the climate of reaction.

Keith Goshorn's detailed analysis of *Repo Man* is also a close examination of the L.A. punk scene of the late 70s early 80s, perhaps the last adversarial youth movement of the century. Goshorn questions the efficacy of such movements in postmodernity; as confrontative, anti-commercial, and "beyond alienation" as punk was, it was easily co-opted and commodified. Punk's stolid resistance to commercialization, ironically resulting in a profound nihilist and self-destructive spirit as it rebuked the terrible reaction of the 1980s, is a good emblem of the catastrophic circumstances of postmodernity.

Scott Bukatman's discussion of "cybersubjectivity" takes a fairly idealist view of one aspect of postindustrial civilization—cybernetics and computer technology—to examine the ways by which its representation in the cinema may offer the subject a new notion of transcendence. Bukatman's argument, drawn in part on André Bazin and Merleau-Ponty, is a continuation of an assault (begun by art criticism, carried forward by cinema studies) on Renaissance perspectivism with its attendant concepts of bourgeois subjectivity. This debate about the emancipatory role of technology, which recalls the Romantic debate about industry, introduces a new dialectic in offering the possibility of a ludic cybernetic culture in place of revolutionary social transformation. In Bukatman's heuristic argument, the culture of "cyberpunk" and the hegemony of a new, technology-supported subjectivity already stand in response to such idealism.

In a kind of response to Bukatman, Philip Turetsky's essay on Gilles Deleuze's concept of the "image-impulse" offers a decidedly pessimistic view of the future of the subject; rather than transcendence, contemporary media technology and representation are involved in disintegration. In his application of Deleuze's ideas to David Cronenberg's *Dead Ringers*, Turetsky argues that the centered, monadic subject has indeed disappeared as much theory asserts. The destruction of subjectivity in the new mediascape has its best metaphors in images of detritus, excess, and decay, the images of postindustrial consumer consciousness. The world of the "televisual body" is now determined by a terrible, naturalistic logic that returns consciousness to the primeval morass of postmodern information.

Jon Lewis' article on Francis Coppola's *Rumble Fish* discusses attempts by mainstream popular narrative to confront the (il)legitimacy of codes and conventions of Hollywood in part by undermining them with increased allusionism and self-reflexivity. *Rumble Fish* is a postmodern "teen pic" (e.g., *Rebel Without a Cause*) that refuses the neat closure and narrative pleasure of that very key postwar genre. In undermining the authority and reassurance of the teen film, *Rumble Fish* becomes involved in a broad assault on assumptions of narrative art, including male charismatic authority, but responds with a nihilism that may repeat postmodernism's insistence on the unrecuperability of society that refuses alternate visions.

Frank Burke's article on *Fellini's Casanova* is the only piece in this book to discuss at length a major director of the high modernist cinematic "canon," an author rather in disrepute before the demise of auteurism. For Burke, *Fellini's Casanova* is a good model of explanation for understanding the postmodern transformation of the subject, as the film marks the hysteria of its protagonist and his creator. The male hysteria in his Casanova makes Fellini a representation of a die-hard and essentially reactionary modernist unable to confront the sexual, intellectual, and economic disempowerment of the traditional male subject in the wake of a wide range of phenomena of the last thirty years, including feminism and postindustrialism.

Catherine Russell discusses the changing representation of violence in the cinema as a significant indication of postmodernity's attitude toward history. Part of her project involves taking on the troublesome issue of periodizing the postmodern and relating it to other cultural movements and historical moments. According to Russell's theorization, the modernist avant-garde cinema, represented most particularly by Godard's *Pierrot le Fou* and *Weekend*, attempted to undermine the representation of violence in cinema (making it artificial and presentational; Godard made us conscious that blood was red paint, not blood), thus overturning the central role of violence in providing catharsis and closure to both narrative and history. Russell notes that at roughly the same time that Godard was working on his responses to Vietnam and new imperialistic violence, Hollywood produced its goriest films ever in *Bonnie and Clyde* and *The Wild Bunch*, works whose apocalyptic violence was very much in a traditional, representational style despite its graphic aspect, which at the time seemed intended to shock the audience into a realization of violence's centrality in American experience. Russell argues that these films spoke to a nostalgic yearning for golden moments of history and used extreme violence to respond to the new threats to consensus and dramatic closure as history itself seemed threatened by a new phase of interpretation and revision. The convulsions of *The Wild Bunch* seem intimately tied to the very impossibility of dramatic catharsis to simulate some sort of historical closure and prop up notions of regenerative violence. Russell then discusses David Lynch's *Wild at Heart* (which has important similarities to *Weekend* and *Bonnie and Clyde*) and Peter Greenaway's *The Cook, the Thief, his Wife and her Lover* in terms of a postmodern aesthetic of decadence that uses a presentational style to celebrate dead popular and political cultures. The graphic violence of these films combine elements of both Hollywood and the European avant-garde to offer a cynical spectacle refusing any notion of history (or a critical cinema) outside of pop images.

A different aspect of spectacle is addressed in Tony Williams' article on *Brazil*, which is treated as a particularly British (Thatcher-era) response to postmodernity and modernist dystopian science-fiction narratives such as *1984*. In Williams' formulation, the dystopia of *1984* is obsolete in postmodernity, whose "spectacle of excess" co-opts and precludes the heroic master narratives and adversarial cultures that Orwell's novel was written under. Williams argues that *Brazil* represents a pre-Oedipal, anti-patriarchal postmodernity of fantasy and plenitude where adversarial discourses simply have no usefulness. Postmodernity suggests, then, a world where power relations must be radically rethought, although it appears impossible to step outside of this moment's ability to absorb such reflection and the utopian impulses underneath it.

My own essay on Martin Scorsese's *Taxi Driver* offers that film as a prelude to American postmodernity in its sense of a coming-home-to-roost of a number of American values, including the myth (well-charted by Richard Slotkin) of "regeneration through violence." The film's protagonist, Travis Bickle, is a kind of composite male ego derived from American history, fiction, and folklore, a postmodern pastiche whose extremely fragile self can be sustained, like society overall, only by various forms of sacrificial, propitiatory violence such as the "last stand" so sacred to the American self-concept. It is not just the "failure" of sacrificial activity to rejuvenate meaning but its naming as myth that has caused extreme doubt about a civilizing process—with its attendant, modernist idea of progress—built entirely on a very contradictory narrative of violence and self-destruction. Even as postmodernity continues to be more questioning and its art more "self-reflexive" concerning such matters, it seems utterly incapable of stepping outside of the mythic consciousness that constitutes meaning through sacrificial violence.

Giuliana Bruno applies Fredric Jameson's oft-cited essay on postmodernism to an appreciation of *Blade Runner*, one of the quintessential postmodern films. *Blade Runner* seems to have used Jameson as a blueprint (or the reverse) for an image of postmodern civilization; Bruno argues that this film, like contemporary theories of postmodernity, marks a major break in patriarchal conceptions of history, memory, the self.

Mick Broderick's essay on the "Mad Max" films of Australian director George Miller discusses one of the most popular movie series of the 1980s in the context of the return-to-myth fixations of postmodernity associated with the renewed popularity of master narrative-espousers such as Joseph Campbell. It is the supreme disingenuousness and postmodern schizophrenia of these films that they both parody and absolutely rely on eschatological mythology and the ultimate "monomyth" of the charismatic male hero. The Mad Max films perhaps more than any other suggest the spirit of apocalyptic wish-fulfillment that characterizes postmodernity at the end of the millennium, as the comfort of the most archaic mythic narratives is so desperately, yet cynically, pursued. As the Mad Max films use *bricolage* to debunk myth, they also do a successful job of restoring myth's consolations.

The title of this book might well be *Catastrophe Cinema* given the consensus about the state of civilization found in the contemporary cinema. It is the faith of this book, however, to confront the inexorable logic of reactionary postmodernity, to accept its major premises, while holding out for the resistance of difference and human intervention, not the inevitable ethos of apocalypticism with which bourgeois consciousness has always attempted to reduce humanity. The difficult critical enterprise that these writers undertake is the most obvious evidence of this faith.

Lula Pace Fortune (Laura Dern), the postmodern body sliding between innocence and sleaze in David Lynch's *Wild at Heart* (1990, shown above) and also the earlier *Blue Velvet* (1986). DeLaurentiis Entertainment, Polygram/Propaganda films. Still courtesy of Jerry Ohlinger's Movie Materials.

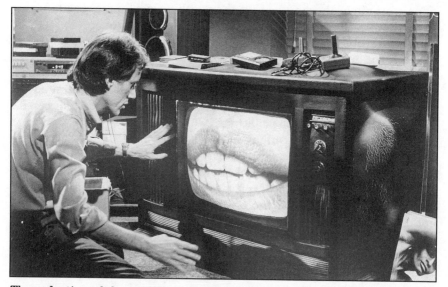

The seduction of the mediascape in David Cronenberg's *Videodrome* (1982). Max Renn (James Woods) becomes obsessed with sadomasochistic TV. Universal Pictures. Still courtesy of Jerry Ohlinger's Movie Materials.

Arthur Kroker and Michael Dorland

Panic Cinema: Sex in the Age of the Hyperreal

WHAT IS SEX IN THE AGE OF THE HYPERREAL? A little sign slide between kitsch and decay as the postmodern body is transformed into a rehearsal for the theatrics of sado-masochism in the simulacrum. Not sadism any longer under the old sign of Freudian psychoanalytics and certainly not masochism in the Sadean carceral, but sadomasochism now as a kitschy sign of the body doubled in an endless labyrinth of media images, just at the edge of ecstasy of catastrophe and the terror of the simulacrum.

1. PANIC SADISM. *Blue Velvet* is the postmodern world. Here, only the predators, like Frank, have energy and can make things happen. Everyone else is reduced to a passive parasite, whether like Dorothy Vallens who is parasited at the level of pleasure of the pain of sado-masochism ("You put your disease inside me") or like Jeff, the detective who lives out the dream that is *Blue Velvet* in the spectacular, and distanced, position of the Kantian judge. The whole *fin-de-millennium* scene alternates between the hyper-kitschy and hyper chromatic colors of a 1950s advertising scene and violent excess. *Blue Velvet* is a perfect cinematic image for a postmodern culture where sex has now disappeared into a fourth order of simulation: Bataille's parodic vision of the pineal eye and the solar anus. Not the body as the sacred object of a power which inscribes, but now a whole media production of body parts for a contemporary cultural scene where indifference spreads. Consequently, hyperreal sex as a detrital vision of panic penises, panic ovaries, and panic erotics.

2. PANIC PENISES. No longer the old male cock as the privileged sign of patriarchal power and certainly not the semiotician's dream of the decentered penis which has, anyway, already vanished into the ideology of the phallus, but the *postmodern penis* which becomes an emblematic sign of sickness, disease and waste. Penis burnout, then, for the end of the world.

And just in time! Because in all of the technologies of sex which make possible a sex without secretions (the computerized phone sex of the Minitel system in Paris; video porn for the language of the gaze, designer bodies, and gene retreading), in all of these technologies of sex, the penis, both as protuberance and ideology, is already a spent force, a residual afterimage surplus to the requirements of telematic society.

Anyway, it was predictable. The male body has always been the privileged object and after-effect of a twofold psycholoanalyical colonization: a *psychoanalytics of reception* which functions, as Lacan insists, by the principle of misrecognition where in the fateful mirror state the bourgeois infant self substitutes the illusion of substantial unity to be provided by a fictive, abstract ego for concrete identity; and secondly, at the *social* level, where as theorized by Althusser, ideology interpellates individuals as subjects. This may be why, in the end, even Michel Foucault said with resignation that the postmodern self is really about sedimented subjectivity, that is, the constitution of the male self as an afterimage of the moral problematization of pleasure and the torturing procedures of the confessional.

Or maybe it is this and more. Not organic, natural sex any longer and not the discursive sexuality so praised by all the poststructuralists, but a cynical and parodic sex—*schizoid and hyperreal sex*—for panic bodies. A schizoid sex, therefore, where sado-masochism of the hyperreal kind operates in the language of a liquid power which, no longer belonging as property to the old language of gender divisions (a male masochism? a female sadism?), operates at the more general level of torturer and victim.

When we have already passed beyond the first two orders of sex, beyond sex as nature and beyond sex as discourse, to sex as fascinating only when it is about recklessness, discharge and upheaval—a *parodic* sex, then we have also broken beyond the analytics of sexuality and power to *excess*, beyond Foucault's language of the "care of self" to *frenzy*, beyond the "use of pleasure" (Foucault again) with its moral problematization of the ethical subject in relation to its sexual conduct to a little sign-slide between *kitsch and decay*. Not then the nostalgia for an aesthetics of existence today or for a hermeneutics of desire (these are passé and who cares anyway?) but parodic sex as about the free expenditure of a "boundless refuse of activity" (Bataille) pushing human plans; not the coherency of the ethical subject (that has never motivated anyone except in the detrital terms of the subject as a ventilated remainder of death) but the excitation of the subject into a *toxic state*, into a sumptuary site of loss and orgiastic excess. Not, finally, a productive sex, but an *unproductive* sex, a sex without secretions, as the site of the death of seduction that which makes sex bearable in the postmodern condition.

Bataille was right:

> The (pineal) eye at the summit of the skull, opening on the incandescent sun in order to contemplate it in a sinister solitude, is not a product of the understanding, but is instead an immediate existence; it opens and blinds itself like a conflagration, or like a fever that eats the being or more exactly the *head*. And thus it plays the role of a fire in the house; the head, instead of locking it up like money is locked in a safe, spends it without counting, for at the end of this erotic metamorphosis, the head has received the *electric power of points*. This great burning head is the image and the disagreeable light of the notion of expenditure. (*Visions of Excess*, 82)

For expenditure is when "life is parodic and lacks an interpretation," that is, the excitation of the solar anus ("the solar anus is the intact anus of her body at eighteen years to which nothing sufficiently binding can be compared except the sun, even though the anus is the night"). And why not? The pineal eye and the solar anus are also always about an excremental sexuality as the third order of simulation into which sex vanishes after the disappearance of organic and discursive sexuality, and after the fading away of the body itself as yet another afterimage of the postmodern scene.

3. PANIC OVARIES. And what then of women's wombs? Is natural reproduction preserved intact at the end of the world or have we already entered into a darker region of the terror of the simulacrum? Now, more than ever, women's bodies are the inscribed focus of a threefold deployment of relational power. In the postmodern condition, women's bodies are the prime afterimage of a strategy of body invasion which occurs in the inverted and excessive language of *contractual liberalism*.

First, the *medical subordination* of women's bodies which results, whether *in vitro* fertilization or genetic mixing, in the alienation of the womb. When the ovaries go outside (and with them the privileged language of sexual *différance*), it is also a certain sign of the grisly technological abstraction of alienated labour into the alienation of reproduction itself.

Secondly, the medical inscription of women's bodies is superseded by the subordination of childbirth to the *ideology of law*. For example, in the Baby M case, the natural mother is reduced to the contractual fiction of a "hired womb"; the meaning of the "natural" is inverted into its opposite number (the actual mother became legally a "surrogate" and the Daddy surrogate—he was always only present as a free-floating seed in a genetic mixing tube—is *juridically* renamed as a real, living father); and, in the end, the entire juridical apparatus is directed towards justifying a new form of legal slavery for women who are poor, powerless, and thus potential victims of this predatory instincts of the ruling elites. A class of professional, middle-class elites, *men and women*, who measure the meaning of the "good" by the standards of petty convenience. Ironically, in the Baby M case, it was only after the natural mother lost custody rights to her baby that the media and the courts began, finally, describing her, not as the "surrogate mother" any longer, but as the *biological* mother. Cynical media and cynical law for a rising class of cynical elites.

Thirdly, panic ovaries are also about all the cases of fetal appropriation where the state intervenes, supposedly on behalf of the rights of the unborn baby, to take *juridical* possession of the body of the mother. A perfect complicity, then, among the *technological* interventions of medicine into the body of the mother (the use of medical technology as an early warning system for detecting birth defects in the fetus); the juridical seizure of the fetus as a way of deploying state power against the body of the mother, and the *politics of the new right* which can be so enthusiastic about the jurisprudence of fetal appropriation as a way of investing the contractarian rights of the fetus against the desires of the mother. A whole hypocritical *fetus fetish* by law, by medicine, and by the neo-conservatives as a way of canceling out the will of the natural mother, and of taking possession of the bodies of women. Margaret Atwood's thesis in *The Handmaid's Tale* about the reduction of women to hired wombs is thus disclosed to be less an ominous vision of the future than a historical account of an already past event in the domination of women.

4. PANIC PARASITES. So it is therefore appropriate, in a hyper-dependent cinema such as Canada's, that sex is portrayed as panic; either castration anxiety (*L'Ange et la femme*, 1977; *Opération beurre de pinotte*,

1985), voyeurism (*Porky's*, 1981; *Meatballs*, 1979) or domination (the long standing rape motif in Canadian cinema from *Le Viol d'une jeune fille douce*, 1968; *Wedding in White*, 1972 to *Loyalties*, 1986). For the triply dominated (economically, culturally, and administratively) Canadian cinema can only achieve expression through virulent extremes of understatement (absence) or overstatement (excess). To take as an example that most Canadian, because hyper-realistic, of filmmakers, David Cronenberg, he represents sex (or in fact any form of interaction) as *viral*, that is, as a meta-androgynous (or interspecies, including human and machines) parasitism, and this from the abdominal parasites of his first feature, *The Parasite Murders* (1975); the vaginal armpit-penis of *Rabid* (1976), to the (off-camera) super-fuck of Joy Bushell by Brundlefly in *The Fly* (1986). Cronenberg's sexual (or affective) universe is one of the relations of the absolute domination of parasitism-plus. In *Videodrome* (1982), cable TV producer Max Renn is aroused by the commercial possibilities of pirating a Pittsburgh-based signal diffusing sadomasochistic sex, until his own body becomes the pirated and vaginal site of *Videodrome* tapes. In a grim illustration of McLuhan's thesis (in *Understanding Media*) that we have become sex organs of the machine, the new flesh of *Videodrome* is shed by Brundlefly in the horrific conclusions of *The Fly* to reveal the meta-human and genetic fusion of cable and insect in the technological nirvana of achieved parasite culture. Thus, of course, Cronenberg's *The Fly* is itself a parodic parasite (a remake) of the 1958 film, and this in turn refers back to the horror film as parasitic literature, here Kafka's "Metamorphosis" and Mary Shelley's denunciation of (the modern) Prometheus whose classical archetype was itself a parasite for punitive vultures sent by the gods.

5. PANIC HEROISM. Seemingly at the opposite end from Cronenberg's hyper-realistic understatement, stands Bruce Elder who in such experimental epics as *Illuminated Texts* (1982) or *Lamentations: A Monument to the Dead World* (1985) offers against parasitism by (the) world (-culture) the (cultural) parasitism *of* the world in a post-Heideggerian lament of heroic solipsism (hyper-realist overstatement). However, here too the sexual (affective) universe presented by Elder is one of sado-masochistic domination (the long voice-over on pornographic photographic pornography in *Illuminated Texts*; the diary passages of ecstatic descriptions of physical illness in both films). Yet if Elder sculpts a critique, an analytics and a therapeutics of the diseases of Western culture, this is possible on the condition of the revelation of the emptiness within (the images of Elder as "a man with a movie camera" at the

end of *Illuminated Texts*) mirrored in the windows of the Auschwitz barracks of a dead culture.

The slide, from Lynch's human predators to Cronenberg's parasites to Elders absent depictions of the stench of corpses that cannot be smelled, fully states the panic of a contemporary cinema which has nothing left to show for itself but the surfaces (and special effects) of its own putrefaction.

6. PANIC CINEMA. Filmmakers have only interpreted the world in various ways; the point, however, is to see *through* it.

Works Cited

Althusser, Louis. *For Marx*. New York: Vintage Books, 1977.

Bataille, George. *Visions of Excess*. Minneapolis: University of Minnesota Press, 1985.

Foucault, Michel. *The History of Sexuality*. Vol. 1. New York: Vintage Books, 1980.

_____. *The History of Sexuality*. Vol. 3. *The Care of the Self*. New York: Vintage Books, 1988.

Lacan, Jacques. *Four Fundamental Concepts of Psychoanalysis*. New York: Norton, 1979.

McLuhan, Marshall. *Understanding Media*. New York: New American Library, 1964.

Shelley, Mary. *Frankenstein*. New York: Scholastic Book Services, 1974.

James Combs

Pox-Eclipse Now: The Dystopian Imagination in Contemporary Popular Movies

Readers of a book on "crisis cinema" may be surprised to see the inclusion of a political scientist. That learned profession is a notoriously cautious one, not noted for much intellectual daring. It was with some trepidation, then, a decade or so ago when I began to go against the grain of my calling and ask the question, what about the movies is political? This was a question, like many others involving popular culture and the mass media, that political scientists had long ago decided was irrelevant and worse, unquantifiable. Still, their cautiousness is well taken, since establishing anything definite and worthwhile about the "politics of the movies" is indeed like nailing the proverbial jelly to the wall. The movies are a sweet if exotic celluloid jelly, and for someone who began as a movie fan (one of my earliest memories is sitting in the first row looking up at a 30-foot high John Wayne in *Red River*) and ended up a movie student, the temptation was irresistible.[1]

The difficulties inherent in a social scientist looking at a subject traditionally the province of the humanities are rather obvious. By trade, we are very good at categories (the Aristotelian influence) and factual evidence (from British empiricism) but not so good at process. Dealing with a subject such as "art and society," relating aesthetic creation with social process, is ceded to the humanities as a subject beyond the purview, and the competence, of political science. Yet that precludes so much: movies, like any kind of popular art, are not beyond categorization (genre, temporal, *auteur*) nor immune from empirical investigation. Too, one cannot commit to a social science without aesthetic considerations, since much of what is important in social process can only be understood that way. And, I contend, if one wants to understand the *dynamics* of politics, developing a vocabulary of "political aesthetics" and examining what is being created at a certain time and place remains one of the best ways to understand what's happening politically.[2]

This may seem a strange conclusion from one who is more influenced by Machiavelli than Hegel, believing as I do that politics is more about interest than ideas, that the exercise of power is not reducible to modes of thought. And I even am unsure as to what "post-modern" means. "Post" became a prefix several decades ago, attached to all sorts of passing nouns—civilization, colonialism, industrialism, feminism, you name it. So just when social scientists thought they had modernity figured out, it was announced that modernity too had passed into history. (I recall also reading a piece about "post-capitalism" in a German journal on the very day that east German television began to accept advertising for Coke, Barbie dolls, and Volkswagens.) Post-modern has become an intellectual adjective attached to everything. I recently reviewed a very good book on the presidency, entitled *The Post-Modern Presidency*, that dealt naught at all with anything attached to post-modernist ideas. It is not all clear what post-modernity is "pre-" since certain dominant aspects of modernity (corporate capitalism, the liberal democratic state, the practices of bourgeois life) seem remarkably persistent. Perhaps post-modernism is our new intellectual myth, putting us on the side of new gods as we witness the twilight of the old ones.

Nevertheless, I think that the concept of post-modernism has some very real political explanatory power, and that those who have done more than just dabble with it are on to something important. If we take a broad view of the conduct of modern social life, especially since World War II, something fundamental has changed to the extent that the canons of modernity have badly eroded. (In fact, I suspect, modernity has been coming apart at the seams since the latter nineteenth-century: it was, after all, a previous generation of poets who wrote about the modern wasteland wherein things were falling apart, and the center not holding; the surrealists and other schools of art didn't help much our sense of objective coherence, but then neither did Einstein and Heisenberg; and James Joyce did do quite a number on narrative structure.) In any case, now the "socio-logic" of modernity has reached a point, for lack of a better term, of absurdity. The economic logic of advanced capitalism has produced prosperity, but also the absurdity of colossal waste and environmental depletion, as well as the excesses of individual greed and narcissistic self-indulgence. The cultural logic has produced diversity, but also the absurdity of the collapse of standards of taste and the inability to sustain creativity. The political logic has produced democracy, but also the absurdity of budgetary insanity and the virtual collapse of a coherent political agenda. If one wishes to use ideological categories, we might say that at the present we have a liberalism that liberates no one, a conservatism that conserves nothing, and a radicalism that is rootless.

The contemporary political situation is one of the sources of the post-modern sense of incoherent floundering and confusion. (Recall that I am drawn not only to an explanation of the cultural determinants of politics, but also the political determinants of culture.) Simply put, we have achieved a world in which nobody is in charge. The "American Century" was considerably less than a hundred years, and the *pax Americana* began to come apart in the 1960s. We are living through the rapid disillusion of complementary empires, the shift of power and wealth elsewhere, and the prospect of bewildering, and highly temporary, political coalitions. I fear now that the world is likely to be more and not less violent for a variety of reasons, not the least of which will be the felt necessity by elites to protect consumptuary practices, such as the profligate use of oil. But that just adds to our sense of confusion, since blood may be spilled for less than noble ideals.

Too, domestic American politics strikes many as absurd. The more we spend on elections, the more diminished the candidates seem, and the fewer people who find it worthwhile to vote. The American political culture is suffused with propaganda, the same principle of hype that created the celebrity culture, advertising, and public relations. A celebrity figure such as Ronald Reagan collapses the categories of politics and culture, transforming the Presidency into a form of performance art. As the official facade of rosy predictions and affirmations of national faith and destiny pervades, the awful truth remains one of oligarchy and incredible wealth at the top, desperate attempts to make do in the middle, and disintegration at the bottom of society. As conditions worsen, we may see more in the way of "symbolic politics," focusing on diverting absurdities such as flag desecration.

Our feeling of dis-ease about the political and cultural present has economic roots, to be sure, but it also stems from the general sense that there is so much bullshit. Harry Frankfurt, chair of the philosophy department at Yale, argues that "one of the salient features of our culture is that there is so much bullshit. . . ." The practice of successful bullshitting arises in a culture that is not so much false as phony, involving media figures and organizational spokespersons in "a *program* of producing bullshit to whatever extent the circumstances require." We use it so much because contemporary "circumstances require someone to talk without knowing what he is talking about." Bullshit proliferates our politics and culture because we now "deny that we can have any reliable access to an objective reality and therefore reject the possibility of knowing how things truly are."[3] Such rhetorical dissimulation gives credence to our suspicion of pervasive phoniness, that American political power, economic prosperity, and cultural unity are not quite what they are represented as by institutional elites.

In such circumstances, it is no wonder that there may well be a great deal of what we might call "functional alienation," in which people continue to live their lives as best they can but without hope of political redress, economic mobility, or stable cultural tradition. Systems of power may persist for a very long time even with an alienated populace if they acquiesce in the legitimacy and functionality of phoniness, accept the political epistemology of inaccessible truth about social justice, and live with the existential state of hopelessness. Media managers may understand and exploit emotional responses to flag burning, Third World dictators, drug dealers, and so forth, but even as we respond we still have the nagging feeling we are being had.

In the most mythic sense, the contemporary state of affairs we deem so changed we term it "post-modern" is such because of the eclipse of the myth of progress. It is harder now to sustain the national myth of benevolent democracy, widely-shared economic prosperity, and stable cultural norms. With the optimistic myth of progress shaken, it becomes easy for us to turn to the alternative myth of the Fall, and seek either scapegoats or redeemer figures ("He'll Make America Great Again"). Further, a sense of living in a fallen present elevates prelapsarian pasts into nostalgic Golden Ages, considered preferable since we now live in an unredeemable present and face a bleak future. If the present is phony and full of simulation and dissimulation, and the future a threat rather than a promise, then past "mythic times" (World War II, the Fifties, the Camelot era) speak to a void of hope. Figures such as Reagan and Bush offer us not so much political as cultural experience, through their self-representation as embodiments of virtues held to be ascendant in the past. As Allison Graham has pointed out, the desire in such an historical moment is for "a recertification of old forms— rather than for a challenging of them, almost as if we have no more stories to tell, no new experiences to share. If the collage is really our only new film genre, then we have become, in essence, a culture trying desperately to rope off, sanction, and harden its myths into an intellectual iconography—trying to say that *this*, then, is the American experience, *this* is our psyche: a static compendium of past motifs."[4] Yet we have every reason to know that this kind of "cultural politics" is phony too, since it so fears the future that it sanctifies these "past motifs" (e.g., the Fifties sitcom nuclear family, the World War II "melting pot" combat unit, even the *Wonder Years* Camelotian innocence) as enlarged into positive mythology while the present is diminished into negative mythology. (In an odd but important way, both Reagan and Bush, and perhaps also Carter and Bill Clinton, enhance our understanding of the post-modern condition, since they too offered us the recapitulation of narratives that are quickly ceasing to make any sense or enjoy any verisimilitude.) If we do not believe in a progressive narrative, then popular art such as the movies seeks alternative narratives that might resonate with audiences, certainly develops confused stories that attempt to incorporate irreconcilable motifs, or becomes subversive to the narrative genres to which it is heir through parody. In such an historical moment, we are no longer "storied," and the stories we are told exist in a kind of limbo, since they possess no logical progression from past to future, or from social problem to sanctioned solution. If we live in a world of incoherence, popular forms of expression such as the movies will likely offer incoherent narratives, in the sense of having become untethered from generic tradition. (The exception, it might be argued, might be neo-*film noir*, at least those films, such as *Body Heat, The Grifters*, and *The Two Jakes*, which use the tradition, but also relate well to contemporary audiences: perhaps it is the case that the very incoherence of the post-modern world makes the byzantine vision of *film noir* all the more relevant).

If our stories lack integrity, becoming confused, parodic, or non-existent, then popular conceptions of heroism become untethered from traditional expectations. The changes in the Western hero over time are evident enough, with much commentary on how the Westerner had disappeared. Actually not: he just became a vigilante agent of revenge in other settings. What has changed is that he (occasionally she, as in *Aliens*) has largely ceased to be a clear agent of the community who acts because he shares their values and wants to see justice done. Now the hero (or, if you prefer, anti-hero) is more likely to be a functional alienate himself, acting out of some private motive stemming from his alienation from society, if incidentally or unwittingly serving a social purpose ("law and order" or somesuch). The Bruce Willis character of the *Die Hard* movies, the Sigourney Weaver character in *Aliens*, certainly Harry Callahan, and even the superheroes of *Batman* and *Darkman* are all in different ways alienates with a purpose, even though that purpose is more or less independent of traditional heroic function and restraint. Such post-modern heroes usually exist in some kind of catastrophic setting, but survive because they see through the organizational

Genocide is justified in defense of the home and corporation. Sigourney Weaver as Ripley in *Aliens* (1986) protects Newt played by Carrie Henn. Twentieth Century Fox. Still courtesy of Jerry Ohlinger's Movie Materials.

or political bullshit and act out their own private motif of action, within the context of heroic roles in which they do not believe, and for purposes with which they profess no allegiance. (If popular audiences will accept heroes only in sardonic terms, perhaps this offers us a clue as to the success of Reagan: the stance of being an outsider acting alone against the government, indeed running in 1984 against the government he headed, turning every criticism or action, even murderous ones, into a joke, and acting with contempt for institution, law, or procedure, all on the assumption that government is either an instrument to be cynically manipulated, or a comic monstrosity to be ridiculed even from its top.)

What is striking about these emerging post-modern images and themes in the movies is that they seem to *posit catastrophe as a given.* It is here, I think, that the movies are most useful to us as a form of art that offers us popular evidence of subtle and changing conceptions of power. Popular movies can be studied as "rituals of power," in which we can see a spectacular vision of trends not only in consciousness, but also in the concomitant forms of power that characterize a society at a given time. Think of the sci-fi movies of the Fifties (*The Day the Earth Stood Still, Invasion from Mars, Invasion of the Body Snatchers*) that constitute a significant cluster of films specific to that political time, the heyday of the Cold War. Although "displaced" into space, they consistently displayed a formulaic ritual of recognizable alien invasion bringing the threat of either annihilation or dehumanization, something that spoke covertly to the political fears of the age. For even though the powerful threat from the surrogate Red hordes was always great and menacing, it was always somehow thwarted, with at least the hope that the status quo of American normalcy would be restored, however tenuously. The *Invasion of the Body Snatchers'* famous added-on ending makes rescue even more ambivalent, but one assumed in 1956 that the peaceable community would eventually be saved through heroic action. But in the wake of the Sixties, genres such as science-fiction and horror became more apocalyptic in the negative sense, with no clear triumph of good over evil and indeed often the vision of the recrudescent power of evil, ineradicable and recurrent as an avenging force in summer camps and on Elm Street. Writing in 1982, H. Bruce Franklin noted that futuristic films since 1970 had become "overwhelmingly pessimistic, when not downright apocalyptic. Whereas the alien and monster films of the fifties showed our worthy civilization menaced by external powers, these movies typically project our awful future as a development, often inevitable, of forces already at work within our civilization."[5] Notice the difference: the earlier Fifties sci-fi flicks posit a crisis that through

American political power and virtue will be averted. The later futuristic films assume a world in which not only will American power not be equal to the task, the fundamental problem is not an externally-imposed "crisis" (cf., the missile crisis, the Iran hostage crisis, and so on) that can be managed, rather it is that the socio-logic inherent in the development of the system itself will lead to a catastrophe that is internally-induced. Since 1982, our movie vision of catastrophe has become more complicated, immediate, and domestic, but not any more hopeful. Movies have returned to the depiction of manageable crises, foreign (*Heartbreak Ridge*, climaxing in Grenada) or domestic (*Wall Street*, climaxing in the prosecution of insider-traders) without satisfying systemic reaffirmation: Eastwood whips the Marine unit in shape, but for a preposterous military endeavor; Michael Douglas presumably goes to jail, but the system of values and practices which gave rise to him remain. Catastrophe lurks in the shadows for a military willing to commit to struggles in which it can become hopelessly entangled, or an economic institution committed to unlimited greed, since the fatal flaw is fundamental and systemic and not an aberration imposed from outside or by an idiosyncratic individual.

As we near the millennium, there is a very real revival of old apocalyptic fears and hopes, ranging from predictions of Armageddon to the harmonic convergence. Such a time brings about both reflection and prediction on the nature and destiny of change, and the years approaching 2001 are no different.[6] (Perhaps postmodernism will be remembered someday as a millennial cult!) But whatever the relationship of the decline of the canons of modernity with the *fin de siécle*, it does give credence to the catastrophic mentality. Survivalism, fundamentalist predictions of the "last days," Presidential musings on the apocalypse, books on an imminent world-wide depression, were searches for signs and wonders—all popular manifestations of the underlying feeling of irresistible change. As Todd Gitlin has noted, "There is *anxiety* at work in these post-modern discourses."[7] Postmodernism cannot help but "participate" in the discourse of such a time, since like much anticipatory thought, both popular and academic, its anxiety stems from the *anticipation of the awful*. Not unlike the Romans of the second and third centuries, A.D., we have seen entropic forces at work and are not sure that their consequences can be forestalled forever, or even for very long. But this anxiety is one of the root causes of ideological allegiance, on the hope that one of the old doctrines might still have the magical power to restore Flint, Brooklyn, or wherever to some desirable state. Since that is not likely to work, the impulse is to elevate the quest to the mythic, seeking the talisman in the movies.

Perhaps the threshold difference between crisis and catastrophic cinema is that in the former things can be fixed, and in the latter they can't. As in the past, we may have crises, but our powers of domination are such that mastery is assured. Alternatively: we are now in such a catastrophic state of decline that even though there may be momentary triumphs we are forced to realize the limits of our powers to rule the world. The former could include, if one's categories are large enough, the Star Wars and Indiana Jones cycles, with their romantic reaffirmation of righteous empire and neo-colonial adventurism. Certainly the revenging and refighting of Vietnam had aspects of reducing that war to another aberration, a momentary lapse of national will and might, rather than a catastrophic event endemic to imperial overreach. The return of the Rambos and suchlike to Vietnam "proves" that without domestic political betrayal, we could have won, demonstrated by our rescue of the MIA's held there (reviving, not incidentally, one of the oldest mythic tales we cherish, the captivity narrative) and massacre of those we could not in fact defeat during the actual war. The more sophisticated 'Nam films do indeed portray it as a catastrophe, but the "return to Vietnam" films with Stallone, Norris, and so on reduce it to something that they now will show us how to fix.

Similarly, domestic catastrophe can be averted through the Reaganesque evocation of the magical past in order to inform and revitalize the fallen present. In *Back to the Future* (1985), for instance, young Marty McFly lives in a postlapsarian world, with town, school, and family disintegrating into irrevocable decay. But, he vows, "history is going to change," and is magically returned to a time of social peace and prosperity (1955), wherein he changes his familial destiny for the better; returning to the present, they were no longer lower-middle class victims but rather prosperous and self-confident upper-middles. But social decay has not been altered in the Reagan Eighties: while the "public household" is being abandoned, the only hope to avoid joining social catastrophe is to cultivate the private household of wealth and consumption. With the presence of abandoned stores, homeless, and terrorists, the present is posited as catastrophic, a time beyond public or political redemption, since that is now deemed as an excluded possibility. What can be enjoyed is momentary private happiness, specific only to the well-to-do. As with Reagan, the past acts upon the present only for those with the means to forestall catastrophe, since public-regarding action has been delegitimated.

In some measure, the same "subtext" pervaded *Field of Dreams* (1989), in which temporal contradictions are overcome in a pseudo-reconciliation of generations, moral lapses, and ideology. But this film also effects a magical cure for private ills in the wake of economic loss, the imminent bankruptcy of the family farm. But the mundane necessity of scratching out a living is forgotten in the wake of mythic union, formed around the parabolic forgiveness for that most heinous of modern crimes, the Black Sox scandal. Like *Back to the Future*, the past informs us only by its instruction for private happiness, since the present is now devoid of political or social awareness. We are granted momentary happiness in a now that celebrates only the magic of the moment, not as an historical linkage that gives us hope for the future. Such films are curiously timeless, at least in the sense that they are futureless. The emotion of their appeal may well be that they offer a respite from catastrophe, a temporal antidote from what we increasingly fear is inevitable. American politics since 1980 can be interpreted as an effort to convince ourselves that we are as a political culture immortal, and that the way to do that is to celebrate the past but forestall the future.

Some movies, however, posit a catastrophic world past even temporary respite and certainly redemption. Even movies wherein some form of heroism has been triumphant will often not see this as functional for social regeneration. *Batman* broods over a dark and decaying Gotham; the kids of *The River's Edge* lack the moral and intellectual tools to understand the meaning of murder; the Martin Landau character in *Crimes and Misdemeanors* understands it, and finds contract murder comfortably justifiable; but then the hopelessly cumbersome and corrupt legal system of *Presumed Innocent* cannot find and punish the true killer. The vigilante justice of *Hard to Kill*, *Blue Steel*, and *Die Hard* wreaks vengeance but serves no identifiable social purpose. In all cases, social institutions—government, law, the police, school, philanthropy, the military—all lack the saving grace of legitimacy and even effectiveness. They are pervaded by bullshit, rendered impotent by corruption, led by self-serving elites, and are usually treated with contempt by those who see through the official mystifications.

Such discomfiting imagery posits a world, then, in which the normative patterns of civilization are themselves in great question. Such a condition can persist for a very long time in reality, but in art the fundamental contradiction at work and play here becomes all too apparent. In terms of political dynamics, what post-modernism is groping for in its own language is what has been called the *dystopian* consciousness. "Dystopian" is a term invented in the wake of those modern writers, most notably Orwell and Huxley, who began to develop alternative visions of the political future but which shared the creation of an awful world. They saw forces in the course of modernity which if unchecked could lead to the exercise of awesome and demonic power.

The experience of totalitarianism gave great impetus to this fearful vision, but the dystopian writers did not think us in the West immune either. Indeed, one of the legacies of the post-Cold War era is the awareness that the totalitarian potential did not die with it. A Romanian dissident in exile, after returning to Romania recently, wrote that now "the two former oppositions of East and West will join together in a new electronic globe that is not a good thing for human beings." Mark Crispin Miller writes that "Big Brother is you, watching." And Jacques Ellul keeps insisting, following Huxley, that the triumph of technique is leading us toward a future of total efficiency and unfreedom.[8] Orwell and Huxley belonged to what we might call the "control" school of dystopian projection; others, such as some science-fiction writers and futurists, belong to the "chaos" school, projecting a future beyond the complete, or even sometimes partial, control of anyone.

Movies of recent times have treated dystopian themes, leaning heavily toward the vision of chaos. But they have amended dystopian narratives in post-modern terms, often imbuing a negative vision of the future with comic or campy motifs. They intermingle the dark and the comic, as if we are at once to take the threat of dystopia seriously and then again not. The heavy weight of the demonic powers foreseen by figures like Orwell are given more sardonic lightness of being. In any case, it might be useful to try to make some political sense out of these varying dystopian images and themes in the movies, since they offer us evidence of how popular art imagines our political future. Let me try these classificatory terms: Caesarian, Gibbonian, Mad Maxian, Orwellian, and Huxleyan.

The popular movie theme of Caesarism refers to the apocalyptic impulse to resist impending political, economic, and cultural change deemed to be catastrophic through the relegitimation of imperial power. This usually takes the form of reactionary politics that reasserts the old ways and glory days, even if they are irrevocably past. Even though in fact the nuclear family of the Fifties is a thing of the past, it must now be defended as an ideal at all costs, including murder. Thus the troublesome mistress must be contract-murdered in *Crimes and Misdemeanors*; the love affair ended with a blunt instrument by the wife and mother in *Presumed Innocent*; and the vengeful (and presumably pregnant) lover of *Fatal Attraction* summarily blown away by another wife and mother in defense of her home and husband. Sigourney Weaver in *Aliens* defends both "home" and the corporation she abhors through defense of the child from the aliens, necessitating and justifying an act of genocide. Acts of violence in domestic defense are complemented in the world through acts of praetorian daring, either by the police defending

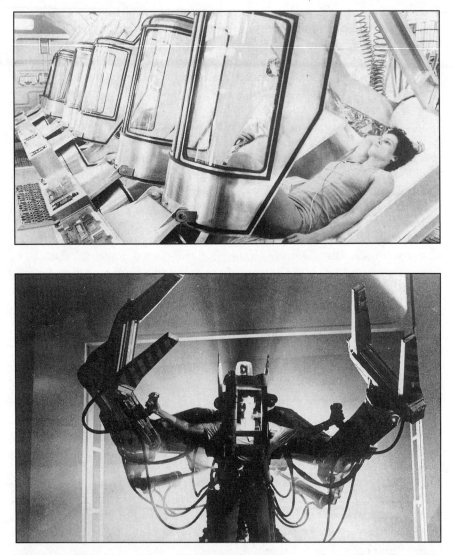

Sigourney Weaver in *Aliens* (1986): the female hero only incidentally serves the interests of the community. (*Top*) Weaver as Ripley wakes up from suspended animation in one machine and (*bottom*) loads herself into another machine, the Power Loader, as if to show how technology extends human capacities to almost unimaginable reaches. With the Power Loader, women heroes no longer need to rely on the physical strength of males. Twentieth Century Fox. Stills courtesy of Jerry Ohlingers Movie Materials.

1980s cinema returns to manageable crises and vigalante justice. (*Top*) Bruce Willis in *Die Hard* (1987); Clint Eastwood (*middle* in *Heartbreak Ridge* (1986), Warner Bros.; and Steven Segal in *The Abuse of Law* (1988), Warner Bros. Stills courtesy of Jerry Ohlinger's Movie Materials.

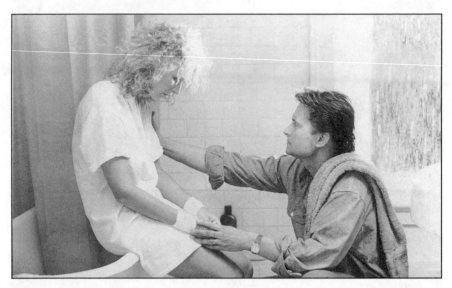

The protection of the nuclear family as a religitimation of state power. Glenn Close as Alex Forrest and Michael Douglas as Dan Gallagher in *Fatal Attraction* (1987). Paramount Pictures. Still courtesy of Jerry Ohlinger's Movie Materials.

A pseudo-reconciliation of generation, moral lapses, and ideology. Kevin Costner in *Field of Dreams* (1989). Universal. Still courtesy of Jerry Ohlinger's Movie Materials.

normalcy against a decaying society (as in *Colors* or *Miami Blues*) or through the reassertion of the martial virtues and military adventurism abroad (as in *Top Gun, Heartbreak Ridge, Iron Eagle, Navy Seals, Death Before Dishonor*, and so on, *ad nauseum*). This has been referred to as the "new Decaturism."[9] In many ways, the same martial impulse was celebrated in the many movies that have appeared with a "medieval" setting, ranging from the *Star Wars* trilogy to the various neo-Arthurian tales (*Excalibur, Deathstalker, Beauty and the Beast*). It is tempting to see in all this a "subtext" of neo-fascism, but that isn't necessarily so. Certainly there is a nostalgia for adventure, mastery, and revitalization of stable male and female roles based on Nietzchean primitivism. Reassertions of masculine domination and institutional power do not add up to a political agenda, but they do suggest a yearning for things to be, as David Byrne sings, "same as it ever was."

By a Gibbonian perspective, I mean a view that things are in imperial decline, and evidence of decay and decadence are everywhere. The people on *Wall Street* or who are *Down and Out in Beverly Hills* are decadent in the manner of the Roman elite of Gibbon's masterpiece—rich, spoiled, useless, incompetent, self-indulgent, and doomed. Those that rule the gigantic *latifundia* in the midst of urban decay, as in *Robocop*, are cynical, greedy, and unconcerned with the plight of the many caught in the midst of decay. The people who run the TV channel on which Max Headroom appears, or broadcast and run the lottery for *The Running Man* show, are providing circuses if not bread for the urban proletariat. But that is the view from the top. The view from the bottom is closer to home. In *Do the Right Thing*, resentment and alienation are just beneath the surface for both lower-class blacks and working-class whites, culminating in an apocalyptic act which is destructive for everyone. The inability of the top of society to empathize with the bottom they have destroyed is made plain enough in the documentary *Roger and Me*, in which the very real Flint resembles the fictional "New Detroit." All these films presume a kind of Gibbonian decline that the elites of society either exploit or cannot reverse, either because of their cynicism or their incompetence.

This post-modern theme is complemented by what we might call the "Mad Maxian" vision, after the Australian trilogy positing a "post-civilizational" world, apparently after a nuclear holocaust. These films show either an urban or "outback" desert, but in all cases any semblance of civilization is gone: Rome has fallen, and the barbarians rule a new Dark Age. The urban wasteland of New York (*Escape from New York*) or Los Angeles (*Blade Runner*), the huddled post-apocalypse enclaves to which the *Terminator* returns, all see a futuristic "urban Gothic" of barbarianism. The desert wastes of the Mad Max films and the many "warriors of the wasteland" see the struggle for marginal survival of a depleted race fighting amongst themselves in vandalous gangs and tribes for the scarce resources left. The savagery of civilization is superseded by an even more primitive savagery in the ruins of a civilization which had destroyed itself. (This image is not only projected into the future: it can be retrojected into the past, as in *Last Exit to Brooklyn*; or applied to another declining political culture, Thatcherian England, as in *Sammie and Rosie Get Laid*; or seen just in a subculture, such as those of *Repo Man* and *Mystery Train*.)

The above movies participate in the "chaos" school of the future. Yet as Robert Heilbroner and other "negative futurists" have argued, chaos and control are interrelated, and more stringent forms of control may be deemed necessary in the future in order for states to survive.[10] Indeed, both Orwell and Huxley envisioned the expansion of state control power. Orwell foresaw the introduction of a technology of pain that would eventually be superseded by such refined controls through propaganda that the "thought police" would be unnecessary. Huxley (as he wrote Orwell) thought that his "brave new world" would be more likely in the long run, as a state based on a technology of pleasure and the most sophisticated and subtle propaganda. Orwell's dystopian vision was translated to the screen in *1984*, but it lacked any post-modernist touch. Similarly, films such as *The Handmaid's Tale* and *The Class of 1999* had Orwellian touches, but were somehow unconvincing. Perhaps the most compelling contemporary vision in the Orwellian spirit was Terry Gilliam's Brazil, a kind of *1984* via Monty Python. In the "not-too-distant-future" of *Brazil*, the state is both sinister and preposterous, characterized by the mechanisms of modernity that have become both demonic and silly—a gigantic bureaucracy that accomplishes nothing except human degradation and punishment, having police and persecutory authorities without moral or political purpose, and the eclipse of individualism and independent consciousness. *Brazil* does share with Orwell the darkly ironic sense that this is what modernity may come to, an apocalypse of control that is forever. In such a world, postmodernity would consist of the total eclipse of the Enlightenment, and the perpetuation of a new political Dark Age based on twentieth-century totalitarian precedents, with the absurdities of rigid controls so well noted by contemporary political writers such as Kundera, Codrescu, and Havel.

Finally, we will mention the Huxleyan vision, simply because it is the dystopian possibility now drawing the most attention, and even deemed by some as the most likely political scenario.[11] Yet it is the one which has received the least cinematic treatment. Why? Perhaps because Huxley's futuristic world is precisely the one that we are creating. Or perhaps because such a techno-paradise that is actually a nightmare is difficult to portray in its full horror, since so many of *Brave New World's* values and practices are what we all do in everyday life. A few movies do come to mind—the second half of *A Clockwork Orange*, *THX 1138*, Woody Allen's *Sleeper*. But little else. It is hard to imagine anyone making a movie of *Walden II*, and Disney Studios appears to have no plans to make a feature film about its futuristic EPCOT center. Nor has a theatrically-released feature film ever been attempted based on *Brave New World* itself. (There was a rather badly done made-for-TV version of it, made for ABC around 1976.) Yet post-modernism senses mightily the advent of the kind of world Huxley foresaw: a weightless culture in which power is masqueraded in propaganda, wherein technique has replaced value, slogan has become truth, and the immediate pleasurable experience has obliterated historical sensibility or humane commitment. Perhaps Huxley's vision is still ahead of our willingness to face up to it, so one of the tasks for post-modernist criticism, not to mention filmmakers, is to treat the full consequences of what we are becoming after modernity.

In any case, there are many contemporary cinematic images of what has been called "the New Bad Future."[12] As we stumble toward the millennium during the 1990's, it may well be the case that we will a wide variety of politically-relevant films that will touch in one way or another the devolution of the logic, and institutions, of modernity. The 1980's were premised on a political promise of national renewal through the good offices of unrestrained capitalism and a dismantled welfare state. Yet now we have every reason to know that both the premise and the promise were phony, burying us further under a mountain of debt and social decay. The euphoria over the Gulf War quickly evaporated despite the official celebrations of "victory" when it became clear that this would likely be only the opening round of a protracted struggle over the control of oil, and that a political and military quagmire of the first magnitude loomed large. (Interestingly, Hollywood, with its ever-sensitive nose, was loath to touch the war against Iraq, knowing full well that the intervention might soon become unpopular or something that should be forgotten, and that tomorrow we might be fighting Iranians, or worse, coalitions of forces that include some of our old allies.) Too, the 1980's deepened the social and environmental problems of both the United States and the world, with the concomitant danger that American society was fragmented into tribes and self-defensive classes, and that our environmental neglect had made the problem beyond redress. (The films of Spike Lee, such as *Do the Right*

Thing and *Jungle Fever*, treat the tribal conflicts in post-modern urban culture, and films such as *Thelma and Louise* depict female solidarity as a class defense, gender pitted against gender in rape and murder.)

With George Bush at the helm, the 1990's may well be the decade of denial, denial that there are consequences to political neglect and delay, economic exploitation and vast inequality, and environmental depletion. But a political system based on denial cannot persist forever, especially since it involves denying the seriousness, or even the existence, of problems so vast that they would daunt the most fearless of leaders. If this is to be the political ethos of the 1990's, then it may be the case that the movies will serve as the major popular form of communication that will offer us guidelines to the New Bad Future, with both dreams of denial that underscore the myth of progress and sublimate catastrophic fears and nightmares of the all too new and bad that is quickly in store for us. As always, the latter will be thought to be subversive, but will be difficult to suppress if they resonate with popular audiences who see in them fantasies that seem both strange and familiar. Perhaps it is the case that the movies help us keep our grip on reality by helping us keep our grip on fantasy. In any event, it likely will be the subversive movie fantasies of a catastrophic political environment in the post-modern world that will offer us strategies for living in a new world that actually may not be very brave at all. Like any other form of power, imaginative power abhors a vacuum; and if all we get from politicians is denial of what we all have every reason to know, then the movies have the opportunity, and perhaps even the responsibility, of becoming the vehicle of our saving imaginative power in a time of denial.

By 2050 or so we will know more fully what post-modernity means, and where the world is going. At the moment, post-modernist criticism serves important political functions by reminding us of the apparent bankruptcy of the narratives that gave impetus to modernity. The movies, as always, give complex and compelling life to the confusion of narratives that characterize the present, but they also give fearful imaginative form to possible dystopian futures which might flow from the present. As in the children's society in *Mad Max: Beyond Thunderdome*, they are still one of our major ways of having a "Tell." Perhaps all cultures need some kind of Tell, a story that sustains them in their conduct. In our time, the post-modernists have pointed to the collapse of our Tell, and how, as the Teller told in Mad Max, it was because of the "pox-eclipse." Now movies are telling us that a pox is upon us, and things as we have known them are in eclipse.

Notes

1. James Combs, *American Political Movies* (New York: Garland, 1990).

2. This has been in the backs of film student's minds at least since Lewis Jacobs' *The Rise of the American Film* (New York: Harcourt, Brace, 1939); to my mind, the poets understand this the best: see Robert Coover, *A Night at the Movies* (New York: Linden Press/Simon & Schuster, 1987); Christopher Durang, *A History of the American Film* (New York: Avon Books, 1978; David Thomson, *Suspects* (New York: Alfred A. Knopf, 1985).

3. Harry Frankfurt, "On Bullshit," *Raritan*, 6 (Fall 1986): 81-100.

4. Allison Graham, "History, Nostalgia, and the Criminality of Popular Culture," *Georgia Review* 38. 2 (Summer 1984): 350.

5. H. Bruce Franklin, "Future Imperfect," *American Film* (March 1983): 48-49.

6. Hillel Schwartz, *Century's End* (New York: Doubleday, 1990); Bill Lawren, "Apocalypse Now," *Psychology Today* (May 1989): 38-39, 42-45.

7. Todd Gitlin, "Post-Modernism: The Stenography of Surfaces," *New Perspectives Quarterly* 6.1 (Spring 1989): 56.

8. Andrei Codrescu, *The Disappearance of the Outside: A Manifesto for Escape* (Reading, MA: Addison-Wesley, 1990); Mark Crispin Miller, "Big Brother is You, Watching," *Georgia Review* 38 (Winter 1984): 710; on Ellul, see James Combs and Dan Nimmo, *The New Propaganda: The Dictatorship of Palaver in Contemporary Politics* (Longman, forthcoming); Robert L. Savage, et. al., (eds.), *The Orwellian Moment* (Fayetteville: University of Arkansas Press, 1989).

9. Harvey R. Greenberg, "Dangerous Recuperations: *Red Dawn, Rambo*, and the New Decaturism," *Journal of Popular Film and Television* 15.2 (Summer 1987): 60-70.

10. Most bleakly in Robert Heilbroner, *Inquiry into the Human Prospect* (New York: W.W. Norton, 1980).

11. Neil Postman, *Amusing Ourselves to Death* (New York: Viking, 1986).

12. Fred Glass, "Totally Recalling Arnold: Sex and Violence in the New Bad Future," *Film Quarterly* 44.1 (Fall 1990): 2-13.

"Right now the most important thing is to get both of my vehicles out of this *bad area*, right?" The urban wasteland of Alex Cox's *Repoman* (1984), Universal Pictures. Shown above, Otto and the dying nuclear scientist. Still courtesy of Jerry Ohlinger's Movie Materials.

A. Keith Goshorn

Repoman and the Punk Anti-Aesthetic: Postmodernity as a Permanent "Bad Area"

I. Repoman and the Postmodern

Repoman, a film written and directed by Alex Cox and released in 1984, still retains a certain currency several years later—in its continued circulation on videotape, in its appearance in late-night art-cinema houses, and even occasionally on international TV slots such as Europe's *Canal Plus*. While *Repoman* was given only minimal promotion and limited release by its own Hollywood distributor, its lasting shelf-life has, perhaps unfortunately, led to its now frequent categorization as an instant "cult" film, inevitably a diminished evaluation. *Repoman* would seem to inhabit an indeterminate position somewhere between a low-budget commercial offering from the margins of Hollywood and a comic document of the common psycho-social milieu shared by a punk subculture and ordinary American workers. It could easily be seen as a narrowly-targeted specialty film catering to fans of a certain genre of early eighties punk/rock music, with that group's particular sense of humor. But I shall argue that there is much more at stake in *Repoman*, and that it is, in fact, on the strength of these surface *dissimulations* by not appearing to be all that it is, that *Repoman* can seduce a broader audience into entertaining a rather sustained socio-political critique of a whole gamut of cultural myths that were proffered by the dominant rhetoric of the Reagan era at the time of its release. By effectively using the shared overlap of the irreverent punk sensibility with a not dissimilar everyday attitude of leering distrust adopted by "service industry" workers in their mutual urban habitat, *Repoman* shows how such apparently "nihilistic" attitudes are both evoked and justified by the absurd demands and conditions of postmodern existence in urban America.

The late-20th century "apocalypse" may or may not have already happened—and the awkward fact that this is hard to determine is itself a feature of postmodernity—but it is obvious in *Repoman* that everyone knows the apocalypse is not going to change anything, that it is still the same faceless game played by "business as usual," and *that* is what creates its dominant tone—as in how to laugh at a bad joke one has already heard too many times. The social ambience conveyed by *Repoman* speaks of something else that is addressed neither by postmodern theorists of crisis and catastrophe or by conservative apologists who proudly maintain that Americans still live in the best of all possible worlds. For most of the people in this film postmodernity is clearly not the end, or the beginning, of anything. There is a sense of the mutual unspoken recognition that "Everybody knows the ship is rotten, everybody knows the captain lied"—as in the lines of a familiar Leonard Cohen song. The apparent "dehumanization" observed by many reviewers of this film can be seen as a comic-ironic device borrowed from the dark parody of urban punk—a survival style which developed semi-consciously as a mirroring device responding to the sickness of contemporary culture. To use Donna Haraway's phrase from another context, *Repoman* helps us to laugh at the "disease that we are."[1] *Repoman* then becomes a comedic vehicle for harshly lampooning the very social icons valorized by the neo-conservative ascendancy, a rare accomplishment in any cinematic mode during the 1980s.

This film resides well on the other side of any contemporary crisis of cinematic representation, but it does involve itself in indirect commentary on the "crisis" condition of the urban *social* beyond its mainstream representation. However, it manages to do so without heavy-handed moralizing and sentimentality. Its ideological critique pokes holes not only in the neo-conservative myth of a "brave new Christian America," but also in illusory strategies of youthful rebellion. Amidst all its bald invectives against mainstream hypocrisies, *Repoman* manages to spoof the follies which result from misappropriating the punk ethos and its confusing signifiers. A nerdy friend of the central figure, Otto, boasts to a group of others at his party that: "We lost our jobs today! Cause we was punkers! Right, Otto? I got so mad I pissed into the community pool!" Or as Duke and Debbi, two young "delinquents," say while running away from the alien presence which has just vaporized their friend: "Come on! Let's go do those crimes! Yeah, let's go get sushi and not pay." Or the film can take a silly but pointed slap at the selfishness of the 1980s yuppie materialist. A wealthy young stockbroker type has his Cadillac repossessed for non-payment while he is shown inside a laundromat trying to convince some poor black women that they should move their wash just so that he can have two machines side-by-side. When he runs outside to try to save his car, the women toss his clothing out on the street and we see that his laundry consists entirely of alligator shirts—the universal emblem of the yuppie mentality. Through its adolescent humor *Repoman* manages to escape a cynical tone in its social commentary, while it often moves so fast that its more serious criticisms can penetrate with laughter before they register offense in their targets. Such an ability attests to a specific potency of popular art-forms.

This is not to say the film is without problems. To endure as a populist intellectual film it must contend with questions of its own inevitable recuperation, ambivalent positions on male sexism, and unsuccessful send-ups of cinematic violence (a blood and guts hold-up / shoot-out scene in particular that reproduces far more than it ridicules gratuitous violence). While trafficking in the anti-aesthetic appeal of punk, *Repoman* simultaneously uses three pseudo-punk caricatures as dimwitted juvenile criminals in order to construct a subplot of questionable value. Yet the violent crimes of these characters bear little resemblance to the very worst behavior of the actual punk subcultures. Somehow, like many of the film's other contradictions, all this seems to come out in the wash—the wash of a reckless, frenzied pace which suits the prevailing "fuck-you" tone of *Repoman*. The film tries hard to live up to the favorite theme of its script, "The life of a repoman is always intense."

The running joke on being "intense" may or may not have any association to the theoretical contention that emotions have been replaced by periodic "intensities" in the postmodern subject.[2] But any analysis of *Repoman* is attended by all of the now familiar postmodern contradictions and controversies over the question of complicity: How can a commercial release by a major studio engaging a mish-mash of conventions borrowed from several genres and full of goofy teenage gags and silly, redundant jokes be considered to have any degree of political adversariality? How can such a claim be reconciled with the fact that its producer was Michael Nesmith, one of the former Monkees, the first prototype of a totally industry-contrived, simulated rock-group, or that its central character was played by Emilio Estevez, the son of a mainstream Hollywood star, Martin Sheen? And does not this character drop out of his peer group of sub-cultural punkers to go to work for a repossession firm whose function is to protect the interests of corporate credit accounts? Wasn't its director, Alex Cox, quoted as saying: "People don't go to the movies to be enlightened—they go to the movies to be entertained."?[3] And hasn't *Repoman* hedged its bets by including more accessible rock music in its soundtrack than just hardcore punk, and by mocking the trio of vulgar pseudo-punks so that it can also play to a larger percentage of that same age group who were adverse to punk?

Regardless of these possible objections, one may still see *Repoman* as a strong oppositional statement in the mid 1980s cinema especially in what it declined to do, refusing to fall in step with the opportunistically reactionary mode of the rest of the American film industry. In coming to terms with *Repoman* as a rather singular example of contemporary cinema, I want to refer the analysis to some of the problematics of post-modern cinema as outlined recently in Christopher Sharrett's definitive summary "Postmodern Narrative Cinema: Aeneas On A Stroll."[4]

If *Repoman* is to be relegated to the status of a "cult" film it is partly because it never got much promotion or exposure in the first place from its major Hollywood distributor (Universal). And this is no doubt at least partly due to the fact that its content ran diametrically counter to the dominant trends of the 80s—trends toward nostalgia, nationalism, sentimentality, "traditional family values" and most of all towards the attempted restoration of individualist phallic glory through images of male competence and conquest. *Repoman*, on the contrary, exults in presenting the ineptness, cowardice, hypocrisy, incapacity, disloyalty, self-inflation, and general stupidity and bumbling of its male characters. With equal irreverence toward the sacredness of John Wayne's masculinity or respect for the father, *Repoman* flaunts its disdain for neo-conservative shibboleths. It managed to do with humor what a serious rhetoric of negation was totally stifled from doing at the same moment of reactionary hysteria over the need to return to traditional values.

In this respect it is worth noting Laura Kipnis' admonition to Left Feminists, and by extension neo-Marxists and others on the left, who have been "increasingly unable to interpellate a popular audience or capture a popular imagination." She echoes an increasing conviction that those who have insisted on holding on to no-longer-appropriate "avant-gardist strategies of negation" which are still "proffered as a counterforce to the spuriously identified subject" have instead merely succeeded in producing their own "Other" in the domain of the popular. Her advice to this "old guard" attitude is to begin to see the popular "as an access to hegemony rather than an instrument of domination." *Repoman* clearly is a gesture away from the former and towards the latter remark. As a popular film, it was able to muster some opposition to the "Reagan revolution" by engaging in "the struggle over the terrain of popular interpellation" and this affirms what Kipnis also calls for, "an acknowledgment that hegemony is won rather than imposed."[5] There are many who might take issue with this last statement, but one could at least safely say that hegemony is always "won" because its agents have maneuvered into a position influential enough initially to impose it, i.e. to gain an advantageous mode of exposure. If this battle then has modulated into a question of access to the "means of projection," then there is not only still an economic dimension but a strategic dimension of the choice of symbolic language and the mode through which it is employed. This is why Baudrillard, for one, always has seemed to be suggesting that the only way to fight against the saturation of the "code" of simulacra images, is to counter with even more seductive and slippery images which can "up the ante," raise a subversive challenge through an even higher level of *simulation* and *dissimulation*. And here finally is where postmodern film theory can actively engage itself and finally exert some actual strategic influence in this struggle over representing ourselves to ourselves.

Nonetheless, I would suggest here that the ability to come up with a critical reading of a given work which interprets its "object" in the conceptual forms of some *au courant* theoretical position does not by any means indicate a relation with the film's public interpellation. At best it may offer itself as another creative theoretical exercise, but it may also entirely miss the popular reception of the film in question. In this sense critical theory of any sort still remains a relatively narrow, elitist pursuit even when focusing on the most widely disseminated artifacts of popular culture, and one must not delude oneself into thinking one is more *engagé* with the public for offering an interpretation of a contemporary film rather than, for instance, a specialized historical analysis of an arcane medieval text. Furthermore, too many scholarly film analyses often reinscribe cinematic oeuvres into not just another medium, but into another discourse altogether. We are all, at this stage, still only engaged in the production of meaning, and still trying to privilege our own. With that in mind, we may proceed with the risks of theoretical review/analysis which prequalifies itself as an act of purely polemical interpretation.

II. Cultural Background

It should be emphasized that the attention given here to the notion of punk as a complex of signs, as an anti-aesthetic style, as a sub-cultural lifestyle, is not merely for the purpose of valorizing its under-appreciated accomplishments in retrospect. I am concerned rather to explore the results of its almost solitary effort during the last fifteen years to create a *counter-public*[6] against the grain of repressive severity cast by the dominant hegemony of neo-conservative momentum as it was building to near-hysteria at the height of the Reagan era. It is important to note in any kind of "cognitive mapping" of contemporary history just who or what movements at least started with an agenda (the degree of eventual recuperation is another issue. . . .) intended and dedicated to *not reproducing* the norms and limits of the dominant status quo. And Punk stands out as perhaps the only youth group in its time that was deliberately trying *not* to reproduce its parent culture. It may be considered an appropriately postmodern phenomenon in that its instinctive gestures resulted in a paradoxical strategy of "mirroring" back to that dominant culture an unavoidable graphic caricature of the worst excesses of that culture in order to register some form of protest and dissent.[7]

It was not actually until the late 1970s that North America received in a delayed reaction the jolt of the punk phenomenon whose momentum had started earlier in Great Britain. Canada was probably a step faster to respond—as it usually is to European emanations—followed by New York in the U.S. But in an important sense, the most fertile ground for the punk movement on a broad scale as both an aesthetic and social phenomenon proved to be the most unexpected site for a profound reception: the sunny palm-tree metropolis of Los Angeles and particularly its lower middle-class suburban towns. As to the reasons for this, one can only speculate on the city's mythical role in the birth (and death) of the American dream, independent of its rapid growth rate continuing in spite of intense smog, crime, congestion, and every other contemporary malaise—all of which created the kind of deflation of the social of which punk was perhaps a symptom. But Los Angeles was also riper than other areas in one other vital respect. Having been under the psychological if not the economic domination of the corporate entertainment industry, Los Angeles never really had a strong or significant underground—social or artistic—relative to its numbers. In more ways than one, even through all the repercussions of the 1960s, it was a *company town*. And perhaps that was why during a brief moment (from 1977 to 1981) the public explosion of punk signs and signifiers, the indiscreet and indeterminate message of the sudden hard-core punk presence shook up the local music, art and social scene in a way quite incommensurate with its actual threat or numbers.

This happened in spite of the fact that it was a movement which was created almost before it existed, not from without as another commercial contrivance, but from within: the beautifully anarchistic rhetoric which characterized the early issues of *Slash*[8] magazine described a thriving scene before it had actually gotten underway, or when it was only an isolated premise emanating from a dank place called the Masque and a few other little known spots. The slanderous challenges of Claude Bessey *aka* "Kick-boy Face," and other writers at *Slash* helped to mark off new ideological turf within the city. They wrote about the bands and the music they admired and wanted to survive while at the same time dismissing the whole rest of the Los Angeles music scene as pathetic, gutless nerds—managing to get the old-boy network of established rock stars and commercial studio musicians worrying about becoming dinosaurs long before they had much reason to worry.

But even with the initial difficulty of such a dramatic aesthetic transition in music and fashion it did not, of course, take too long for the industry's instinctual marketing machinery to overcome its earlier disgust and avoidance and to set about the predictable commodifying and mercantilizing of as many punk signifiers as it could grasp. Almost with a collective sigh of relief, this slightly delayed but typical exploitative market response then began to give us everything associated with "New Wave" and all the countless black, white, and pink department store knock-off fashions which ever since have saturated consumer offerings and entertainment imagery. In an instinctual aesthetic response of "disappearance"[9] the "real" punks tried to counter this sanitizing domestication by adopting ever less-identifiable non-fashions and nondescript attire as they witnessed the escalating co-optation of their own signs, abandoning black leather and returning to cast-off items from the early 60s that did not yet have public nostalgia value or readily apparent, commercially viable signification.

Yet the dozens of punk bands and their excited followers, seemingly bursting out of nowhere, enjoyed a brief moment when they were the new game in town. Their burgeoning gatherings attracted the attention and animosity not only of musicians of older musical styles who began to worry about being eclipsed, but that of the local police departments as well. At a time when it was becoming harder for cops to vent frustrations on Blacks and Latinos in the traditional local manner, the multi-racial and androgynous-looking punk crowds became known as the "new niggers" for the L.A.P.D., a label the punks had no trouble wearing (a role they could not resist.) Charges of police brutality in breaking up punk gatherings became routine in the alternative press, and for a moment there was all the energy of another counter-culture movement feeling its strength in repression and defining itself against the upwardly mobile materialism of the surrounding majority. Spikey

hair and torn jeans on one end and upwardly-mobile alligator shirts
on the other created perfect *Others* for one another within the North
American cultural landscape of the Reagan/Mulroney era.

By the mid 1980s, however, punks had already become common
enough and numerous enough to begin to blend into the surroundings:
they had gained a familiar, recognizable category of difference and lost
their capacity to *epater les bourgeois*. There is no need here to recount
the subsequent history of the punk music scene which will continue
to be ever-more documented and studied. However, in the medium of
cinema there is relatively little "product" widely available which reflects
the influence of the punk movement in/on the film industry. Beyond
such specific films featuring bands or stars like the Ramones' *Rock n'
Roll High School,* Cox's later *Sid and Nancy,* Dennis Hopper's *Out of
the Blue,* or a few seldom seen quasi-documentaries like Penelope
Spheeris' *The Decline of Western Civilization* (and her later greatly
compromised Roger Corman production *Suburbia*), there is little
cinematic evidence of this brief moment in contemporary cultural history.
Of the many reasons for why the punk legacy should receive further
critical attention only one concerns me here: its distinction as possibly
the twentieth century's last significant example of a spontaneous public
opposition, and perhaps the last social movement of youth to adopt
intentionally an *overt* adversarial posture. Presumably, any future
adversarial movements will have learned certain crucial lessons from
this movement's fate and thus also will have learned to advertise their
resistance on a different level of semiotic logic, in a less direct and less
vulnerable manner.

After Dick Hebdige's rather singular and lonely 1984 study, *Subculture: The Meaning of Style,* there have been more and more voices
stepping forth to acknowledge the historical significance of punk, among
them Simon Frith, actually a long-time leftist music critic, Arthur Horne
in *Art Into Pop* (1988), Dave Laing in *One Chord Wonders: Power and
Meaning in Punk Rock* (1985), and Lawrence Grossberg, in some of his
writings on music and popular culture. Andrew Ross, responding to Greil
Marcus' uncategorizable paen to the punk phenomenon *Lipstick Traces:
A Secret History of the Twentieth Century* (1989), reminds the guardians
of canonical studies that "Punk, in many respects . . . was the moment
when it became inescapably clear that the traditional concerns of the
avant garde would henceforth be addressed and worked through in
relation to popular culture."[10] To the extent that *Repoman* sought to
utilize or exploit the psychological and aesthetic strategies of punk, it
should be reconsidered within the dynamics of the previous statement,
as part of a greater inquiry into the possibilities for popular cinema

to assume any of the past modernist hopes for art as public conscience, or agent of social awareness.

To say that *Repoman* employs a certain punk sensibility is not to say it is a punk film, or is even primarily about punks or an attempt to represent their subculture—even if it is occasionally more successful in portraying some of its characteristic attitudes than some relatively straight-forward documentary attempts. One thinks here of Penelope Spheeris' film, the nevertheless quite memorable and valuable quasi-documentary *The Decline of Western Civilization*. (And again one must distinguish the general punk ambience and the character of Otto from the three overdrawn punk caricatures wearing "designer punk" attire). *Repoman* is still an external, somewhat appropriative construction with all the latent concerns of market imperatives. If *Repoman* captures a certain sensibility and psychological mood, one could yet argue that another underappreciated "cult" film—David Lynch's early black and white experimental work *Eraserhead*—is a more appropriate visual statement of the "industrial sublime" that emerged simultaneously with the punk anti-aesthetic.

Although they will probably never receive great exposure, there are, in fact, quite a number of relatively "authentic" punk films and video shorts made by and for persons more or less within the punk scene. Notable among these *courts métrages* are: "Louder-Faster-Shorter" directed by Mindangis Bagdon (1978) which chronicled the San Francisco punk scene and its main bands, "Human Fly" by Alex de Lazslo (1978) which featured The Cramps in the cellars of New York, a bizarre clay animation "Dirt" by Mike Connor (1978), two by Richard Gaikowski "Moody Teenager" (1980) and "Deaf-Punk," about the Club for the Deaf in San Francisco who used to rent their space for punk nights, two by the mysterious and often veiled Residents "Third Reich 'n Roll" (1975) and "The Skinny Man" (1979), "The Man in the Black Sedan" by their associate Snakefinger, the elaborate video shorts by the well-known group Devo, especially their first: "Devo-The Truth about De-evolution" (1978), and finally some interesting clips by associates of the Boston group "Ground Zero." Many of these engage in attempts to satirize and visually deconstruct the dramatic excesses and pretensions of Hollywood production style, but the humor is also often more oblique and difficult for the unexposed/inexperienced to follow than is the relatively accessible comedy of *Repoman*. It takes exposure to only a few of these shorts to realize that for all its merit *Repoman* has more in common with mainstream Hollywood than with the artsy-punk avant-garde which flourished for several intense years in major North American cities.

Nevertheless, relative to depictions of punk in other commercial releases—including Cox's own *Sid and Nancy*, which seemed to be trying unsuccessfully and self-consciously to represent "punk-as-it-really-was" in the Sex Pistols' London—*Repoman* seems to establish a greater degree of credibility. This is perhaps because all it does is to establish a certain psychological ambience through which everything recklessly hurtles and thereby manages to do some justice not only to punk irreverence but also to the gritty urgency of the urban "wasteland" of late twentieth-century capitalism. In some respects the Los Angeles of *Repoman* is equivalent to the 21st century Los Angeles of *Blade Runner*: we can easily recognize a few identifying landmarks in each, but both serve to allegorize the social/material condition of the whole culture in their respective periods, indicating its most advanced state of development/decay/devolution. *Repoman* shows us the *other* side of L.A. in the late twentieth century—those great anonymous expanses that are usually avoided in favor of the typical Beverly Hills/West Side vision of affluence. It is of course this latter which is typically allowed to represent the American experience in many staple TV and film productions for international and domestic consumption. Part of the film's strength is its everyday "realism" even amidst its deliberately ridiculous and implausible narrative themes and sci-fi genre appropriations. *Repoman* utilizes much actual non-studio footage of the city and stages one of its scenes in a local Sunset Boulevard dive/club using a local band (The Circle Jerks) from the same indigenous peer group represented within the film. Except for the *Repoman* theme, sung by relatively mainstream rocker Iggy Pop, most of the music used in the film was done by groups from the local L.A. punk scene. And in keeping with the social milieu it represented, the film employed local Latino punk musicians Tito Larriva and Steven Hufsteter of the group the Plugz to arrange its musical score. All of this helped to lend this unabashedly rough film a feel of credibility and "authenticity" that slicker Hollywood films typically lack.

A direct dependence on a rather specific genre of music is crucial both to *Repoman*'s immediate appeal and to its presentation of a particular mood which existed during a certain brief period of popular music history. Judging by the continued circulation of its videotape, there are a great many who can still empathize with the energy of that moment, perhaps some more easily now than at the time of its release. *Repoman* works best when its soundtrack is well-synchronized with its action, as in one of its better moments when a neo-mod scooter gang appears across the screen, leisurely weaving down all lanes of a dark boulevard, orchestrated by an instrumental track that gives the feel of cruising excitement in night-time L.A. However, there are some awkward low-spots when music is conspicuously missing, others where its return is too abrupt, and some when it is employed in a rather cliched and predictable manner. (*Repoman* is not afraid of being dumb or stupid.)

But *Repoman* is not constructed as if by stringing together a series of MTV-style videos as is ever more frequently the case in Hollywood studio formula-films, thereby further erasing the line between film and television, between "cinema as art" and cinema as an extended form of the commercial advertising spot. Furthermore, I would disagree with Sharrett's perception that "rock and roll . . . is depicted as absolutely co-opted and commodified"[11] in *Repoman* just because, Kevin, an awkward borderline punk/nerd figure, is heard earnestly singing a 7-Up commercial jingle over and over. (This incident, in fact, is what causes Otto to boil over and lose his patience with his/their compromised position as "happy face" chainstore workers, provoking their subsequent dismissal.) Critics also can easily misconstrue Otto's singing of a song which he repeats in a slow, resigned cadence as merely "a modified version of a TV theme song":

> We got nothing better to do
> Than watch TV, have a couple of brews—
> We're gonna have a TV party all right
> Tonight!
> Don't care about anyone else
> We don't wanna know
> We're gonna watch
> Our favorite shows
> SATURDAY NIGHT LIVE
> JEFFERSONS!
> DALLAS!
> GILLIGAN'S ISLAND!
> FLINTSTONES.[12]

This is actually a song from Black Flag, one of the most influential Southern California hard-core punk bands. Their group logo, ubiquitously stenciled and postered around the city, consisted of the symbol for "anarchy" superimposed over a black flag background which simultaneously played upon the trade name for a certain brand of cockroach killer. This kind of double parody is also what is employed in the above-mentioned song when the tame and passive activity of watching TV is described in the intense rap of the hard-core sound. But for Otto, just having had to accept the loss of his girlfriend to some other guy (the script calls for her to sleep with not one but two other males at the party), this is a moment of questioning his connection to a particular circle of friends as he begins to look for a change of scenery. This is a legitimate moment of angst, then, and not reducible to a weightless example of the collapse or co-optation of adversarial subjects (or music) into commercially constructed subject positions.

Beyond its continual utilization of and historical grounding in a popular music form, *Repoman*'s potency lies in presenting a sense of the threadbare absurdity of living in the contemporary urban desert and trying to pretend there is a justification for doing so beyond economic necessity. Some of the repomen talk of their plans for escaping their position if they gain the large reward offered for the alien-filled vehicle, while Otto unsuccessfully appeals to his family high school graduation fund for an exit to elsewhere. He is already well aware of his pitiful status as a youthful wage earner in the American service economy: after losing his job as a can-stacker in an all-night chain grocery, his minimum wage options are given as a night watchman, an "asbestos worker," or a "french fry maker." It is made apparent to the viewer that Otto is living in the West Coast American version of the "no future" world that spawned the punk movement among British youth. This is the dys-topian "desert of the real" as described by Baudrillard, where everyone is living on a sparse diet of recycled promotional myths propped up by endlessly circulating worn-out signifiers. Besides the backdrops of blank industrial buildings, freeway overpasses, and oil refineries, its visual emblem in *Repoman* is the frequent appearance of cans with generic "food" and "drink" labels. The film plays with this in a number of ways, like having Otto's mother suggest he not eat his "Food" dinner directly out of the can, but to "put it on a plate, son. You'll enjoy it more." Bud, the middle-aged repoman who draws Otto into his sphere, is beset by the not-uncommon fear that sooner or later "Gonna' be some bad shit coming down one of these days. Catch all these dildos with their pants down." Bud already has his escape route planned out, his hiding spot picked out, and his survival supplies stashed. But what *Repoman* presents is not how grim this wasteland is, but the different strategies its inhabitants have for dealing with it, for surviving in it (though seldom changing it), and the subsequent effects on their attitudes and relations with others.

If the average working person—lower or middle class—manages to sustain his/her forward inertia, it is often done through the acceptance of a traditional social myth, religious narrative, or, increasingly in today's media culture, some collection of contemporary promotional cliches that keeps the proverbial "carrot" in place and which may also justify a refusal to dwell too long on the *collective* problems of the social. Punks, on the other hand, founded a life-style not just upon mocking the proprieties and conventions of the bourgeoisie (the former avant-gardist stance), but by simultaneously partaking of its current junkfood culture while becoming immune and indifferent to its most salacious aspects, playing with its defects and thus offering a parodic celebration of the defunct dream of modernity, its detritus, its pollution, its decay. The intense indifference of the punk "anti-aesthetic" is not easily explained, but is related to making a bad joke out of everything that is threatening in one's environment in order to defuse its potency, or to relieve one's anxiety. This is something more than fatalism, more than the *mise-en-scene* of paradox and parody, and, as the common observation has it, is certainly moving "beyond alienation."

Yet this is not "reified alienation"—but rather something closer to "dance music for the apocalypse." All of this is why punks generally got along with the "straight" world far better than the previous youth counterculture of the sixties (with which there are far more connections than is often recognized.) Thus I can only partially agree with the contention that *Repoman* "uses the sarcasm of punk/new wave to demonstrate the disappearance of the demarcation line between adversarial and mainstream culture" merely because "Otto's punk haircut is appropriate to his job as grocery clerk and to his night life as slam-dancing punker."[13] Otto shows his disgust for the privilege of this "lovely" job which he is told he should "feel lucky to have" by hurling a "fuck-you" to his boss and then hurling his too-cheerful co-worker into a pile of stacked cans. (Furthermore, the objection above weakens when we realize that California has always allowed more free self-expression in its mainstream working-place attire than the rest of the U.S.)

Yet the dawning recognition of the "no future" cast to the postmodern experience portrayed in *Repoman*—another "L.A. junkyard"—is not suggestive of a "new wilderness filled with potential,"[14] the inherently conservative redemptive reading as perceptively noticed by Sharrett often existing just beneath the text of other contemporary science fiction films. The only possible redemption here is by elements and tendencies completely exoteric or esoteric: the dangling signifier of the elusive "aliens" and Miller's hilarious but serious vision of a "lattice of coincidence laying on top of everything." After a brief Arizona desert sequence, the film deliberately opens with a shot of the phallic glass spires of downtown Los Angeles (corporate prosperity) followed by a quick shot of an idealized pastoral green landscape, and then zooms in on the smog and grime of the daily world that is actually inhabited by the great majority of the millions who live in the Los Angeles basin. Except for the final parodic spectacle of the old Chevrolet Malibu ascending as spaceship, the film remains focused on the tired post-industrial landscape as a rather pointless rat-race.

Nevertheless, it cannot be denied that there is a certain fetishizing that has resulted from the punk anti-aesthetic that ironically has helped to create a not-inconsiderable degree of reenchantment in this vision of the rusting, decrepit ruins of the "industrial sublime," or in the sense of the "nuclear sublime" as a comic sense of accommodation to living in the shadow of imminent destruction. That all of this subsequently can be, and has been, appropriated into numerous marketing devices is also undeniable. (Even in the 1990s we can see sixth and seventh generation take-offs in MTV videos still borrowing on the original anti-aesthetic style and stance established by punk, though in ever more diluted and stylized forms).

But *Repoman* itself at least keeps clear a critical distinction here between punk and "new wave." Most of what has been merchandised, especially the safe, sanitized industry version of punk music that was known as "new wave" and its visual and aural suffusion into commercial entertainment and advertising, remains always already on the side of the simulacrum of promotional culture and its business-world propriety. But there is no sanitized "new wave" music in *Repoman*, even if the soundtrack is not entirely comprised of the raw hard-core punk sound that was indigenous to the social scene that Otto inhabits. Furthermore, the film goes out of its way to skewer a local Los Angeles radio station which had originally been a main source of airplay for local music from the early punk scene but which became progressively recuperated by corporate formula-rock and strict rotating playlists, all under the banner of squeaky clean "New Wave" music. This station, mentioned by name in the script, is heard through a disc-jockey's voice on Bud's car radio— "the mellowest of the mellow sounds KROQ continues with another Nelson Riddle medley played by Mantovani's strings—A send up of a Beverly Hills-style "new waver," with department store punk fashions, would have fit well into the humor of the film, but "new wavers" were for quite some time literally afraid to leave the safety of the affluent West Side to venture into the section of Los Angeles where the "real" punk venues existed. Except for the three caricatured members of Duke's trio, the punk aesthetic portrayed in the film is indicated by Otto's deliberately de-stylized attire of Southern California hard-core, on-guard against the constant co-optation of signs and fashion by the omni-present culture industry centered in Los Angeles.

These "real" punks were characterized by a closer resonance with the racially-mixed working-class neighborhoods where they often lived, not only in their attire but in their attitude. In his first visit to the office of Oly's repo-yard, Otto paradoxically earns a degree of respect and establishes his credentials by pouring out the beer he is handed directly onto the floor while proclaiming in disgust: "You're all repomen!" It is this attitude which gains their approval—and after a moment of angry disbelief Bud and Oly respond in unison: "Kid, you're allright!" and proceed to offer him a job. The subtext, of course, is that in some respects the repomen are natural punks themselves. The sympathetic connection between Bud and Otto is based upon a natural rapport which exists through some degree of shared affect and use of language, euphemised in their mutual appreciation of all things "intense." What may be mistaken for mere sarcasm throughout the film is actually the typical existential mood/stance of a great deal of disenchanted urban America: a tough, sullen edge fostered by the grim daily realities and lack of simple amenities which have been long lost to constant harsh competition in late-capitalist society. (A dark and profane sense of humor is its only saving grace.) Punk has tried instinctively to play with this *mechant humeur*, sometimes succeeding but sometimes succumbing to the same level of discontent and ill-will. When this happens, then there is no "demarcation line" left between the mainstream and the punk gesture towards an adversarial culture. What is perhaps not evident at first in a fast-action film like *Repoman* is that the audience's perception and the critic's "spin" will more so than usual depend on how they are able to read the multiply-coded spoken language of the film.

In a noticeable departure from more typical Hollywood productions, the film both presents and "unpresents"[15] this cultural ambience as a reflection of the postmodern condition which can be read as a general allegory of the effects of late capitalism. The sustained comic depiction of existence in the suffused glow of post-industrial decay is the film's strongest aesthetic accomplishment. Chief repoman Bud makes one of the key thematic statements early in the film when he tries to enlist young Otto's help in getting his (supposedly) pregnant wife's car out of this "*bad* neighborhood." ("Right now the most important thing is to get both my vehicles out of this *bad area.*") The allegorical joke unfolds from there that for everyone in the film, daily reality is lived out in this same greater "Bad Area." But apropos of a postmodern film, this "bad" is a reversible signifier and simultaneously resonates with a local pride in how bad their town is, in the sense of Black street slang as *tough / formidable / too cool / hard to beat*. Life in postmodernity then becomes readable as a sort of perpetual "bad area."

But not surprisingly, mainstream critics like Pauline Kael perceived the film as set in "a scuzzy sci-fi nowhere" with buildings that "don't look like they have anything inside worth protecting," and everywhere beset by a sense of "stagnation," inhabited by "dazed sociopaths" and totally lacking in "civility or courtesy"—which yet, all in all, was reducible by her to a likeable "low-budget nihilistic fantasy."[16] The trouble with this kind of journalistic criticism is that the reviewer typically concludes that such unflattering pictures surely must refer to somewhere else, some "problem area" and never to the general society of which he/she is a part. Such a view is intrinsic to a promotional culture moving ever closer to a world of pure simulacra—a culture where images as floating signifiers become consumable images of difference, stripped from effective reference to a disappearing "Real," where "concrete reality" amounts to nothing more than the particular comfort/discomfort of one's perspectival privilege. A film like *Repoman* can become only a "nihilistic fantasy" for those with adequate insulation from the daily experience of another "perspective," but it can also be full of urgent and relevant social criticism for those who need or care to look for it— once again underscoring the ultimate importance of critical interpretation. Indeed, in postmodernity the making of the artwork (a film or any other) becomes only the first level of production—the subsequent packaging, presentation, promotion, and finally the public interpretation become equally important in the production of public meaning.

III. The Popular As A Critical Mode

A complete history of all the contemporary issues subjected to comic critique in *Repoman* is literally too extensive to detail here. Its criticism goes beyond conventional social/political satire and develops a running staccato humor to take the place of a serious negationist rhetoric in order to radical with a vengeance certain deserving targets found on the American social landscape of the 1980s.

The film is most relentless in its send-up of Christian fundamentalist televangelism and it features its own televangelist "the Reverend Larry." The early tip-off to his significance is in the opening scene when we see the motorcycle cop hiding behind one of his promotional billboards in the desert which advertises "Reverend Larry's Gospel Vigilante Hour"—the two forms of neo-conservative authority as law and religious order collapsed into one. Reverend Larry is frequently heard *voice-over* in the background exhorting his flock to "Give me your money NOW!" for his most important campaign against contemporary evil:

The Lord has told me personally, yea! For I walk with the Lord,

Amen! Larry, he said, you and your flock shall see the PROMISED LAND! But only if you first destroy the TWIN ABOMINATIONS of Godless Communism abroad and Liberal Humanism at home! Joyous Hallelujah! SMASH 'EM DOWN!

Not only are Otto's parents perpetually stoned-out in front of the television set, depicted as total victims of the Reverend Larry's influence, but we are shown how the televangelist has enlisted their financial aid to "send bibles to El Salvador" in the familiar American right-wing mixing of politics and religion. We later learn how his mother and father also have exhausted all their money, including Otto's graduation savings, by giving it away in return for having their names put on Reverend's "Chariots of Fire Honor Roll." But what most infuriates Otto is when we hear how the Reverend Larry exhorts his TV-land followers to call a toll-free number to turn in people—especially "idle youth(s)—who have "failed to register for PATRIOTIC CHORES." Later, he also tries to use his TV show to weasel in on the quest for the reward money for the alien-filled Malibu. We hear him on a TV screen in the hospital issuing an urgent request: "A very sad unchristian thing just happened. A sweet old lady's car was stolen. It's a Chevy Malibu. Brothers and sisters, please, if you've seen this car, just call this toll-free number . . . praise the Lord." The Reverend Larry receives his final searing indictment in the last scene of the film when he is revealed as the sniper in the police helicopter who ruthlessly mows down Bud when he refuses to leave the Malibu.

The direct commentary in the film on vigilante surveillance of citizens by other citizens, even urging families to spy on family members echoes a concern with the Reagan era's smokescreen politics as exemplified in the "WAR ON DRUGS" campaign. In such as atmosphere, Otto's parents predictably are manipulated by FBI agents searching for Otto and subsequently do not hesitate to tell them where their son can be found. In one of the most consequential deletions from the original script which did not survive the final distribution print, Otto is shown—shortly after hearing that his T.V. zombie parents have turned him in—dousing their house with gasoline, torching it with them inside, and then casually walking away from the flames in the middle of the night. (More than one such incident did occur in the U.S. in the hysterically reactionary mood of the 1980s, although, to be sure, this serious incident in *Repoman* was to be introduced in the vein of dark comedy peculiar to the film.) Such cuts not only modified the intensity of the social commentary delivered by the film, but significantly skewed the intended picture of Otto's own rage and resistance to the mainstream social experience. As a result Otto is then perceived by some left critics as only weakly resisting his circumstances, ineffectually defiant, and eventually recuperated—thus any oppositionality is "subsumed under the larger idea that Otto 'joins the team,' "[17] a misreading which will be addressed later.

To further address the neo-conservative issues of the Reagan years, the primary family unit in *Repoman* is shown to be virtually non-existent—absent in Kevin's home where his punker friends gather for parties just as it is at Otto's, where his parents are totally lost to a zombie world of television consciousness. If there is a crisis in the dissolution of the nuclear family, the film does not follow the bourgeois tendency in typical Hollywood films to turn away from the social sources of the anxiety, but looks it straight-on while laughing down the sorry state of things it forces us to starkly reconsider. Another important scene unfortunately deleted from the final release focused on Otto in a moment of extreme need (the night before he burns the house down) trying to curl up on the couch between his parents; instead of comfort he only succeeds in getting himself tangled up in cobwebs, a further comment on the dead state of his family life. And, as mentioned, part of Otto's apparent attraction to the repoman job is due to the willingness of Bud to show an interest in him, to try and impart *something* to him, which is more than his own father seems capable of doing. Furthermore, nineteen-year-old Duke decides to become an armed criminal just after being thrown out of the family home by his parents. At several points in the film, families are heard fighting in the background. In short, *Repoman* blatantly denies the reality of the much-propagandized "return to traditional family values," the very cornerstone of the 1980s neo-conservative ideological rhetoric. The film instead offers witness to their absence.

It does show throughout, however, some other traditional American values that are thriving: omnipresent, dehumanizing competition and blind material greed—the very processes through which the former traditional values have been eradicated, and evidence of the continuing blind faith in a system that systematically erases the values in whose name it has been constructed. This absence of close family relations has been, of course, frequently exploited in the period's advertising campaigns, such as those which have attempted to sell insurance by showing idealized close father/son relationships to enunciate the patriarchal corporate message, "I'll always be there for you."—i.e., in promotional culture, any social lack can always be purchased in the form of a simulational surrogate, in this case the consumer's purchase of corporate security.

Along with fundamentalist televangelism and the return of close
family values, the other most relentlessly targeted myth in the film
is the masculine ego, the male personality with all its myths and fragile
self-assumptions. This also can be seen as fully commensurate with the
punk sensibility which based much of its public posturing on a parodic
or self-lampooning mockery of male tough-guys and phallic images—
particularly those of the established rock star performance pretensions.
A staple part of many a punk group's stage "act" was a send-up of their
"mastery" of musicianship, or a deliberate mockery of the characteristic
macho posture of *braggadocio* and *bravado*. Bud, like most of the
repomen, is preoccupied with the signs and measures of what it is to
be a "real" man: He warns Otto, "Bein' a REPO MAN'S A DAMN
TOUGH MAN'S JOB ONLY A MAN CAN DO. It ain't for pussywhips
or pissant punks." And Lite tells Otto he once passed up a chance to
manage a well-known rock band because managing a pop group was
"no job for a MAN." The props Bud uses, however, to confirm his male
image are costly; his advice to Otto—"When a *man* takes up *Commanders*
. . . he puts all other smokes aside"—is always followed by a fit of
consumptive coughing. When Otto tries to act cool and tough by smoking
Commanders, he only ends up burning himself after placing a second
Commander behind his ear to impress a girlfriend. Adulation of the
favorite right-wing patriotic symbol, John Wayne, is slagged (albeit
rather homophobically) in one key scene after Plettschner, the pathetic
"Rent-a-Cop," refers to the "Duke" as "the greatest American that ever
lived!" This is followed by Miller's solemn revelation that:

MILLER	John Wayne was a fag.
REPO MEN	THE HELL HE WAS!
(*aghast in unison*)	
MILLER	He was too, you boys. I installed two-way mirrors in his pad in Brentwood. He came to the door in a *dress*.
OLY	That doesn't mean he was a homo, Miller. A lot of regular guys like to watch their buddies fuck. I know I do. Don't you?

The males who fare worst against writer/director Cox's satire are
those who try to pump up their masculinity or hide behind their uniform.
Plettschner is shown sitting around the repo-office doing his knitting
even while making his snide tough-guy remarks. He explodes at Otto
for cursing him, bragging that the kid hasn't "earned the right yet"
to challenge a real man like himself who has "been in two wars, worked
five years in a slaughter house, and ten years as a prison guard in

Attica"—to which Otto can only reply "So what?" The final blow
delivered to weak masculinity hiding behind a badge and a uniform
comes when Plettschner cowers outside in the dark "like a chicken-
man" as he watches the FBI agents try to rough-up the secretary
Marlene. But she is easily able to neutralize these two male bullies,
even flatten them with a few swift karate chops. Examples abound of
these agents' bumbling, cowardice, and even vanity—an inclusion that
cannot help but resonate with the disclosures of the Reagan
administration's bumbling revitalization of covert "para-legal"
operations partially exposed in the Iran-Contra scandal. Practically every
male in the film is foiled at some point in his attempt to demonstrate
any kind of competent mastery, the very basis on which their identities
are invariably founded. Even young Otto is shown continually having
trouble with finding the right key to open doors. Baudrillard has offered
a relevant summary of the contemporary masculine plight: "The object
man is only a subject stripped naked, an orphan of desire, dreaming
of a lost mastery—neither a subject nor truly an object of desire, but
only the mythical instrument of a cruel liberty."[18] (Significantly the
only male to receive any kind of vindication by the end of the film is
precisely the one [Miller] who has turned away from any attempts toward
traditional phallic or rational mastery.)

But if the male image takes quite a beating in *Repoman*, we should
take note that women are not exactly presented in an admirable light
either: Marlene, the receptionist/secretary for Oly's repo-business, plays
both sides by sharing hot-line information and working secretly with
their competitors. Agent Roger, as the head of a covert government
agency, is a cold and ruthless cyborg, exceeding her male counterparts
as a compassionless being. Debbi, Otto's former girlfriend, is portrayed
as totally insensitive, demanding, and opportunistic, although she is
the brains and authority behind the trio of punks-turned-robbers. Leila,
the UFO devotee, appears as sincere and earnest but is totally naive
and easily taken in by the ruse of the government agents. Otto's mother
is barely alive, seen only vegetating in front of the television screen
tuned in to Reverend Larry's gospel-vigilante crusade. The film's token
little old lady is even shown as a cranky shrew. The "repo-wives" make
a brief appearance as identical brainless caricatures—"fixed grins,
lipstick, drunk, and extramaritally horny." But the unflattering depictions of women are not nearly so undermining as are those of the males,
and if there is a message to be gleaned from all this, it would seem to
be simply that it is very difficult for anyone to be pleasant, admirable,
or honorable in the contemporary urban environment. (As shown here,
the situation may be tragic or it may be comic, but it is no longer

recognizable as any kind of *crisis*—this is advanced postmodernity, and thus fully "post-crisis.")

Finally, it should be said that there is noticeably little pandering to the gaze in *Repoman* as all of its characters seem to disqualify themselves as enviable or desirable objects in the course of the film's over-all deconstructive momentum. Any and all of the characters can provoke laughter, but idolizing or even admiring them is almost entirely denied the spectator. With no reverie of the fanciful gaze allowed, with little room for identification with "star" qualities, and no nostalgia for another time evoked, our attention is solicited elsewhere—not to some lost "original context" but towards the immanence of what is wrong in this world—towards what is both pathetic and often very funny.

Whatever narrative vehicle exists to carry along the flow of images and action in *Repoman* is almost incidental, even if at the same time we are not exactly given up to the play of "sheer text" because there remains a minimal sense of grounding "realism" which leaks through from the continual allegorical resonance of the multiple social issues earlier referred to in this analysis. Yet there is actually more of a traditional narrative unfolding, along with a closely connected sub-plot, than is apparent on first viewing. The intertwining stories of a young punk kid's inadvertent employment with a company of automobile repossessors, coupled with a zany sci-fi quest for an old car with "hot aliens" in the trunk, do serve a basic purpose of setting-up jokes and fast action scenes. They are hardly what the film is about, but they do provide its many surfaces for varied projections of interpretation, rather than over-directing a barrage of intended meaning. It is mostly from this sense of non-saturation with determinant, univocal meaning that the film can be considered postmodern.

Appropriately, *Repoman* treats its shaky narrative with inchoate kineticism as the film seems to careen along, reveling in its dangling threads and sloppy edges, but all this is only in keeping with the general tone of punk irreverence. What it does accomplish is the creation of a mood, a state of psychological ambience, an existential pulse all of which serves to evoke an intense sense of the condition of contemporary urban life, the plight of the individual subject perpetually short-changed.

It has been noticed, even by journalistic critics of *Repoman*, that "There is nothing at the center . . ." of *Repoman*—inadvertently confirming the film's distinctive postmodern feel. But while it does show the rather arbitrary construction of groundless subject-positions founded upon nothing but this or that floating signifier found in late twentieth-century America, the film also engages in a minimal amount of old-fashioned character study to portray its peculiar cultural context. Oddly

enough in one of his most vulnerable moments, Otto becomes the carrier
of an unspoken code among his peers when he appears stoically to accept
the fact that a woman (his girl-friend) can sleep with whomever she
wants. When he is confronted with this at a party, he does not succumb
to the typical male response of starting a fight with the other man or
abusing the woman, but rather leaves in disgust after first pushing the
hapless Kevin down the stairs when the latter tries to tell the two new
lovers to get out of his parents' bedroom. No matter how much personal
pain it may cause him, Otto's departure cannot be simply written off
as his rejection of "The loose morals of the hard-core scene." At the onset
of Otto's next relationship with the young UFO-cult devotee, Leila, he
is more than ready to jump into the back seat of the car for some light-
hearted "quickie" sex. The joyous, light-hearted manner in which this
incident is presented would also seem to be a counter-comment aimed
at the attempted imposition of a new repressive sexual austerity which
was being proselytized by the religious Right during the time of the
film's original release.   ˋ

On the other hand it is more difficult to understand the inclusion
of a later sexual encounter between Leila and Otto at her place of work.
When Otto shows up in the middle of the day and requests an audience
with Leila in the back room, only to demand that she strip down for
another quick encounter, he receives only an angry rejection. Otto's
coarse response is to pull down his pants and say: "The least you could
do is give me a blow job." For this he receives two sharp slaps in the
face before she is called back to work. The scene passes ambivalently
somewhere between a gesture of innocent comedy, a condemnation of
Otto's crude sexism, and a possible tacit acceptance of such deliberate
rude behavior as contemporary irreverence toward sex. In the earlier
party scene where Debbi sleeps with Duke after rejecting Otto, other
more explicit, offensively sexist remarks made by the third lover were
removed from the final release, adding to the film's rather ambiguous
posture towards gender relations. The strongest commentary on relationships is saved for the final scene where Leila yells at Otto not to get
into the ascending Malibu-become-spaceship: "What about our
relationship?!" Beaming widely as the glowing vehicle takes off, Otto's
only reply is to say "Fuck that!"

A parody of scientific schizophrenia is embodied in the mad figure
of the lobotomized, over-radiated nuclear scientist "J. Frank" who is
at once a refugee, an apologist and a victim of the U.S. government's
atomic research center at Los Alamos, New Mexico from where he has
escaped with his cargo of "hot aliens." Through his literally "split-brain"
discourse we learn of the fate of those who work on neutron bomb projects

"so immoral they drive you mad." This testimony is interspersed with hilarious defenses of the healthy virtues of nuclear radiation from which he is simultaneously dying. Focusing on the little-acknowledged existence of street level populist opposition in the Reagan years, we also hear the savvy Black repoman "Lite" discoursing upon how he certainly never would be in the U.S. Army or fight in its insane wars: "Fuck, no way. Nobody gotta do that shit. Not in this country. New I.D. don't cost no more than a pink slip [phoney car title]. Know what I mean?"

What has been invariably concluded by mainstream journalists, academic reviewers, and even radical critics is that there is to be found in *Repoman* a sense of the "loss of affect" and the "death of the social." For some this translates as merely "a total lack of humanity"—but that is only the peculiar view from the outside/outsider who cannot read the shifting fast-rap-banter of the film and the particular affectional tone through which it is spoken. This limited vision then sees only the posing and the postures of an Other described as "druggy burnouts," "dazed sociopaths," "soreheads," "deadbeats," and "rusted out punkers."[19] Yet standing a bit closer, one might sense that there is actually plenty of affect passing among certain characters, even if it is self-reflexively spoofed by the large rusty barrel labeled "Personal Affects" that Miller, the junkyard mystic, scrapes around the concrete yard to collect contents from the repossessed cars. But the affect that exists is deeply-coded in the various styles of the several groups appearing—and it certainly is the case that these are *conflicting* codes that do not communicate with each other: Otto and the other punksters, the Happy-Face UFO followers, the repomen of Oly's yard, the free-lance duo of the Brothers Rodriquez, the trio of amateur punk criminals, and the FBI goons. In this respect, there are several meanings at odds with each other if not imploding in dissonant cacophony.

Whatever sense of the *social* there is to be found in the film will only be seen as it perseveres in isolation among these conflicting, colliding and completely incongruent codes and senses of the "Real" held by the several groups represented. The obvious detriment of such a plurality of language games "without mutual conversation" is that too often respect and consideration for others is granted only when it coincides with the particular narrow code to which one adheres. The FBI group, easily read as a send-up of a Reaganesque "covert action" group, is led by the icy cyborg Agent Rogerz with the glittery steel hand. She is most memorable for her characteristic remark while forcing Leila to torture Otto: "*No one* is innocent!"—the film's indictment of the arrogant hubris of such "above the law" government agencies. In the final scene there is a brief exchange between two of these covert operatives, who declare that their profession is "more than a job, it's more like a calling." In spite of Bud's speeches about respecting the civil rights of the "Repo Code," he obviously will use whatever ruse he can to separate a targeted car from its owner. Lite, on the other hand, doesn't need such self-deceptions; he defends the Brothers Rodriguez by correcting Otto with a reminder that "They ain't scumbags. They're car thieves just like us." While their trade may be objectionable to nearly everyone else, there is a sharing of some social civility among the repomen themselves. However, it is a very tenuous male camaraderie that is also always threatening to fall apart. Its highest cohesion is reached when they go out together like a police department "S.W.A.T." team to beat up the rival Rodriguez Brothers.

Unlike most large-budget features, *Repoman* is not afraid to part company with artistic conventions and does not attempt "to steer clear of a presentationalism which would suggest a new political awareness of the spectator."[20] Its comic bathos indirectly attempts to export a new political awareness which is clearly not continuing "to advance dominant ideology," even if it does demonstrate that "previous notions of ideological consensus no longer exist."[21] Importantly, the film makes no moralizing judgments about such social "fragmentation" and its perceived detrimental effects. Contrary to both bourgeois liberal and neo-conservative uneasiness over an increasing multiplicity of disconnected public spheres, *Repoman* merely presents this condition as the acceptable everyday reality it clearly is in a city like Los Angeles. In such environments, as perhaps most noticeably reflected in the diversity of the L.A. popular music world, there are simply many contradictory codes and styles co-existing side by side, regardless of what they think of each other or how much they are able to inter-communicate. This is simply postmodern urban reality, and Los Angeles is an appropriate example for showing how tolerable such a "crisis" can become. Judging any sense of public "panic" becomes a matter of subjective, even aesthetic, interpretation. As expressed through Bud, a *crisis* to be avoided by some is merely an *intensity* to be sought out by others. This same recognition is one of the profound lessons of the punk anti-aesthetic: what is ugly for some can become beautiful for others—and a case in point for the purported null-ification of "the question of beauty and ugliness"[22] in the postmodern era, already deemed a *fait accompli* by Baudrillard and many others. At the same time *Repoman* is not representing a realistic picture of anything as it continually mocks its own free-wheeling travel in an only half-serious realm of science-fiction camp, occasionally engaging in humorous intertextual citations such as the hail of ice cubes at the end which recalls the hailstorm and black rain of Peter Weir's *The Last Wave*.

Repoman may be set in a context perceivable as some kind of "waste-land," depending on one's criteria, but it has little relation to the typical fare of Hollywood's dystopian and crisis film genres. The "crisis" of this urban cultural context has been so constant, so much a continual daily reality that few can perceive it as such. Thus, there is virtually no sense of "panic" to be found in this life-world, except for perhaps the frenzied bumbling of the covert government agents and, of course, the momentary panicked excitement which surrounds the escalating search for the Malibu and its "hot alien" cargo. Or one could also say that the recognition of daily "intensities" occurring in the life of a repoman, as valorized in Bud's rhetoric, is his way of marking off discrete intervals of meaning from an existence that is otherwise characterized by indifference and boredom. Such a stance furthers the hard postmodern urban cool that develops beyond even *reified* alienation, beyond panic and frenzy and desperation. Indeed, if such a moment ever occurred here, it has long been forgotten or it has become so much the norm that it is no longer even recognizable as such. Instead, this new urban experience will be registered against a drone of boredom and indifference to events that once might have caused at least some amount of concern or alarm. It is the special virtue of *Repoman* to make us laugh empathetically with this version of the postmodern condition, as, for example, when Bud speaks to Otto while leaving a liquor store:

BUD	tense situations. When you get five or six of 'em a day, gets to the point where it don't mean shit. I've seen men stabbed. Didn't mean shit. Guns don't mean shit either. That's when you got to watch yourself.
	(Bud pays for the drinks.)
BUD	Here, I'll handle it pal. Settle down.
	(he picks up the purchase.)
BUD	Have a nice day. I mean night. Day, night, doesn't mean shit.

This may be a way of saying that one is "immune" to such "realities" because I've "seen it all"—which is also to say that one is beyond the staged sensationalism of either TV news or cinematic violence, which one knows at this point to be only a product promoted by some other business in some other part of town. Otto can easily relate to this because punk bands often used to stage deadpan mockery of spectacle and gore in their live shows, as a way of communicating to their cohorts as audiences something on the order of: "we know what games are being played—we're hip to the scam that's coming down." This is an existential posture that has been earned, through repeated exposure to promotional strategies in the society of the spectacle, and a subject position of survival that cannot be dismissed as another gesture of transcendence or evasion of anxiety.

Postmodern urban subjects at such a phase may then be seen as significantly disconnecting from programmatic responses to the diet of the spectacle. Even Bud's mock-serious rambling banter about belief in the "sacred trust of credit" or his mimicking of promotional copy about commercial products ("When a man takes up *Commanders*, he puts aside all other brands") may reveal a degree of self-reflexive awareness about his manipulable position as subject-become-virtual-screen for the projection of promotional images.[23] We wonder if Bud is fully aware of the folly in his statements and if he is simply enjoying playing a certain role, while simultaneously being the comedian who makes fun of his own naive and earnest beliefs—knowing quite well how his identity is continuously being created from and dissolved into the cultural text. Some of his remarks are too priceless to believe otherwise: "You aren't a commie, are you? I don't want any communists in my car, no christians either!" On the other hand, it may seen that the fully socialized and conventional aspects of his persona are in such radical disjuncture with other aspects of his behavior (smashing the coin telephone with a tire iron when it doesn't work, driving down the middle of the concrete river bed, frequent consumption of cocaine and amphetamines on the job) that he might well be considered some kind of precarious schizophrenic. Perhaps a more defensible reading would be that Bud is another example of Deleuze and Guattari's self-affirming "schizo"[24] engaging in sane responses to an insane environment as an act of at least partial liberation. Bud is, indeed, the most appropriate voice for singing the *Repoman* theme song: "Riding down the river on a slab of concrete, I heard a witch doctor say: 'Why don't we go out for Whoppers!'"

I would contend, however, that Bud's character, and the similar contradictory persona of others in the film, are simply presentations of what are by now common everyday subject-positions for many inhabitants of the contemporary urban metropolis. Such contradictions comprise many of us by now, and to show the continuity of such mainstream working people with officially "deviant" and/or "subcultural" postures and the attitudes of punks like Otto is one of the film's special achievements. To acknowledge this is not to diminish the adversarial gesture of the latter, but to reaffirm the "Big Lie"[25] of the reactionary rhetoric of the Reagan era. At the height of the "War on Drugs" hysteria, for instance, millions of Americans still engaged in illegal and "un-

American" practices as many had already been doing for years, regardless of their public responses on the matter, or even regardless of their self-professed political preferences. (Postmodern schizophrenia reaches its heights when individuals manage to justify their private personal behavior yet can join in a public uproar to condemn the same practices for the collective social.)

Likewise they can also harbor contempt for the bland and soulless self-image held up to represent ordinary or traditional Americans. This revelation is again spoken by Bud in perhaps the best one-liner of the film: "Ordinary people, God how I hate 'em!" *Repoman* also chose rather deliberately to send-up pious attitudes towards drug usage, the favorite whipping-boy of neo-con propaganda. In one of the more humorous put-downs, the Brothers Rodriguez are shown in their warehouse apartment discussing with Marlene the reasons for the Chevy Malibu's high bounty-fee for repossession while a joint of marijuana circulates in the room. They muse that perhaps the car is worth so much because it is full of drugs, and then remark that "Hermanos Rodriguez don't approve of drugs!" Marlene counters by saying that "Neither do I, but it's my birth-day," and urges them to go ahead and find the car. The other repomen at Oly's yard are much more open about their drug use, with Bud swearing to Otto that "Ain't a repoman I know that don't take speed"—necessary, of course, because the successful repomen are the ones who "Get home at three A.M., get up at four." After that they take off to try and score some "pharmaceutical meth" that one of Otto's friends is selling. Explicit scenes of Otto smoking "joints" and of the passing around of a marijuana bong pipe at the punk party were modified from their original description in the script, although not Otto and Bud "snorting" cocaine off the dashboard of the car. Duke and Debbi are shown "doing" lines of coke before doing their robberies. However funny or absurd such episodes are made out to be, there is always the very undramatic implication that all types of drug use are just an ordinary aspect of daily life for working people as well as for "adult weirdos" and teenage subcultures, just one more item in the necessary diet of consumer culture. This is perhaps a more appropriate referent for Sharrett's observation of the "disappearance of the demarcation line between adversarial and mainstream" culture in *Repoman*. Mainstream working people and subcultures now often do take the same drugs, but they are more likely to be "maintenance and survival" drugs for getting through the day. In this sense the general culture has already passed through (or retrogressed behind) the earlier phase of purely "recreational" drug use, and any continued use of "transcendental" psychedelic drugs as a means of psychic exploration or psychic transformation has passed for the moment into the ever-more discrete and esoteric realms.

Although *Repoman* is clearly not involved in the tracking of Otto or anyone else in a conventional quest for individual meaning, Otto is nevertheless the central figure of significance, (in spite of the fact that it is Harry Dean Stanton's Bud who is the acknowledged star upon whose shoulders the film is in many ways carried.) It is Otto whose social and psychological development are in the process of negotiation, and it is his ideological values and life direction that are at stake—he is the representative "subject in process." We watch as he is bounced and pulled between the critical influences in his life: his fading parental figures, hilariously under erasure as permanent "couch potatoes" (passive TV addicts) become televangelism zombies, his former peer-group pals (Kevin, Duke, etc.), all losing their credibility, and the new and un-expected factor, his repoman job with its allure of action and intensity. But the latter only becomes a viable option for him because of the elder advisor/father figure in the person of Bud through whom he is more or less introduced into a contemporary rite of initiation.

In this context Otto's persona has already been solidified through immersion in the tough and irreverent existential stance of the punk scene, and he is acting from this subject-position quite effectively, given the restraints of his age and social conditions. Like any teenager, his problem is more one of finding an acceptable milieu, someplace where he can feel at once at ease, engaged, occasionally excited, and as if he is being given a tolerable degree of "slack," precisely what he didn't have at his previous job.

Following the unfolding of this simple history is virtually the only gesture towards providing a narrative vehicle to those requiring one. And those looking for young Otto to undergo some transition to maturity or increased responsibility or wisdom from his rites of passage are sure to be disappointed. The closest they will get is the observation that after the *second* incident in which his mentor Bud is shot and wounded— unlike the first—Otto does go to comfort him instead of running away. But it is important not to forget that these scenes are only constructs for delivering the general black humor of the film.

A frequent critical response to Otto's quick change of appearance from a slam-dancing punk to the rather "square" detective/used-car salesman look of a repoman has been to treat it as indicative of a conversion, a recuperation. But it is hardly fair to condemn Otto for his "acquiescence" to the life style and values of the repoworld, his "shift from subculture to the arrogant, depoliticized petit-bourgeoisie."[26] More relevant than such a strong interpretation is to recognize that as a sixteen- or seventeen-year-old boy, Otto only can be expected to be eager for new experiences, for the promise of a few thrills and excitement. Otto is also at least momentarily taken in by the crazy/wise schizo-rap of Bud in whom he senses a degree of mutual recognition and camaraderie, not only as a surrogate father figure but as a sort of middle-aged punk himself. Otto is more naive and inexperienced than completely "soulless and utterly adaptable." He is genuinely concerned when he asks Bud in all earnestness, "Do you think all repomen follow the code?" Following a repossession episode in which Otto experiences urban gunfire for the first time, his remaining middle class sensibilities show through his punk veneer when he protests to Lite "You're crazy Lite. You can't just shoot into people's houses. Maybe you shot the guy."

Otto is a subject caught between the forces which insert one into the "already-semiotized text" and the instinctual impulses to resist it. Otto's subject-position is too indeterminate to be reducible to formerly recognizable categories—not to the earlier "rebel without a cause" persona as a victim of modern *anomie* anymore than to that of being simply *alienated*. Perhaps he is truly "beyond alienation" as has been suggested, but he is not concerned about "fitting in," either. It does seem clear that he has long ago abandoned any serious ambitions toward fame, fortune, or respectability, and it is possible to conclude that Otto has previously been enough of a "real" punk to have some time ago forsworn participation in the "straight" world of careers and upward mobility. The point to be made is that Otto never really takes his repoman job seriously, he is only looking for something a little more exciting than the pseudo-thrills of television, especially just after he has been burned by his former girlfriend in the punk scene. (His lack of loyalty to the career repomen is underscored by his willingness to abandon Bud when he is wounded and lying in a pool of his own blood during the liquor store hold-up scene.)

Where then, does Otto fall within the cinematic expectations of a protagonist? Postmodern theorists are undoubtedly right to point to a trend towards the "disappearance of the protagonist."[27] But in *Repoman*, this may indicate something more than a "depoliticized a-historical consciousness" which has, after all, long been the world-view of the bourgeois public, as that of commercial cinema. If a total saturation with promotional signs and images leads to the hollowed-out social landscape of simulacra culture, this process arguably may be further advanced in a multi-media capitol like Los Angeles than anywhere else. It may then be that there are no real "actors"[28] (in Alain Touraine's sociological sense) left as individual agency is ever-more dominated by economic forces, promotional market manipulation, and mere arbitrary chance luck for the human carcass whose image happens to fit a certain image-role/product. In this sense *Repoman* laughs at the resulting dance of folly as (mostly male) figures struggle to claim some ground of personal identity with the increasing recognition that there are no heroes or few human models left worthy of emulating. Thus, we come back to the question of the "star" now without any kind of a viable star's role to play (discounting for now all the desperate, reactionary and self-defeating attempts to resurrect the male hero for which Rambo stands as the ever-more absurd-looking Hollywood paradigm). In a recent analysis of Fassbinder's *Querelle*,[29] Sharrett has provided a pertinent discussion of the uncontrollable escalation in the past few decades of screen-star candidates outdistancing their generic history. He points out how Martin Sheen can already seem like a more "authentic" elder star than more recent classes of Hollywood clones, even if Sheen was but originally brought forward as a simulation of the lost adversarial figure of James Dean (who along with Elvis Presley and a few others, now circulate as mere "trash archetypes.")[30] It is not the loss of stars themselves that are of critical concern here, but the loss of a tradition of outsiders or adversarial figures as stars. What then are we to make of the fact that Emilio Estevez, as Otto, is the son of Martin Sheen? It is possible to see his role in *Repoman* (as punk outsider) as a potentially strong adversarial figure in the making. Estevez seemed to have the minimal charisma and adequate disdain for normativity in the dominant social to begin a career as an oppositional/adversarial advocate. Unfortunately, any hopes for such potential advocacy (in his screen career) of this seemingly fading cultural tendency appear to have been squashed rather quickly by his subsequent positioning in ever-lighter, more commercial roles.

Harry Dean Stanton's role as Bud is much more ambiguous and ambivalent than Estevez's Otto. Bud may be read as a kind of proto-typical banal character cut from the same cloth as a million others, but one who nevertheless unconsciously manages to create his own unique style, caught somewhere between cool and fool, too funny to be pathetic. Bud is not "clearly deranged" as journalistic reviewers saw him. He is the ordinary kind of guy who can mouth all the platitudes of the day—and make them sound at least momentarily believable (no matter how contradictory.) His repertoire is a pastiche of random impressions, fragments of promotional messages, and snippets of news and political slogans that have stuck in his mind and have somehow been sewn together as his own working ideology. It is with this serious schtick that Bud sermonizes to Otto on their first outing as co-workers (in between their snorting of lines of amphetamine laid out on the dashboard): "It's what I call the Repo Code, Kid. [*sniff*] Don't forget it. Etch it into your brain. Not many people got a code to live by anymore." Above all, his pride is in the difference between the repoman's ethic and all those bland others: "Ordinary person spends his life avoiding tense situations—*Repoman* spends his life getting into 'em." Bud also exhibits a normal working class pride that rails against the rich, because he knows that "millionaires never pay their bills."

At the same time, there are to be found in him echoes of a right-wing survivalist mentality, and a host of prejudices against all those incompetents like the "Marina Faggots" who won't know what to do when the "heavy shit comes down someday!" But he also serves the film's purpose as the spokesman for setting up its own serious jibes at retrogressive attitudes which flourished during the Reagan era, such as indifference to the plight of the homeless or believing those persons have *chosen* such a fate. When riding through a skid-row section of downtown L.A. with people sleeping on the sidewalks, Bud muses to Otto: "A lot of them are on the run, don't even use their Social Security numbers. . . . If there was only some way of finding out how much they owe and making 'em pay. . . ." But Otto (Cox?) defends them with a liberal's compassion: "Oh for Christ's sake, Bud, they're winos. They don't have any money. You think they'd be bums if they did?"

In the end Bud is erased by his own greed and hypocrisy. Failing to follow his own sterling advice to his young apprentice that "Only an asshole gets killed for a car!" Bud goes down in a hail of bullets from a police helicopter after leaving his hospital bed trying to beat the others to the reward money for the alien vehicle. In this failure to live up to his own code—especially when depicted as one of the last explicit "believers" in the film-there is an unavoidable implication of the failure of all social codes and ethics. In this final scene Bud also faces up to his own disillusionment with the work he has done for years, to his faulty belief in his job: "Shit . . . eleven years of repoing cars and what have I got . . . shit." A last important but finally obscured social comment packed into this scene (explicit in the screenplay but only implicit in the final cut) is that the person commandeering the police helicopter who orders Bud to get out of the glowing Malibu and then brutally shoots down the already heavily bandaged figure turns out to be none other than the Reverend Larry. As legalized assassin, the televangelist can now be seen as conterminous with the general greed, corruption, and lawlessness of social and legal authority. But as usual in *Repoman*, the seriousness of such implications also is subverted simultaneously by the absurd trappings of the scene—in this case Bud remarks just as he is shot: "COME AND GET ME COPPER! I'M WELL ARMED AND I

KNOW WHERE YOU LIVE!. In the end it is hard to say whether Bud
is more a comic than a tragic caricature in his representation of the
contemporary individual who is programmed to value codes and
traditions, and in struggling to articulate them finally realizes the futility
of his/her pathetic gropings towards meaning.

IV. Problems of Resistance and Recuperation

This final scene overturns all previous narrative momentum far more
than it provides any sense of closure with the unexpected ascension of
Miller and Otto in the Old Chevy Malibu-become-alien-spaceship. This
rather bizarre ending, replete with intertextual references and
commentary on the genre of science fiction fantasy, is nevertheless up
to something more than facile self-referentiality with the medium. The
film also engages in an easily overlooked reversal when it places its
former "fool" into the position of the only male with any claim to mastery,
the only cool head in a crisis, and the only person who knows what to
do in an unprecedented situation, the only one other than Otto who
is truly ready to deal with the possibility of an *elsewhere*.

Sharrett has argued that "the trashing of traditional representational
narrative strategies," by Hollywood's commercial adoption of "formally
avant-garde techniques of temporal and spatial displacement and indeter-
minacy" became a familiar appropriation which has served ultimately
to advance "the disappearance of the protagonist."[31] He contends that,
subsequently, this has been a key factor in "the emergence in art of
a depoliticized, ahistorical consciousness that can be seen as a
culmination to the bourgeois world view." But if this is the case, we
must look to something other than the figure of a conventional heroic
protagonist to introduce themes of transformation and difference. When
all potential male star/protagonists are shown to be exhausted or
incapable of traditional heroic action, attention does turn elsewhere,
not to a still disenfranchised woman, but at least to a man who
exemplifies none of the traditional qualities of patriarchal masculine
heroes—machoism, lust, power, conquest, mastery, narcissism, etc.

In *Repoman* we are caught off-guard at the end by the quiet
emergence of Miller, the junkyard mystic/fool, as the only person who
remains cool in a real crisis. Although presented as a sympathetic
character, a slight touch of idiocy skews his cosmic insights into a weird
freewheeling rap that is even too much for young Otto to take seriously.
He is precisely the type of character which the normative hegemony
of the neo-conservative eighties relished in excoriating—not only as a

non-productive, worthless fool, but in their most damning judgment and for quite transparent ideological reasons, as a "60s burn-out." In the early part of the film Miller is given lines that deliberately make his cosmic rap collapse into ridiculousness while he stirs trash fires of repo-debris and stirs up his own brew of late-twentieth century urban metaphysics. Later he is shown mimicking the posture of a wacky shaman dancing around and chanting a cure for Otto's head wound. Miller deepens his inscrutable fool persona by uttering such sage remarks as the reason he has never learned to drive is because "The more you drive the less intelligent you become."

Yet all this can be read as a set up, because ultimately we are forced to consider that Miller not only signifies but reaffirms *radical difference*. Miller stands as the sign of the subject who has been completely unmoved by the liberal/conservative mainstream consensus in its recent momentum to convince all that "utopian or radical options are naive or outdated."[32]

However "incoherent" Miller's rap, however "spaced-out" he sounds, Miller yet signals a trace of another kind of transcendental subject—a quietly adversarial and totally unrecuperated one whose legacy has been under threat of erasure both from the neo-conservative right in their determined revisionist history of recent public experience, and also from traditional left criticism still under the influence of analytical rationalism and the continuing hegemony of productivism as guiding mythology. Miller's schizophrenic interpretation of daily consensus reality—which introduces strange metaphysical theories of other planes of existence— is a warped echo of the much-maligned 60s counter-cultural opposition which sought to undermine the reigning rational epistemology with a mixture of arcane and occult teachings gathered from around the anthropological globe and from the mythological past. In being portrayed as a fool, Miller also signifies the sorry social status in postmodernity of any human belief in new frontiers, in the possibility of better alternatives, in the possibility of an *elsewhere*.

As a contemporary male figure, he stands out among others in the film for his gentleness and freedom from the power-seeking, muscle-flexing tendencies of the phallocentric ego. In spite of his articulation problems, Miller the junkyard/fool comes off as not so far away from the humble Taoist sage or the contemporary seeker of paralogical, paraphysical solutions, now valorized by the advanced wing of post-structuralist thought in trying to recognize the importance of the *unsayable* and the *unpresentable*. His character is ultimately the greatest marker of *difference* in *Repoman* because he provides a comic hint that there is forever something "eluding the grasp of the comprehending subject."[33] As such he stands beyond the slapsticks sci-fi hi-jinks revolving around the chase for the Malibu, the Happy Face people, etc., and as such his figure points to the emerging postmodern sense of a need for political grounding in something other than purely *human* metanarratives. Lastly he stands as the antithesis of the "fully artifactualized subject"[34] represented in the film by the clandestine FBI Agent Rogerz and her stainless-steel hand.

This final scene of the ascension of a glowing car into the night sky does not imply closure and a return to stasis, nor does it need to be written off as an absurd, parodic send-up of other science fiction genre endings— but it may stand as just a goofy allegorical hint of the barely surviving idea that a different order of being may exist, an elsewhere that is beyond the power and determination of the current social, political, and semiotic systems. In our current situation it can only help to add a little laughter and stimulation to our desperate attempts at "dreaming forward."

Commercial cinema so far has not done very much with the available cultural text of the punk phenomenon. Other than a few films which zeroed in on its daily rituals, commercial cinema was far more inclined to appropriate the detached signs of punk, emptying its signifiers for use in a purely decorative manner and thereby succeeding only in adding to the ever-broadening options among postmodern "production styles." *Repoman* is worth remembering for the degree to which it did not do this.

But the question eventually arises as to whether the punk sensibility and its peculiar anti-aesthetics provided any kind of viable social alternative, as a life-style or adversarial mode of being, or whether at best it provided a means of existential survival, a manner of tolerating the crass environment of postmodern decay. The answer would seem to be both. Punks did propose a new way of inhabiting the postmodern body, and they did create different exercises in contemporary *masquerade* and *carnival*. They even proved again that it was possible to look mean and vicious and yet be rather kind and polite (certain skinhead groups excepted). If the transition to a post-apocalypse culture has already occurred without notice in a gradual erosion of the social, psychological, and physical landscapes—the "slow drive to delirium"[35]—perhaps we should not be so quick to criticize those living and fighting on the front lines who seem to have created only mere "survival" strategies. Punks have also been one of those peculiar species who have managed to outlive their "public death." As Donna Haraway has said of other marginalized and socially discomforting groups (single working mothers and displaced third world primitives in recently industrialized nations, etc.), punks are among those people already written off who yet "refuse to disappear on cue"[36] even after their day in the media sun has long since set. The fact that the signs of this movement have endured for nearly two decades—longer even than those of the much larger movements of the 60s adversarial culture—can indicate either that its social and aesthetic message is still relevant, perhaps still being absorbed, just as much as this undoubtedly indicates that its signs of difference were tremendously marketable for popular culture. The fact that its images were readily recuperable into the mainstream marketplace, and therefore were ever-more widely distributed, can just as well be taken as a mark of its success in capturing the public imagination, in interpellating a popular audience. Is it not preferable to have succeeded in disseminating even a diluted message of resistance and *difference* to the greater masses than none at all? Perhaps. Or did punk only sing the last raucous chorus of the swan song of the twentieth century avant-garde impulse? In any case it is becoming more apparent all the time that "in the realm of popular culture, the example of punk music . . . has come to stand as a celebrated test case of the problematic of cultural politics."[37] *Repoman* then also becomes a test case for introducing elements of the punk sensibility and its public message into the least-politicized but potentially most powerful form of popular media, the commercial cinema.

The punk sensibility shares another affinity with Haraway's unique social criticism, her notion of a new oppositional human/cyborg politics that recognizes our unavoidable connection with machines as well as with nature in the necessary struggle against the all-too-perfect, controlled and controlling communicational systems of *phallogocentrism*. Not too differently from what the punk movement had always seemed to understand, her cyborg politics "insist on noise and advocate pollution"[38] of those too "beautiful" and would-be perfect organizational systems. And like her proposed mutant cyborg bodies, punk was not afraid to embrace the face of the "monstrous"—celebrating instead what the mainstream fled, trying to interject the face of the unacceptable Other into the normalcy required by the sterile business-as-usual culture of late capitalism. Punk then also can stand ironically as a referent of partial hope and affirmation for postmodern meta-theories, like Baudrillard's, which contend that all ". . . closed, or meta-stable, or functional, or cybernetic systems" are "eventually waylaid by laughter, instantaneous subversion (and not by a long dialectical labor), because all the inertia of these systems works against them. . . ."[39] In the beginning, at least, this was the unconscious, implicit hope of the punk movement: resistance by destabilization of conventional aesthetics and sign systems.

Yet how could an intendedly subversive avant-garde movement know that its own attempts to expose, scandalize or deconstruct some existing social practice or institution ever foresee how and in what way it would already have inscribed in its gestures a blueprint for its commodification and subsequent semiotic recuperation for a safe, rather than a disturbing or disrupting, interpellation into the general public culture? If Baudrillard is accurate in claiming that the great "achievement" of western modernity is not the *commodification* of everything, as is often claimed, but rather the *semiotizing* of everything in the world primarily through marketing aesthetics,[40] then we must entertain the notion that avant-gardes who struggle to reclaim difference ultimately only may serve to reinfuse the health of capitalism's semiotic hegemony. What can we say about punk if its ultimate fate has not been to mirror back the urgent emptiness and ugliness of the "no future" wasteland as it instinctively attempted, but rather to help aestheticize and semiotize, and thus partially anaesthetize us to, the unsightly decay and pollution of the carcass of capitalist modernity that everywhere chokes the post-industrial landscape? If its purpose was partially to overturn the naturalizing judgments a previous generation had made in protest against this same visual deterioration of the urban environment a few years before, (i.e. the 60s generation's deification of the natural and the beautiful), then perhaps it succeeded all too well.

Was the punk movement but another unwitting victim of postmodern complicity, ultimately complicit with that very process to which it was opposed? That uncanny capacity of advanced capitalism to be able to co-opt anything and everything, and especially that which reveals its difference most emphatically, is precisely what postmodern theory tries to analyze as the process of *recuperation*. It is often remarked that this ability is the greatest strength of advanced capitalism. Baudrillard's by-now quite familiar theoretical treatment of this situation has tried to explain how: "Everything that gets inserted into the definalized space-time of the code, *or tries to interfere with it* is disconnected from its own finalities, disintegrated and absorbed—this is the well-known effect of recuperation or manipulation: cycling and recycling at each level" (italics mine).[41] Of course it is all too easy to form an impression, after such observations, that the current system is unstoppable, that it will continue to out-determine any attempts made to alter its own indeterminant course. But is this recuperative capacity actual, or only apparent in its recent success as a culture of triumphant promotional simulacra? Baudrillard's own discourse seems increasingly to imply, even as he is taken to task for his purported "nihilism" and "pessimism," that there are still some possible adversarial strategies left, even if they require previously unimaginable positions and new methods of "para-logical" thinking and "paraphysical" strategies. But he immediately qualifies the statement above by pointing to a more intriguing one: "All dissent must be of a higher logical type than that to which it is opposed!"[42]

It may be that in its now reified forms and postures, the punk gesture was co-optable because it failed to rise above the same logic it opposed: even at its "reversible" best, the punk subculture's primary signifiers depended on their recognizable difference from mainstream norms. If there is to be another more potent and biting movement of radical youth, it will have to introduce a presentation or engage in a collective seduction that is beyond the present capacity of the commodifying/semiotizing *code* of late capitalist functionalist aesthetics. The question then raised is whether that is possible while still maintaining an attractive and seductive currency in the domain of the popular? *Repoman* finally may be seen as an interesting postmodern gesture, already dated, ambivalently resting somewhere between celebration and exploitation, while testing the waters of possibility and complicity in the domain of the popular, perhaps the only realm that matters in postmodernity.

Notes

1. Remarks from presentation at University of California, Davis, February 18, 1989, Conference on Critical Theory: "Discourse and Praxis in the Humanities and the Social Sciences."

2. Fredric Jameson's commentary on postmodern intensities has recently brought much attention to such ideas in the anglophone world, although various French thinkers have been discussing this notion for the past few decades.

3. From an interview cited by Lawrence Van Gelder, "At the Movies," *New York Times*, Dec. 4, 1987: C-10.

4. *Canadian Journal of Political and Social Theory*, 12.1-2 (1988). Also relevant is Sharrett's more recent "The Last Stranger: *Querelle* and Cultural Simulation," *Canadian Journal of Political and Social Theory*, 13.1-2 (1989).

5. Laura Kipnis, "Feminism: The Political Conscience of Postmodernism," in *Universal Abandon*, ed. Andrew Ross (Minneapolis: University of Minnesota Press, 1988), 164.

6. By "counter-public" I mean to distinguish a group whose life-style and practices are noticeably different in aims and values from the mainstream public "norms"—and not just a "special interest" group or movement dedicated to specific prerogatives without further opposition to the direction of the general culture.

7. It should be remembered that such strategies do have historical antecedents from at least as far back as *Les Incroyables* in late 18th century Paris.

8. *Slash* also evolved into a record label and managed to deal mostly with local groups who met their own standards of punk purity, although a few of their bands like "X" did become internationally successful in a commercial sense.

9. "Disappearance" as a social and political challenge, particularly on a collective level, has been theorized by both Jean Baudrillard and Paul Virilio.

10. Andrew Ross, "The Rock 'n' Roll Ghost," *October*, 53 (Fall, 1989), 44.

11. Sharrett, 97.

12. Alex Cox, *Repoman, The Screenplay*, ed. Dick Rude (Boston & London: Faber and Faber, 1984), 28. Note: from here on citations from the script will be as printed in this version and will not be specified by page.

13. Sharrett, 97.

14. Sharrett, 81-102.

15. See Frank Burke's remarks: ". . . a strategy which . . . not only asserts the impossibility of representation in a post-essentialist context but also frees the spectator from presentation, hence from the domination of the text, in "Aesthetics and Postmodern Cinema," *Canadian Journal of Political and Social Theory*, 12.1-2 (1988).

16. Pauline Kael "The Woman Question," *The New Yorker*, Aug. 6, 1984: 73-74.

17. Sharrett, 97.

18. Baudrillard, *Fatal Strategies* (New York: Semiotext(e), 1990), 123.

19. Kael, 73-74.

20. Sharrett, 81.

21. Sharrett, 81.

22. In this sense punk furthers the aesthetic statement first made (in this era, perhaps) by Andy Warhol's "Campbell's Soup Can" art which, according to Baudrillard, began to collapse not only the traditional distinctions between the beautiful and the ugly, but the real and the unreal, the transcendent and the immanent, etc.

23. See Baudrillard, *The Ecstasy of Communication* (New York: Semiotext(e),), 11-27.

24. See Gilles Deleuze and Felix Guattari, *Anti-Oedipus: Capitalism and Schizophrenia*, Vol. I, Preface by Michel Foucault. Trans. Robert Hurley, Mark Seem, and Helen R. Lane (New York, Viking, 1977).

25. This well-worn political term has recently been picked up again by grass roots activists on the left during the 1980s to describe what they feel was the diversionary role of Reagan Administration's "War on Drugs."

26. Sharrett, 98.

27. Sharrett, 100.

28. See Alain Touraine, *The Return of the Actor*, trans. Myrna Godzich (Minneapolis: University of Minnesota Press, 1988).

29. Christopher Sharrett, "The Last Stranger: *Querelle* and Cultural Simulation," *Canadian Journal of Political and Social Theory*, 13.1-2 (1989).

30. Sharrett, "The Last Stranger," 119.

31. Sharrett, "The Last Stranger," 100.

32. Sharrett, "The Last Stranger," 80.

33. Mark C. Taylor, "Descartes, Nietzsche and the Search for the Unsayable," *The New York Times Book Review*, Mar. 10, 1988.

34. From Donna Haraway's 1989 lecture—see footnote (2) above.

35. A paraphrase of Baudrillard utilized to describe the postmodern spiral into the universe of simulation by William Chalowpka, University of Montana, Political Science Department at "The Disappearance of Art and Politics," Conference Missoula, Montana, 1989.

36. Donna Haraway, "A Manifesto for Cyborgs: Science, Technology, and Socialist Feminism in the 1980s" in *Feminism/Postmodernism*, ed. Linda J. Nicholson (New York and London: Routledge, 1990), 219.

37. Ross, "The Rock 'n' Roll Ghost," 109.

38. Haraway, 218.

39. Baudrillard, "Symbolic Exchange and Death," *Selected Writings*, ed. Mark Poster (Stanford: Stanford University Press,), 123.

40. Baudrillard, Public lecture delivered at conference "Modern Communication and the Disappearance of Art and Politics."

41. Baudrillard, "Symbolic Exchange and Death," in *Selected Writings*, p. 122.

42. Baudrillard, 122; actually a citation from Anthony Wilden, *System and Structure: Essays in Communication and Exchange* (London: Tavistock, 1977), xxvii.

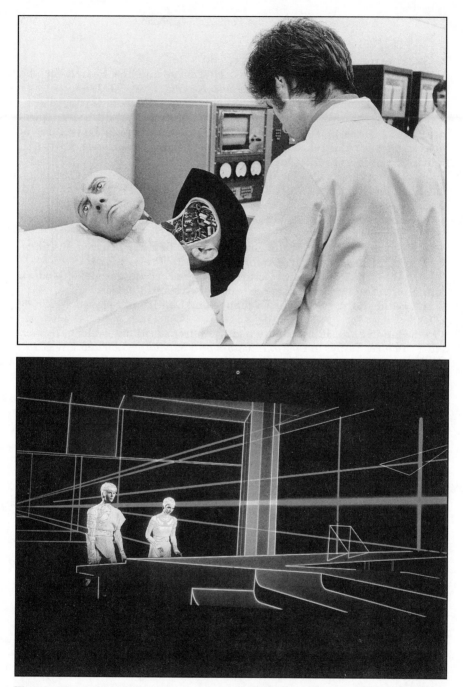

The simulacra enters into cinematic fantasy (*above*): *Westworld* (1973). MGM. (*Below*) the cybersubjectivities of virtual reality: *TRON* (1982). Disney. Stills courtesy of Jerry Ohlinger's Movie Materials.

Scott Bukatman

cybersubjectivity & cinematic being

In their imaginations they saw the cinema as a total and complete
representation of reality; they saw in a trice the reconstruction
of a perfect illusion of the outside world in sound, color and relief.
—André Bazin, 1946

But in the computer country, they dream of eliminating the
interface, of breaking down the barrier of the screen and
eliminating the distinctions made between this side and that side.
—Karrie Jacobs, 1990

By now the image is becoming familiar—but not quite. A figure stands
in a kind of high-tech bondage. Wires and cables snake from gloves and
sensors to a pair of hard-crunching computers off to one side. The head
is enshrouded by an elaborate apparatus that blocks the subject's eyes
and ears. The figure stands in an uneasy crouch, reaching out to grasp
the invisible air. This is not, however, some sensory deprivation
nightmare. The subject is comfortably ensconced in *virtual reality*, a
cybernetic paraspace comprised of real-time interactive data. The cables
are connected to sensors, providing a computer with information
regarding the subject's bodily orientation. The helmet apparatus feeds
visual and auditory information about the virtual environment. Dual
mini-monitors permit a simulated parallax, and 360° sound creates a
totalizing ambience. The subject can hear a sound behind her, turn to
see its source, walk towards it, and even (with the aid of a Dataglove)
pick it up, while to the outside observer, of course, there is nothing there.
Virtual reality significantly extends the sensory address of existent media
to provide an alternate and manipulable space. Multiple users can enter
the same virtual reality, and play virtual catch, or otherwise interact
on this virtual plane. They can appear to each other in different forms,
or as different species or genders—a simulated, but powerful, poly-
morphism is at work here. To be installed into such an apparatus would
be to exist on two planes simultaneously; while one's objective body

would remain in the real world, one's *phenomenal body* would be projected into the terminal reality. In an ecstatic exaggeration of Merleau-Ponty's phenomenological model, world and body comprise a continually modifying feedback loop, producing a terminal identity without the terminal—a *cybersubject*.

Virtual reality technologies have attracted much attention at the beginning of the 1990s, and it is evident that the age of simulation, endlessly explored by cultural theorists, is far from over. At this point, the discourse surrounding the immersive interface of virtual reality far outstrips the achievement. The VR apparatus is still bulky and inconvenient—far from the desired ideal of a transparent interface technology. At the same time, the computational requirements are so intense as to put the experience out of reach for all but the wealthiest clients—entertainment companies or the military, for example (and this essay can simply point to the *realpolitik* questions of *who* is building *what* kind of realities for *whom*). There is every reason to believe, however, that the technology will improve to the point of widespread feasibility and affordability within a decade. Yet, even now, the mere existence of *virtual reality* makes possible a full interrogation of some issues crucial to human and social existence. Using *cyberspace* as a common synonym for the simulated spaces of virtual reality,[1] journalist Howard Rheingold in "What's the Big Deal About Cyberspace" has written that "cyberspace feels like one of those developments that come along unexpectedly and radically alter everyone's outlook forever after" (450). Such ontological and epistemological structures as the nature of the human, the real, experience, sensation, cognition, identity and gender are all placed, if not under erasure, then certainly in question around the (still largely) discursive object of virtual reality and the postulated existence of perfect, simulated, environments. Virtual reality has become the very embodiment of postmodern *disembodiement*.

The polymorphous possibilities of virtual reality have produced a range of responses, from the merely prurient to the unabashedly utopian. Most journalistic accounts of VR, and even many of the comparatively conservative pronouncements by affiliated scientists and technicians, stress the fundamental newness of the experience, and yet its precursors are clear, from videogames to graphical computer interfaces (GUI's) to, of course, the cinema. In fact, one is frequently reminded, in studying the VR sensation, of the meditations of André Bazin upon "the myth of total cinema." The prehistory of cinema was dominated by a desire for "a total and complete representation of reality," he wrote. The inventors of the medium, those other scientists and technicians, "saw in a trice the reconstruction of a perfect illusion of the outside world in sound, color and relief" (Bazin, 20). By such standards, the silent cinema, the monochromatic cinema and the flat cinema represent a set of compromises with what the medium ought to be. "In short," Bazin proclaims, from within this perspective "cinema has not yet been invented" (21).

Virtual reality represents an attempt to eliminate the interface between user and information—"transforming data into environment," as Karrie Jacobs puts it (69). The interaction with information takes on a "direct" sensory quality which appears to eliminate the interface entirely. Thus, the intensified spatial experience of virtual reality, with its simulated immersion into an interactive and nonnarrative alternate space (with a promise of simulated touch and odor to follow) can easily be assimilated to the same dream that Bazin isolated in 1946, the dream of a total cinema.

There are a range of experiences—in literature, cinema, games and even theme parks—that permit the intricate activity of interface that is increasingly essential in the new order of things. However, a distinction needs to be made among these interfaces with the electronic world that are produced through different media. We must distinguish between an interface that incorporates some form of direct sensory engagement (games and theme parks, for example), and an interface that operates through an action of narrativization (literature). These represent two distinct modes of subject address, although—and this is essential—they often occur in tandem. The cinema itself combines them, incorporating its intensified phenomenal experience of vision with the guidance, *telos* and closure of narrative. Computer games almost inevitably combine narrative progression with "virtual" sensory pleasures. Repeatedly, the operations of narrative constrain the effects of a new mode of sensory address, and so the fascination with the rise of virtual reality systems might represent a possible passage beyond narrative into a new range of spatial metaphors. The richer the sensory interface, the more reduced is the function of narrative. In this context, *TRON*, a film released by the Disney studios in 1982 (before the advent of cyberpunk science fiction), becomes a fascinating cyborg object, poised as it is between the demands of narrative experience and the "pure" spatiality generated by virtual reality systems (this will be explored below).

1. envisioning terminal space

To engage with terminal culture means to somehow encompass it, but the methods for doing so are not entirely apparent. In her book on electronic media and postmodern culture, Margot Lovejoy constructs a crisis of knowledge which is precisely a crisis of *vision*:

> As yet, though we live in a culture in which images are the dominant currency of communication, we have been unable to form an adequate picture of the future. Despite the new electronic power to create instant image flow, the ability to see the more diffuse Postmodern connections . . . has become more difficult. . . . It is harder to visualize a multinational identity than a local entity. We can only see the world by forming a picture through various specialized mediations. . . . We now lack a convincing vision. (247-248)

To narrate electronic culture thus depends upon our ability to visualize it. The lack of a vision adequate to the datasphere has led to a set of allusive attempts to reconstitute the space of the computer in human—biological or physical—terms; in other words, *to permit terminal space to become phenomenal.*

In one attempt to *envision* the space of the computer, the Museum of Modern Art hosted "Information Art: Diagramming Microchips." Sponsored by INTEL, the show displayed enlargements of computer-produced diagrams reminiscent of urban sprawl (this resemblance is no coincidence—chip and city are designed for ease of circulation and a maximization of available space). It was unsettling to see well-heeled patrons of the arts scrutinizing these complex surfaces, as though the chip, now susceptible to vision, was somehow also susceptible to knowledge. "Despite their ubiquity," the catalog read, "there is an element of mystery to integrated ciruits. They are mysterious because they are sensorially inaccessible to us" (McCarty, 6). But the enlargement and aestheticization of the chip does not render them any *more* accessible. The exhibition thus became a celebration of the manifest inertia and inscrutability of the microchip, rather than a rationalist revelation of its function.

Computer modelling is another exemplary envisioning of terminal space. In the sciences, engineering and design, what Timothy Binkley calls "the virtual camera" becomes a means of representing the "spaces" of abstract numbers and equations in forms similar to the tangible and perceptible objects of everyday life. "The virtual camera is an imaginary object ensconced in the abstract space of a hyperreal world whose features are described numerically using mathematical tools." The virtual camera transforms abstract numerical space into a *coordinate* space within which the "models" can be represented and manipulated. Visible objects in this hyper/cyber/reality are nothing more than the result of *computational geometry* (Binkley, 20).[2]

Of all the representations of electronic space, none has the ubiquity of the Mandelbrot set. This fantastic informational "object" of infinite complexities is the result of a relatively simple algorithm, iterated numerous times. Shapes spiral about one another, forms repeat at every level, and new Mandelbrot sets are discovered lurking in almost every region, each one surrounded by its own halo of infinite detail. This object has become the icon of fractal geometry and chaos sciences. The Mandelbrot set, as the archetype of both this chaotic orderliness and the modeling power of the computer, has taken on an almost mystical significance—a cybernetic mandala, if you will.

This mysticism becomes evident in a "scientific" video presentation of computer-generated fractal images (strongly associated with chaos studies) called *Nothing but Zooms*. Through its New Age music and program notes ("A whole new world awaits you and personal change you might not have expected is yours for the taking"), the terrors of the randomness of chaos are transcended. The videotape becomes a visual rite of passage, a means of centering the self. By its very mechanics, the zoom provides an optical center regardless of the objects photographed, but these sequences repeatedly end on a newly located (and fully immanent) center: another Mandelbrot set, for example. Circularity and symmetry thus become fundaments of the visual exploration, and the "chaos" of a disorderly, decentered, electronically-constituted reality is recontained within a framework of narrative telos, spiritual probing and the physiology of perception. *Nothing but Zooms* serves to anchor the terrors of chaos in its reassuring activity of visualization.[3]

2. fun in cyberspace

The Data Glove is only one of the virtual environment tools offered up by the technology of the computer. Most prevalent are the games which line the shelves of every computer store. When Case jacks in to cyberspace in *Neuromancer*, he enters a realm which "has its roots in primitive arcade games" (Gibson, 51). In Steven Levy's history of the minicomputer, *Hackers*, games are very significant. "Games were the programs which took greatest advantage of the machine's power—put the user in control of the machine—made him the god of the bits and bytes inside the box." After buying a new game, a kid could "go home for what was the essential interface with the Apple [Computer]. Playing games" (Levy, 304). Levy's glibness does not hide the validity of his observation. Games are far more than an idle recreation for many "users"; they in fact represent the most complete symbiosis generally available between human and computer—a fusion of spaces, goals, options and perspectives. "To see tomorrow's computer systems, go to the video game parlors!" the acclaimed systems designer Ted Nelson declares (Nelson, 235). Games literally test the user, and in more than just eye-hand coordination.

The first computer game, developed by hackers in 1962 was *Spacewar*, a simulation that presented flat outlines of starships doing battle by spitting little pixels at each other while vying for position around a gravitationally powerful "sun." The next was *Adventure*, a text game which described surroundings and action. The adventurer could, by typing simple instructions ("GO NORTH"), move in different directions, examine a range of objects, learn secret words, and interact with other characters. In *Virtual Reality*, Howard Rheingold correctly observes that "*Adventure* is a virtual world in a conceptual way," rather than a sensory one (Rheingold, 23). Both games remain paradigmatic of computer gaming, and the most intriguing games have combined the kinesis of *Spacewar* with the interactive narrative format of *Adventure*. Games become metaphors for hacking itself—the process of experimenting with computer structures in a non-formal and often intuitive manner.

There was, and is, a ludic quality encouraged by hacking away in the minicomputer universe, since the computer provides a realm in which many things are possible, and with minimal risk. Seymour Papert's research on computers and education stresses the computer environment as a closed, formal system, separate from the everyday world. This is uncannily close to Johan Huizinga's definition of *play* from his philosophical treatise *Homo Ludens*: "a free activity standing quite consciously outside 'ordinary' life as being 'not serious,' but at the same time absorbing the player intensely and utterly. . . . It proceeds within its own proper boundaries of time and space according to fixed rules and in an orderly manner" (Huizinga, 32). The recent *Cosmic Osmo* by Miller and Miller provides an interactive, animated environment where children (and adults) can wander, Alice-like, through an unfamiliar solar system, playing games, communicating with characters, recording their own music (and playing it back); all without endangering anyone (including the computer system). The game fosters experimentation with the virtual objects in its worlds, while the forking paths of the non-linear experience replace the traditional syntagmatic structure of the story. Although restricted to the space of the screen, "games" such as *Cosmic Osmo* point towards the more enveloping alternate worlds of virtual reality systems. Jaron Lanier's VPL Research developed an early virtual world derived from the Mad Hatter's tea party. A user can follow the instructions to "Eat me" or "Drink me" and experience the same abrupt scalar disruptions once known to Alice alone.

Games present a range of options for the player that center upon different types of interface—input/output devices, real-time, spatial simulation—and consequently offer a range of subject positions. With each new advance, the imbrication becomes more total; the symbiosis more pronounced. In short, games provide a metaphorical interface with the electronic realm of the computer in and of themselves. Through the translation of percept into movement, the players' thoughts—to paraphrase Merleau-Ponty—are given their place in the world. Through play, a kinetic interaction is established between subject and object: the *perceiving* body becomes a *phenomenal* body.

3. narrating terminal space

While one might anticipate a wave of virtual reality fiction, in which a host of anachronistic fantasies are played out within virtual worlds (as on the holodeck in *Star Trek: The Next Generation*), so far there been only a slow trickle. Perhaps one explanation lies in the fact that narrative *already* functions as an immersion within a simulated existence. Reality, as writers such as Jean Baudrillard and J. G. Ballard continually argue, is becoming fiction, and "the writer's task is to invent the reality." As Ballard reminds us, foreshadowing the emergence of virtual reality technology: "We live inside an enormous novel" (5).

The crisis of vision in electronic culture leads to a further understanding of the narrative and discursive strategies of science fiction. John Clute has written that the crisis of vision in the Information Age in fact underlies science fiction itself:

> No longer has information any tangible, kinetic analogue in the world of the senses, or in the imaginations of writers of fiction. Gone are the great arrays of vacuum tubes, the thousands of toggles that heroes of space fiction would flick *almost* faster than the eye could see as they dodged space 'torpedoes,' outflanked alien 'battle lines,' steered through asteroid 'storms'; gone, more importantly, is any sustained sense of the autonomy, in space and time, of gross visible individual human actions. And if 'actions' are now invisible, then our fates are likewise beyond our grasp. We no longer feel that we penetrate the future; futures penetrate us. (Clute, viii)

Theorists of the genre note the privileged phenomenological status of science fiction:[4] in otherwise diverse works it is the experiences of space and perception that enable a tentative definition of being for both protagonist and reader/spectator. Samuel Delany and Teresa de Lauretis argue that the process of reading or experiencing a work of science fiction already constitutes a process of dislocation which resists a totalization of meaning, and this is redoubled in the thematic concern with spatial orientation and exploration. A new phenomeno-logic is required by the "qualitatively new techno-logic" (Sobchack 1988) which we now inhabit, and science fiction has become a crucial cognitive tool. In many works science fiction produces a range of *narratives*, those explicatory semiotic mechanisms, about *simulation*, that phenomenon of the post-referential era. There is an ongoing attempt to explore and map the new terminal spaces, to establish an electronic cartography within the paradigms of the simulated and the spectacular. It is interesting to note two narratives that predate the technologies of virtual reality, but which anticipate its tropes. A film with some relevance to the relationship between cinematic narrative and virtual reality is Michael Crichton's *Westworld* (1973). The central, memorable, concept concerns a fabulous theme park where visitors can interact with lifelike simulacra. In *Westworld* you can pick a gunfight with Yul Brynner, while jousting and other debaucheries are available over in Medievalworld or Romanworld (only *Westworld* is at all convincing—probably because of the familiarity of the Western cinematic tradition and its backlot sets).

Westworld's central notion of an electronically simulated, interactive environment anticipates the advent of virtual reality systems but without the aesthetic or political contexts of cyberpunk SF, *Westworld* lacks an effective language. Where it should revel in the hyperreal, the film unfortunately settles for the banality of an overlit, television-drama aesthetic (only Brynner's performance produces the essential feeling of immersion in a hypercinematic fantasy).[5] The plot, predictably enough, involves a failure of the "foolproof" technology, as the renegade robots slaughter the hapless guests. A similar dystopian vision marks Ray Bradbury's "The Veldt," in which a nursery offers a range of simulated environments to amuse the children. The children trap their parents in a "simulated" African veldt, and leave them to be devoured by the all-too-real "simulated" lions. In these cautionary science fictions of the spectacle, the subject is actually devoured by the "reality" of simulations technologies.

One touchstone for scientific research as well as philosophical reflection on this technologically disembodied reality has been the writing of the cyberpunk movement in '80s SF. A street level science fiction that foregrounded a perverse and convincing urbanism, cyberpunk was concerned with the intimacy of the contemporary interfaces that exist between human subject and electronic technology. From William Gibson's *Neuromancer* (1984) and Bruce Sterling's Shaper/Mechanist fictions to the Max Headroom phenomenon and the replicants of *Blade Runner* (1982), the post-alienation discourse of cyberpunk produced a range of techno-Surrealist mappings of technology onto the form of the human. Organism and machine dissolved their boundaries in an ecstatic act of cybernetic-neurological fusion and redefinition. The dramatically decentered spaces of cyberpunk fictions were not the expansive realms of far-flung empires or enormous starships, but rather the invisible spaces of electronic circulation or microscopic nanotechnologies.

The implosive SF of Gibson's *Neuromancer* yielded a stunning representation of the invisible arenas of electronic activity. The themes and language of *Neuromancer* were uncannily anticipated by Fredric Jameson's essay on postmodernism, and the novel presented a remarkable consolidation of the themes and issues of terminal culture. In this saga of battles fought within a spatialized world of data— *cyberspace*—Gibson coalesced an eclectic range of generic protocols, contemporary idiolects, and a pervasive technological eroticism combined with a future-shocking ambivalence. *Neuromancer* is set in the 21st century, when the world is dominated by the high-tech *zaibatsus* (multi-national corporations) of Japan, Germany and Switzerland. Fortunes are to be made in the illegal retrieval and sale of data, and Case (a closed object, a container, a hard case) works on the black market. Data is a protected commodity, and cybernetic security systems can only be circumvented by people like Case, a cyberspace cowboy neurologically *jacked into* the world of the computer. Armed with the proper ICE (intrusive counter-electronics), Case can negotiate his way through the most elaborate systems. But Case blew a job and his employers damaged his nervous system for revenge: he can no longer jack in. "For Case, who'd lived for the bodiless exultation of cyberspace, it was the Fall."

Cyberspace is a powerful imaging of the data spaces of electronic culture. "We can only see the world by forming a picture through various specialized mediations," writes Lovejoy, in a phrase which recalls Gibson's definition of cyberspace as a *consensual hallucination*—a software mediation—whose function is precisely to provide that vision of, and entry into, the invisible—but actual—world within the computer. That "consensual hallucination" is the designated space where access is permitted to the invisible power structures and data linkages of the Information Era.

4. the phenomenology of cyberspace

A phenomenology of science fiction locates a signficant attempt to redefine the imperceptible (and therefore absent to consciousness) realms of the electronic era in terms of the physically and perceptually familiar. The motive is to render the electronic fields present to consciousness—to turn them into phenomena—and therefore susceptible to human intentionality. Husserl's phenomenological reduction shifted the philosopher's attention *toward* the cognitive processes of consciousness and *away from* the veracity of any given external conditions.[6] This has evident benefits for a phenomenology of such an abstract, fictional, and non-physical space as that being defined here.

Cyberspace is an abstraction which, diegetically and extra-diegetically, provides a narrative compensation for the loss of visibility in the world, the movement of power into the cybernetic matrices of the global computer banks, and the corresponding divestiture of power from the subject. In the very real context of cybernetic disembodiment, in which the human is barred from perceiving or manipulating a terminal reality measured in nanoseconds of time and imploded infinities of space, the need to reconstitute the subject's phenomenal being is overwhelming. The passage of the diegesis from physical space into the pixels and bytes of an "invisible" terminal space addresses the massive redeployment of power within telematic culture. This occurs first of all through a revelatory act of envisioning that space: a movement which both decenters and recenters the subject in a ways that recall the work of Merleau-Ponty, who wrote: "Vision alone makes us learn that beings that are different, 'exterior,' foreign to one another, are yet absolutely together, are 'simultaneity'" (Merleau-Ponty 1964, 187). The otherness of cyberspace abides as an ultimately *defining* metaphor, an attempt to recognize and overcome the technological estrangements of the electronic age, and a preliminary attempt to resituate the human as its constitutive force.

5. cinematic cyberspaces

Science fiction cinema had already demonstrated an awareness of the computer as the new space of dramatic interaction, without quite understanding how to cope with that dramaturgical displacement. Display screens and digital graphics dominate the mise-en-scène in *Alien*, *2001* and *Blade Runner*. In films as different as *Scanners*, *Wargames*, *Brainstorm* and *TRON*, climactic scenes feature a character involved in a frantic quest for information or control through the computer terminal. That the hurried and hushed pecking of fingers on keyboards lacks the visual interest of car chases and special effects pyrotechnics is evident. Jameson's comments regarding the representation of these instruments of reproduction are interesting:

> they make very different demands on our capacity for aesthetic representation than did the relatively mimetic idolatry of the older machinery of the futurist movement. . . . Here we have less to do with kinetic energy than with all kinds of new reproductive processes; and in the weaker productions of postmodernism the aesthetic embodiment of such processes often tends to slip back more comfortably into a mere thematic representation of content. (Jameson, 79)

What Jameson misses here is the significance of the transformation of these reproductive environments of data storage, circulation and retrieval into dramatic and kinetic environments of cybernetic accommodation. "Weaker productions" these might be, but in their insistence upon envisioning these spaces of reproduction, they are clearly significant, and function as something more than "mere thematic representations of content." Dramatically and philosophically, however, tense heroes tapping keys is an ineffective engagement with a new and ontologically significant set of electronic technologies. The spectator's identification with a powerful surrogate, an identification which flows across the boundary of the cinematic screen, finds itself blocked by yet *another* screen. Behind the terminal lurks the real power, the real activity, the drama of present reality. The screen-surrogate (character and/or camera) must therefore, somehow, cross that screen to engage more directly with Dataist existence. In David Cronenberg's *Scanners*, the camera tracks across a circuit-board as a telepath instigates a spectacular computer melt-down. In *Brainstorm*, tense terminal intercutting yields to an out-of-body cybernetic experience. These are primitive prefigurations of the cyberspaces which permit a reintroduction of the dramatic motility which had disappeared into the invisibility of electronic space. To return to Jameson's terms, the essence of the drama is the investment of all kinds of "new reproductive processes" with the "kinetic energy" of a prior technological moment.

6. TRON

Neuromancer resembles *Blade Runner* in its bleak, impacted urbanism (as well as in the density of its informational system), but it is *TRON* (Lisberger, 1982) that represents the most sustained cinematic attempt at mapping cyberspace. The Disney ethos of *TRON* seems so at odds with the dominant attitudes of the cyberpunk subgenre that it remains largely unassimilated, even unremarked, in accounts of cyberpunk fiction. The film exists in a kind of cybernetic vacuum, yet remains a deeply consequential gesture towards accepting and cognizing the existence of cyberspace, and towards endowing its existence with phenomenological significance.

As in *Neuromancer*, the narrative involves a penetration of the terminal frontier—the barrier of the screen is broken down as Flynn, the hacker protagonist, finds himself translated into the virtual space that exists inside the banks of computers. There he must do battle with the evil Master Control Program (a kind of cybernetic Ming the Merciless) in order to liberate the billions of bytes of dominated data. *TRON* was unanimously criticized for the juvenalia of its videogame-level script, the banality of its characters and the coldness of its conception. However, if its narrative is often incoherent or inadequate, and its characters lack "substance," then these failures can perhaps be regarded as indicative of the film's struggle to define a new space; its failures then become symptomatic of the very ambiguities and uncertainties which cyberspace represents. The film wavers between narrational and spectatorial dominants, creating a provocative aesthetic counter-tension. The film also oscillates between the familiar, character-centered structures of "classical" Hollywood cinema and a non-subjective terminal identity generated by the hyperbolic trajectories of its computer-simulated camera positions. *TRON* represents the point of interface between a cinematically-constituted experience of Being and the cybersubjectivities of virtual reality.

TRON was the first commercial film to rely on entirely computer-generated images and sequences. Although much of the film is only computer-*enhanced*, sixteen minutes of footage represented the state of the art of computer animation techniques (circa 1982).[7] Computer-generated effects, such as those found in *TRON* or *The Last Starfighter*, are characteristically too perfect to be accepted as facsimiles of the real world—the surfaces are smooth and undetailed, reflections perfectly focussed, movements unswerving and non-inertial. The perfect coordinate space of the terminal field allows a precision of perspective that eludes the ordinary eye. As Sobchack has written, "electronic space constructs objective and superficial equivalents to depth, texture and invested bodily movement" (Sobchack 1988, 13). The new "depthlessness" that Jameson proclaimed as characteristic of postmodernism (Jameson, 60) receives its surest—but least critical—figuration in these translations, abstractions and reductions of the real world. The body, with its analogic imperfections, is exempted from this digital world—*contra TRON*'s narrative strategies, this is precisely a disembodied space.

A phenomenology of the cinema demands the recognition of the linking of cinematic vision to emergent technologies. Spectatorial identification often functions in terms of the *projection* of a purposive human consciousness, and the *introjection* of a technologized space which the camera mediates and assimilates to the terms of human vision. The incorporation of computer-generated graphics into the cinematic field in films like *TRON* or *The Last Starfighter* poses no unique analytical difficulty, since the cinema has traditionally been interlaced with new technologies of vision and motility, and thus with extensions of consciousness and subjective empowerment. The cinema *already* constructs a space of accommodation to unfamiliar technologies. As Walter Benjamin wrote, the film corresponds "to profound changes in apperception" (Benjamin, 240). But the specific mode of vision constructed through computer graphics both weakens and extends the perceived power of the subject in a unique fashion.

Cognizing Power in the cybernetic landscape: David Warner in *TRON* (1982). Disney. Still courtesy of Jerry Ohlinger's Movie Materials.

7. cyberkinesis

The disengagement from the physical body of the referent further extends to a new mobility. The simulated objects of this virtual world are presented through a camera movement which is itself simulated. The "virtual" camera in these digital sequences exists apart from the narrative. Here there are no literal point of view structures, no inscription of subjectivity. Merleau-Ponty has, of course, written about the significance of subject motion:

> the normal subject penetrates into the object by perception, assimilating its structure into his substance, and through this body the object directly regulates his movements. This subject-object dialogue, this drawing together, by the subject, of the meaning diffused through the object, and, by the object, of the subject's intentions—a process which is physiognomic perception—arranges round the subject a world which speaks to him of himself, and gives his own thoughts their place in the world. (Merleau-Ponty 1962, 132)

The relevance of this passage to *TRON* and *Neuromancer* is extensive. The subject penetrates the object via an act of perception which reciprocally endows the subject with a bodily presence.[8] Intentions and meaning are translated into activity within a world defined through that very subject-object interface. Cyberspace is an analogic environment that permits the subject to "assimilate its structure into his substance." In so doing, the subject experiences "a world which speaks to him of himself." Further, "his own thoughts" are granted "their place in the world."

Merleau-Ponty writes that "for us to be able to conceive space, it is in the first place necessary that we should have been thrust into it by our body" (Merleau-Ponty 1962, 142). Gibson writes: "Headlong motion through walls of emerald green, milky jade, the sensation of speed beyond anything he'd known before cyberspace" (Gibson, 256). The spatiality of *TRON* or *Neuromancer* exists to permit bodily mobility and, hence, subject definition. The human becomes the dramatic center, the active agent in a spatiotemporal reality from which he—and it is always "he"—has been rigorously excluded.

The computer-controlled camera brought a precision of movement previously undreamt of in cinematic history, enabling the swooping maneuvers amid the canyons of the Death Star in *Star Wars*, but the precision of the computer-generated image, which includes a simulation of camera movement, inscribes an even finer control. From an encompassing angle far above the games arena, the "virtual camera" moves smoothly down into the path of an oncoming light cycle and eases beneath it, rotating and fast-tracking to follow the cycle towards its destination. This is not a trajectory associated with the physical limitations of a human perspective, and instead represents an ecstatic terminal vision—a transcendence of bodily limitations.

In these sequences, the camera serves to give the viewer a *place* in virtual reality, a place defined almost solely in terms of spatial penetration and kinetic achievement. If Merleau-Ponty is right, and the ability to conceive space depends upon our being "thrust into it by our body," then *TRON's* cinematic movement constructs an effective space of accommodation. More directly than even *Neuromancer's* breathless prose, *TRON* propels its viewers into a once-inconceivable space. The viewer experiences a motile power without analogue in the physical world, but it is rarely inscribed as explicitly subjective. Camera movement is partly tied to vehicular movement, although often in elaborate counterpoint, but is also somewhat autonomous, swinging from high angles to low in a giddy display of its own computerized power. As explicitly as in the early history of film, the viewer identifies with a hyper-omniscient camera, which is now associated with the virtual realities of postmodern technology.

In his psychoanalytic phenomenology of the cinema, Christian Metz has argued that cinematic identification occurs around the filmic apparatus itself—specifically, with the camera. This identification is frequently disguised by the operations of narrative and the spectator's concomitant secondary involvement with his or her screen surrogate, but in many films the power of the camera is nevertheless displayed, however fleetingly. *TRON's* cyber-kinesis, radically distinct from human bodily movement, hyperbolizes the identification with the camera— although, in this case, the "camera" is really a fiction—it's a virtual camera, moving about in a virtual world. The space is the fiction.

8. life in cyberspace

TRON opens with a complex trajectory among phenomenal spatial levels before settling into a sustained presentation of life in cyberspace. The film intercuts with increasing speed among three spaces: Flynn in the so-called real world, Flynn's computer-program "analogue" at the high-tech controls of a cybernetic tank, and the computer-generated chase between the tank and pursuing security vehicles. Three levels of action are thus introduced, each with its own distinct phenomenal quality. The first and third levels, representing physical and cybernetic spaces, are familiar tropes in *Neuromancer*, but the middle level, featuring the Flynn-program, offers something else; namely, the Disney stock-in-trade, anthropomorphism. In Disney's cyberspace, actuarial programs are as boring as the insurance salesmen who use them, and debates rage regarding the existence of the "Users"—those mythic beings in another realm.

Through *TRON*'s strategies of anthropomorphism, the problem of configuring the space of electronic culture for human appropriation and assimilation is largely sidestepped by a narrative which avoids any hint of "otherness." Computer programs are human—in fact, computer programs seem to be white, heterosexual and chaste.[9] Electronic space is a fully bodied space, and thus a space of denial. Visually, however, the film almost decimates its own crude anthropocentrism. The film is almost unrelentingly flat, an effect exaggerated by its panavision proportions. Once Flynn has been translated into the memory banks of the computer by the unscupulous Master Control Program, there is no reassuring intercutting to the stability and familiarity of the aforementioned "real world." Sobchack writes that the deflated space of *TRON* "presents this new electronic subjectivity and terminal space as nearly 'absolute,'" noting that "the category of the 'real' (that narrative 'real world' mainframing the computer program world) is short-circuited and loses power" (Sobchack 1987, 257).[10]

TRON (and *Neuromancer*) transform the virtual field of the Cartesian coordinate system of spatial definition into the Newtonian spaces of concrete forces and forms. This is no idle metamorphosis—it serves to reduce cyberspace to the definitions of bodily experience and physical cognition, while grounding it in finite and therefore assimilable terms. Merleau-Ponty had raised objections to the detachment of Cartesian coordinate space by noting that he is inside space, immersed in it; space cannot be reconstructed from an outside position (Merleau-Ponty 1964, 178). Cyberspace, with its aesthetic of immersion and implosion, maintains the mathematical determinism of the coordinate system with its grids, perspectival reductions and geometric disembodiment, but at the same time it superimposes the experiential realities of phenomenal space upon the abstractions of this Cartesian terrain.

9. bodies of data

The virtual space of *TRON* does not so much annihilate as require the *refiguring* of the subject. Rosalind Krauss has analyzed the "radical development" of minimalist sculpture in terms that might be analogous.

On one level, minimalism continued the project initiated by Rodin and Brancusi, who relocated the "point of origin of the body's meaning" from "its inner core to its surface":

> [T]he sculpture of our own time continues this project of decentering. . . . The abstractness of minimalism makes it less easy to recognize the human body in these works and therefore less easy to project ourselves into the space of that sculpture with all of our settled prejudices left intact. Yet our bodies and our experience of our bodies continue to be the subject of this sculpture—even when a work is made of several hundred tons of earth. (Krauss, 279)

While it might seem ludicrous to apply such terms to a Disney film, some comparisons do suggest themselves. Cyberspace is precisely non-corporeal, and so it is precisely non-subjective. If cyberspace is an interiorized space, then it is not the interiority of *psychologized subjectivity*, but rather of a fully *technologized* (cultural) space that overlaps and restates the vocabularies of a postmodern urbanism.[11] In the terms that Krauss offers, the radical aspect of *TRON* might be located in its "relocation of the point of origin of the body's meaning" from a psychological essentialism to the parameters of a techno-cultural configuration. Even when the work is "made of" millions of bytes of information within the banks of a computer's memory, "our bodies and our experience of our bodies continue to be the subject" of that work. The excess of surface apparent in *TRON's* paraspace emphasizes a terminal decentering of human experience and definition. As Jameson wrote, in the days *before Neuromancer*, "this latest mutation in space—postmodern hyperspace—has finally succeeded in transcending the capacities of the individual human body to locate itself, to organize its immediate surroundings perceptually, and cognitively to map its position in a mappable external world" (Jameson 1984, 83). The point of origin of the subject is relocated, away from an *a priori* interiority and towards the modes of a technologically produced cybernetic culture.

The cyberspatial explorations of *TRON* and the cyberpunks can, I think, be posited as legitimate attempts to encode "our bodies and our experience of our bodies," even if the abstractness of their spaces make it "less easy to recognize the human body . . . and therefore less easy to project ourselves into the space." Finally, it should be noted that Krauss's understanding of sculpture, a medium of spatial and temporal physicality, of bodily engagement with a spatiotemporal object, reveals an underlying narrative impulse which then becomes explicit in the more evident narratives of *TRON* and *Neuromancer* (although, in these non-sculptural works, the surrogate experience of narrative still *replaces* direct bodily engagement).

10. narrative containments

Many works of science fiction present narratives about simulation, and here it is clear narrative initiates the dislocation of the human in the terminal non-space, but also becomes the means of inscribing that space as a possible site of human projection.

These two terminal fictions rely on existent narrative paradigms to ground their space in a structural familiarity, but at the same time, neither narrative quite succeeds *as narrative*. First, narrative fails to entirely ground and explain space—a phenomenal excess remains. This excess is exemplified by the paraspatial rhetoric of Gibson's prose, and also by the dizzying simulated motion of *TRON's* virtual camera.[12] Narrative ultimately narrates its own failure and supercession by the overwhelming phenomenological imperatives of terminal space.

The narrative encourages an identification with Flynn in order to enhance the phenomenological effects of its electronic spatiality. Therefore, the narrative itself operates as a further analogy for the viewer's perception of, and imbrication with, a cinematic cyberspace. Perhaps this very redundancy obviates the imperatives of narrative, leaving it a formal structure without conviction. *TRON* thus exists as a cyborg entity; part "organic," part "cybernetic;" partly destabilizing, partly reassuring; an interface between different cinematic functions and varying subjectivities. In its kinesis it provides an elegant example of Merleau-Ponty's "physiognomic perception," that subject-object interface; while its narrative, with its anthropomorphic assimilations, serves the ostensibly similar function of speaking "to him of himself," giving "his own thoughts their place in the world."

At the same time, however, the narrative of *TRON* promises no *need* for accommodation. Rather, within the diegesis cyberspace is posited as coextensive, and indeed *synonymous*, with physical reality—simulation replaces reality but the banality of both realms renders the substitution moot. In *Neuromancer*, a hyper-technologized everyday reality requires all the trickster skills of the cybernetic tactician just to survive: the headlong kinesis of cyberspace is only the literalization of an already-cyberneticized existence, while in *TRON* cyberspace is a theme park which is just as comfortable as the adolescent, Disneyfied "real world." The narrative denies the need for accommodation while the special effects construct an undeniably new and important space into which it thrusts the spectators, propelling them towards a perceptual accommodation with the demands of a terminal reality.

Ultimately, however, *TRON's* narrative *prevents* the total refiguration of cinematic space, and the film never attains the thorough debstabilization of space and spectator that one associates with, for example, *2001*. Michael Snow's non-narrative epic *La Région Centrale* (1971) provides a useful comparison. Here, a remote-controlled camera, situated in the Canadian wilderness, reconstructs both physical landscape and spectatorial perception. As in *TRON*, the camera attains a freedom of movement (about its own axes) "which can mechanically perform more motions than the subtlest of film-makers, holding it by hand," could ever achieve. The world depicted, as P. Adams Sitney notes, is a function of the camera's own technology: "The whole visible scene . . . becomes the inner circumference of a sphere whose center is the other central region: the camera and the space of its self" (Sitney, 383-384). *TRON* also produces a spatial representation that alludes to the hidden or invisible technology through which that space was envisioned. *La Région Centrale*, however, forces the viewer into radical modes of perceptual engagement, and without a reassuring human presence to fix the spatial deformations. Snow's film presents a technological space in which the horizon is thrown out of balance, a decentering and *cinematic* space phenomenally different than human spatiality. *TRON* is not quite so extraordinary.

The significance of *TRON* lies in these fluctuations between the imperatives of spatial exploration and narrative explication. While the special effects produce a cybersubject, the narrative anchors a more traditional subjectivity that appears ever-more anachronistic against the datascapes of terminal reality. Philosopher Don Ihde has noted the contradictory desires to possess technology but to also remain unchanged by it: "Such a desire both secretly rejects what technologies are and overlooks the transformational effects which are necessarily tied to human-technological relations. This illusory desire belongs equally to pro- and anti-technology interpretations of technology" (Ihde, 75).[13] *TRON's* provisional figurations articulate precisely this desire.

11. caveat emptor

The contradiction that Ihde locates has provocative implications. In cyberspace, the duality between mind and body is superceded in a new formation that presents the mind as itself *embodied*. The body, here, exists *only* in phenomenological terms: it perceives and it moves. This might explain the uncanny applicability of Merleau-Ponty's model of subject-construction to the postmodern paradigms of cyberspace: the mind is embodied, yet escapes the materiality of bodies, of flesh. Through the construction of the computer, there arises a mind independent of the biology of bodies, a mind released from mortal "limitations." Unlike the robot forms of modernity, wherein a mechanical body substituted for the organic, the invisible processes of cybernetic information circulation and electronic technology construct a body that is at once material and immaterial—a fundamental oxymoron, perhaps, of postmodernity.[14]

The redefinition of the subject under the conditions of electronic culture responds to the fear that the human has become obsolescent; last year's model. Now the human proudly takes up a position within the machine, but almost always from a position of mastery: by entering the machine, the machine becomes a part of the human. The subject is, and is not, afraid to leave its body behind. The computer can become a new body, with its electronic sensorium extending far beyond human capacities, and yet some residual form of the body is retained in almost every instance.[15] If there is an ambivalence regarding the status of the body, however, no such hesitation marks the attitude towards the mind. Cyberspace is a celebration of spirit, as the disembodied consciousness leaps and dances with unparalleled freedom. It is a realm in which the mind is freed from bodily limitations, a place for the return of *the omnipotence of thoughts.*

In *Totem and Taboo*, Freud cites Frazer's *The Golden Bough* on the subject of magic ("Men mistook the order of their ideas for the order of nature, and hence imagined that the control which they have, or seem to have, over their thoughts, permitted them to exercise a corresponding control over things"). For Freud, there is at the heart of magic a desire to believe in the omnipotence of thoughts and the power of will: "A general overvaluation has thus come about of all mental processes—an attitude towards the world, that is, which, in view of our knowledge of the relation between reality and thought, cannot fail to strike *us* as an over-valuation of the latter" (Freud, 85).

To illustrate the phenomenon of the omnipotence of thoughts, Freud refers to "the evolution of human views of the universe":

> At the animistic stage men ascribe omnipotence to *themselves*. At the religious stage they transfer it to the gods but do not seriously abandon it themselves, for they reserve the power of influencing the gods in a variety of ways according to their wishes. The scientific view of the universe no longer affords any room for human omnipotence; men have acknowledged their smallness and submitted resignedly to death and to the other necessities of nature.

"None the less," he adds, "some of the primitive belief in omnipotence still survives in men's faith in the power of the human mind, taking account, as it does, of the laws of reality" (88).[16]

If it is true, as Freud notes, "Primitive men and neurotics . . . attach a high valuation—in our eyes an *over*-valuation—to psychical acts" (89), then here we must observe the prevalence of narratives about "psychical acts" that occur in the genres of science fiction and fantasy. Within a worldview now dominated by the "scientific" paradigm, thoughts are re-invested with their originary omnipotence. Cyberspace represents the return of the animistic view of the universe *within* the scientific paradigm. Consciousness becomes separated from the body—it becomes a body *itself*—as its power spreads throughout the global electronic space of terminal culture. In this sense, then, cyberspace is a refusal of the reality principle and any other limits on subject power. The power of human will is hardwired into the system. If I have described the subject in cyberspace as a purely perceptive and kinetic subject, then I should also note that Freud has discussed "the animistic soul" in terms of "its volatile and mobile quality, its power of leaving the body and of taking possession, temporarily or permanently, of another body." All of these are "characteristics which remind us unmistakably of the nature of consciousness" (94). Thus the penetration of consciousness into the cyberspatial matrix is an extension of the power of the will recalling the "animistic" conception of the universe that precedes the emergence of the mature ego.[17]

12. the hypercinema of virtual reality

Brooks Landon has astutely noted that cyberpunk, ostensibly a literary subgenre, is non- or even anti-narrative in its practice. The trajectory through different cyberspaces, from the narrative metaphors of *Neuromancer* and *TRON* through the ludic explorations experienced through computer games, Disney's worlds and virtual reality technologies, traces the path of an increasingly direct interface operating between technology and body. Despite the headlong *rush* of Gibson's prose in *Neuromancer*, the reader's body nevertheless remains distinct from the techno-surrealist evocations of another reality which is nevertheless uncomfortably like our own. In *TRON*, the viewer is thrust into a technologically and phenomenologically distinct space through the synaesthetic effects of cinematic kinesis, but this radical maneuver is always contained, explained and grounded by the operations of a particularly conventional narrativity. Ultimately, narrative itself comes to seem a clunky and intrusive interface, an anachronism from an earlier era.

The supercession of narrative by the direct sensory engagements of virtual reality represents the culmination of a fantasied form of representation that no longer seems representational. In this sense, virtual reality becomes the fulfillment of that drive towards what André Bazin once termed "the myth of total cinema," a cinema without boundaries. The subject's senses are engaged by a simulacrum of reality so perfect that its technological origins can be comfortably denied. While Bazin emphasizes the impossibility of this long-standing fantasy, it can still be acknowledged that the promise of virtual reality does—*to a certain degree*—obviate the need for a narrative paradigm that has heretofore primarily permitted the exploration of space by the spectator's screen-surrogate.[18] The body in virtual reality transcends the need for a surrogate character to experience the diegesis *for* him or her, or for a narrative to ground the exploration of an unfamiliar space. Instead, an illusion of direct, immediate (and seemingly *non-mediated*) engagement is produced, while spatial exploration is at last acknowledged as an experiential end in itself.

Virtual reality (in its present, primitive, form, and as anticipated by Gibson's kinetic, frenetic, cyberspace) effectively models a slyly reductive version of the phenomenology of Merleau-Ponty as it exemplifies the hypercinematic fantasy Bazin described. This occurs, in both cases, within the paradigmatic postmodern fiction of an invisible, electronic space which must be rendered visible and penetrable to a human subject that still retains its relevance. The cybersubject's immersion in myriad virtual realities thus represents both a *fantasy* of cyborg empowerment and a *real* tactics of adaptation to the exigencies of terminal reality. Within these spaces of accommodation, narrative *and* virtual, the body moves towards a more complete interface with the electronic, as the human becomes ever more fully inscribed, defined, and delimited by forces of electronic culture.

Notes

1. John Walker of Autodesk, Inc. (a manufacturer of one VR system) writes, "I define a cyberspace system as one that provides users with a three-dimensional interaction experience that includes the illusion they are inside a world rather than observing an image" (444).

2. Electronic space thus projects a Cartesian ideal in the form of a perfectly coordinated and potentially infinite space and objects within that space become functions of the coordinate system. "[T]he 'image' is only a matrix of digital codes in a data space" (Lovejoy, 291). The visual field is simply a translation of numerical data—it could as easily be presented acoustically or as ASCII codes—but retains a functionally and, indeed, a

reality, despite that. J. David Bolter notes that the phenomenon of computer space is based both in mathematical logic and empirical, physical, reality (Bolter, 97).

3. Vivian Sobchack has noted a recuperative impulse behind chaos studies, specifically in its obsession with the order which had eluded perception but which is now suddenly manifest in all things (Sobchack 1990). She notes, for example, that James Gleick's *Chaos—the* popular work on the subject—continually stresses the lonely, iconoclastic figures of the non-conformist, interdisciplinary avatars of chaos studies. Chaos is thus narrativized, personified, and granted the spiritual high ground—the horrifying limits of orders are banished.

4. Including, for example, Annette Michelson, Fredric Jameson, Mark Rose, and Vivian Sobchack.

5. The film also provides some digitized footage to indicate the android gunfighter's point of view, further anticipating *The Terminator* and *Robocop.*

6. "The universal *epoche* of the world as it becomes known in consciousness (the 'putting it in brackets') shuts out from the phenomenological field the world as its exists for the subject in simple absoluteness; its place, howver, is taken by the world as given in consciousness" (Husserl, 125).

7. These processes do not require the use of any physical models or drawings—everything can be generated, including the effects of depth, light, and shadow, through CAD programs, and the movement effects and spatial alterations con be calculated and displayed by the computer. The procedures remain powerfully labor-intensive, but it is computational power and time which is at issue, rather than the man-hours of traditional animations process. *TRON* was produced before the advent of the technique of ray-tracing, which is now *de rigeur* for all such simulations. Ray-tracing "simulate[s] the behavior of light as it passes through and reflects off surface so that highly realistic images can be artifically synthesized" (Friedhoff, 101).

8. "Normal" as distinct from those suffering from apraxia or agnosia, to whom Merleau-Ponty refers at the outset.

9. As in *The Wizard of Oz,* Flynn encounters his real-world friends in cybernetic forms.

10. It should be noted that the narrative, in terms of audience engagement, is so slight, and so insufficiently developed, that its subversion is almost a moot point. The script (replete with such lines as, "Forget it, Mr. High-and-Mighty Master Control! You're not making me talk!") and incompetent pacing and character direction are undboutedly responsible for the film's rapid box-office demise, rather than the "alienating effects" of its electronic effects. For the purposes of analysis, however, such flaws provide useful grist for the mill, and are much in keeping with the notion of a "failure" of the human within the context of a newly, and increasingly, cyberneticized existence.

11. For more on science fiction and the postmodern metroscape, see Bukatman 1987.

12. Narrative's failure is also found in the crudeness of these narratives —the tough-guy posturing of *Neuromancer* or the cuddly anthropomorphisms of *TRON*—crudeness that can now be read as axiomatic of their project.

13. Thanks to Vivian Sobchack for directing me to Ihde's work.

14. Psychoanalysis might offer some insight into the power-fantasy represented by a mind with complete control over the forms and events of the external world. *Neuromancer*, for example, is very susceptible to a reading based in an understanding of the mechanisms of projection and introjection. Thus, Case's alienation at the beginning of *Neuromancer* is the result of his realization that mind does not equal body—thought is not constitutive of, or coextensive with, physical existence. The reality principle has intervened, but in *Neuromancer* this act of maturation appears as a fallen state. Thanks to Richard Allen for these provocative ideas.

15. Sometimes, as in *TRON* or John Varley's story, "Overdrawn at the Memory Bank," the narrative centers upon the recovery of the protagonist's "meat" body.

16. Freud, 88. One cannot help but note that Freud's anthropology has imposed a model of psychological development on the process of cultural change. The "evolution" that he describes is fully analogous to the growth of the infant through childhood: the original belief in the power of will (which, in fact, predates the full emergence of the ego), the surrender of power to the parents (who may still be influenced "in a variety of ways") and the final (albeit provisional) acceptance of the reality principle.

17. Gibson seems aware of this: witness the emergence of voodoo mythology as another paradigm for cyberspatial existence in *Count Zero* and *Mona Lisa Overdrive*, the sequels to *Neuromancer*.

18. I am not, however, arguing that this phenomenological function is the *only* purpose of narrative, nor even that it is the *privary* purpose. That narrative, and especially cinematic narrative, possesses a phenomenological component, however, seems beyond dispute, and it is to this component of narrative that I refer.

Works Cited

Ballard, J. G. (1985) "Introduction to the French Edition." *Crash*. New York: Vintage Books.

Baudrillard, J. (1983). "The Precession of Simulacra." *Simulations*. New York: Semiotext(e) Inc.

Bazin, A. (1967). "The Myth of Total Cinema." *What is Cinema?* Berkeley: University of California Press.

Benjamin, W. (1969). "The Work of Art in the Age of Mechanical Reproduction." *Illuminations*. New York: Schocken Books.

Binkley, T. (1989). "Camera Fantasia." *Millenium Film Journal* 20/21: 6-43.

Bolter, J. D. (1984). *Turing's Man: Western Culture in the Computer Age*. Chapel Hill, NC: University of North Carolina Press.

Bukatman, S. (1987). "The Cybernetic (City) State: Terminal Space Becomes Phenomenal." *Journal of the Fantastic in the Arts.* 2.2 (43-63).

Clute, J. (1987). "Introduction." *Interzone: The Second Anthology.* New York: St. Martin's Press.

Csicsery-Ronay, I. (1988). "Cyberpunk and Neuromanticism." *Mississippi Review* 16 (2/3): 266-278.

Delany, S. R. (1984). *Starboard Wine: More Notes on the Language of Science Fiction.* Elizabethtown, NJ: Dragon Press.

De Lauretis, T. (1980). "Signs of W[a/o]nder." *The Technological Imagination: Theories and Fictions.* Madison: Coda Press.

Finch, C. (1984). *Special Effects: Creating Movie Magic.* New York: Abbeville Press.

Freud, S. (1950). "Animism, Magic and the Omnipotence of Thoughts." *Totem and Taboo,* James Strachey, trans. New York: W. W. Norton & Co.

Friedhoff, R. M. and W. Benzon. (1989). *Visualization: The Second Computer Revolution.* New York: Harry Abrams.

Gibson, W. (1984). *Neuromancer.* New York: Ace Science Fiction Books.

Huizinga, J. (1970). *Homo Ludens.* London: Temple Smith.

Husserl, E. (1986). "Phenomenology." *Deconstruction in Context: Literature and Philosophy.* Mark C. Taylor, ed. Chicago: University of Chicago Press.

Jacobs, K. (1990). "Design for the Unreal World." *Metropolis.* 10: 40ff.

Jameson, F. (1984). "Postmodernism, or the Cultural Logic of Late Capitalism." *New Left Review* (146): 53-92.

Ihde, D. (1990). *Technology and the Lifeworld: From Garden to Earth.* The Indiana Series in the Philosophy of Technology. Bloomington, IN: Indiana University Press.

Krauss, R. (1977). "The Double Negative: a new syntax for sculpture." *Passages in Modern Sculpture.* Cambridge, MA: The MIT Press.

Landon, Brooks. "Bet On It: Cyber/video/punk/performance." *Mississippi Review* 16.2/3 (1988): 245-251.

Leary, T. (1990). "The Interpersonal, Interactive, Interdimensional Interface." *The Art of Human Computer Interface Design.* Brenda Laurel, ed. Cupertino, CA: Apple Computer.

Levy, S. (1984) *Hackers: Heroes of the Computer Revolution.* New York: Dell Books.

Lovejoy, M. (1989). *Postmodern Currents: Art and Artists in the Age of Electronic Media.* Ann Arbor: UMI Research Press.

McCarty, Cara. (1990). *Information Art: Diagramming Microchips.* New York: Museum of Modern Art.

Mead, S. (1985). *OBLAGON: Concepts of Syd Mead.* Japanese publication.

Merleau-Ponty, M. (1962). *The Phenomenology of Perception.* Trans. Colin Smith, trans. London: Routledge & Kegan Paul.

_____. (1964). "Eye and Mind." *The Primacy of Perception.* Northwestern University Press.

Metz, C. (1977). "The Imaginary Signifier." *The Imaginary Signifier*. Ithaca: Cornell University Press.

Miller, R. and Rand Miller. (1989). *Cosmic Osmo*. Menlo Park, CA: Activision. Software for the Macintosh Computer.

Nelson, T. H. (1990). "The Right Way to Think About Software Design." *The Art of Human-Computer Interface Design*. Brenda Laurel, ed. Cupertino, CA: Apple Computer.

Papert, S. (1980). *Mindstorms: Children, Computers and Powerful Ideas*. New York: Basic Books.

Rheingold, H. (1990). "What's the Big Deal About Cyberspace?" *The Art of Human Computer Interface Design*. Brenda Laurel, ed. Cupertino, CA: Apple Computer.

_____. (1991). *Virtual Reality*. New York: Summit Books.

Sharpe, W. and L. Wallock. (1983). "From 'Great Town' to 'Nonplace Urban Realm': Reading the Modern City." *Visions of the Modern City: Essays in History, Art and Literature*. Sharpe and Wallock, eds. New York: Hayman Center for the Humanities.

Sitney, P. A. (1979). *Visionary Film: The American Avant-Garde 1943-1978*. New York: Oxford University Press.

Sobchack, V. (1987). *Screening Space: The American Science Fiction Film*. New York: Ungar Press.

_____. (1990). "The Scene of the Screen: Towards a Phenomenology of Cinematic and Electronic Presence." *Post-Script*, 10:50-59.

_____. (1990). "A Theory of Everything: Meditations on Total Chaos." *Artforum International*, 19 (October): 148-155.

Walker, J. (1990). "Through the Looking Glass." *The Art of Human-Computer Interface Design*. Brenda Laurel, ed. Cupertino, CA: Apple Computer.

Philip Turetzky

Televisual Bodies: Television and The Impulse Image

1. Body and Image

"Television is a Mystery."[1]

The mediascape marks our bodies in their spatio-temporal assimilation to television via the domination of certain types of image. It is not only the humiliating content of images of the body beautiful, their rhetoric and allure that encumbers us, but perhaps more so the fragmentation of our bodies due to the type of image that television surreptitiously imposes on every image that it contains. This type of image is the impulse-image. What belongs to the destiny of this image belongs as well to that of television as a technology enframing our bodies.

The impulse-image was first described by Deleuze as a special type of image in his taxonomy of the images belonging to the cinema.[2] The impulse-image is a form of the movement-image, which is differentiated within the sensory-motor connection and suspended between the affection-image and the action-image. However, images are visibilities; ways in which light is organized and in which spatio-temporal arrangements and interactions are organized by the distribution of light. So if "medium" is taken to include all modes of visibility, images may appear in other media. The same image may appear not only produced by different forms of equipment, but, as Foucault has shown us, within the workings of different technologies of power. Although, like signs, images are not constituted by the material that supports them, the material medium and its spatial disposition are not entirely neutral regarding what types of images they accentuate. What sort of visibility and distribution of space is emphasized among technologies of power will tell us much about the functioning of these technologies.

Television is both a piece of equipment and a technology of power; it produces images and as an object forms spatio-temporal arrangements that function to support power relations. George Trow recognized these power relations when he focused on the ability of television to enforce its scale on all possible contents, resulting in a leveling effect. But Trow admits that "No one has been able to describe the scale as it is experienced."[3] By shear juxtaposition within this scale and by combination through the cynical "and,"[4] as the only logical connective television allows, every image becomes just one more image without rank or emphasis. The failure to grasp the scale that television imposes is due partly to the relative neglect of the fusion between television and bodies, but due mostly to a failure to perceive the type of image that dominates television and through which television dominates: the impulse-image. The parameters of the impulse-image redefine every image that appears on television. The scale of the small screen imposes the harsh fragmenting co-ordinates of naturalism and degenerate or

Bodies turned on themselves: *Dead Ringers* (1988). Morgan Creek Productions. Still courtesy of Jerry Ohlinger's Movie Materials.

repetitive moments of time on every image that appears within it and on the bodies it absorbs. This coalescence of television and bodies forms a televisual body: the site of the contemporary apocalypse. The static violence of the impulse-image always already enframes the images on the screen which trumpet the revelation of the ultimate triumph of good over evil in the celebration of the good life. Hence, the destiny of the impulse-image in entropy and repetition becomes the final revelation of the force of television.

The impulse-image will best be understood first in the context of the cinema, and only then as it appears when imposed in the context of television. The cinema presents us with alternatives to the impulse-image. The lack of dominance of this one sort of image in the cinema makes the isolation of the properties of this image stand out as properties of a particular sort of image rather than as features peculiar to the medium. Once these properties are isolated, then the question to what extent television is dominated by the impulse-image can be posed. This is the question whether the impulse-image must dominate the television image, and whether the technologies of power in which television as impulse-image enters as visibility, allocation of space and temporal destiny must arise out of the television as apparatus.

2. Dead Ringers: Bodies and the Impulse
Toward Technical Refashioning

> the dissociation not only of the limbs but of all the parts of the body is very common and considered normal.[5]
> —Stuart Ewen, *All Consuming Images*

While Deleuze analyzed the impulse-image in the films of Stroheim, Buñuel and Losey, we shall take a film of the contemporary cinema for our exemplar. It is here that bodies are most rigorously brought under the signs of fetish and symptom that mark the impulse-image, and thereby brought under the regime of the impulse-image which will later inform our analysis of television. The impulse-image has generally been relegated by Hollywood to a particular genre, that of the horror movie, while action-images have tended to dominate most mainstream films. Yet as more and more mass market films are produced with video in mind, this tendency is reversing both itself and the trend noted by Deleuze when he says that generally in the work of American directors "the action-image represses the impulse-image, which is too indecent because of its brutality, its very restraint, and its lack of realism."[6] Action-images require decisive actions which resolve real problems in a determinate context or which disclose real aspects of a real situation. The violence of impulse-images pulverizes the real connections that determine a real situation and thereby destroys its coherence as a determinate context which can support and encompass the consummation of an action.

David Cronenberg, known primarily as a director of horror films, has produced an impulse-image film that avoids both Hollywood's repression of the impulse-image and the traditional horror film genre. Cronenberg's *Dead Ringers* is an exemplar of the impulse-image as the destiny of bodies; bodies turned on themselves. Bodies are the site of both the origin and the return of the impulse; bodies as "both radical beginning and absolute end."[7] In *Dead Ringers* bodies are moved by impulses to their own perfection as bodies and at the same time are the material on which these impulses act.

The impulse-image is the image of naturalism, the incomprehensible, indifferent and harsh world that appears in the novels of Zola and Stephen Crane. Naturalism is manifested in the space mapped out by four co-ordinates and by either of two transfigurations of time. The four co-ordinates of naturalism are originary worlds, derived milieux, images and acts of impulses, and perverse behaviors in the derived milieux. An originary world is a formless mass composed of the unstructured juxtaposition of innumerable bits and pieces derived from determinate realistic contexts of action; derived milieux. A determinate milieu is a coherent realist background against which individual actions make sense as directed toward comprehensible goals and constrained by causal regularities. A determinate milieu is defined by a definite social, historical and geographical ordering of space and time. A derived milieu is a fragment of a determinate milieu, pieces of which are wrenched from this definite organization of space and time. By themselves, these fragments look like real objects, actions and emotions, but since they are separated from a determinate context they make no sense in relation to their surroundings. The unstructured juxtaposition of indefinite numbers of these fragments forms an originary world: originary both because it is given immediately and because it is a primal source out of which temporary monstrous combinations coalesce and back into which they decay. An impulse is an active force present in an action once it is separated from any determinate milieu that could provide the action with a coherent sense, cause or rational justification. Impulses are always directed toward a single end. So while it has a sort of intelligence, an impulse acts blindly, regardless of the ends served by any other forces or interests. An impulse breaks up a determinate milieu, takes what it needs until it exhausts the aspects of a milieu that it can turn to its own ends, and leaves the rest as unconnected detritus. The fragments an impulse takes for its purposes are symptoms of the impulse, those it leaves behind in the originary world after the impulse disrupts and destroys any coherent scene of action are fetishes. The impulse must exhaust the milieu. It seeks a change in the milieu or a new milieu. An impulse will impact a milieu only in so far as the pieces of the milieu can serve as a means to the ends of the impulse. Hence, impulses manifest perverse behavior in derived milieux. What is left of coherent action after the impulse's monomania takes possession of a determinate milieu is perverse behavior, not only cannibalistic, masochistic, sadistic, and necrophilic behaviors but also more subtle spiritual perversions. This leads to a static violence that amounts neither to an action nor to an affect. This static violence prevents the formation of a determinate milieu with its coherent, even ethical, organization of social and historical causality and obligations. It also prevents the affective expression of qualities which would require the coherence of reflection.

Static violence is maintained by the two tendencies of time which traverse the four co-ordinates of naturalism: a predilection toward repetition and a degeneration down the line of the steepest slope. Both of these are forms of degeneracy. The latter is a path of deterioration, an inexorable entropy, decaying from a social, moral or even metaphysical state when the force of the impulse exceeds the capacity of the any determinate action to cope with it. Repetition, on the other hand, projects a more subtle nihilism. Even though an original metaphysical, moral or social state is restored, it is restored in an exact repetition. This repetition undermines the values and rankings that separate good from evil. Since good and evil exchange endlessly as the cycle repeats, neither can claim preeminence. Good becomes no less a deviance and perversion than evil.

In naturalism nature is an originary world, a basic *physis*, out of which all things arise and to which they all return. This emergence includes the products of human beings, ". . . the originary world does not oppose Nature to the constructions of man: it is oblivious to this distinction, which is valid only in derived milieux."[8]

Cronenberg's use of empty, almost exclusively interior sets, grey and blue light, and the sterile environment of the clinic display the identity of the human order and the natural order as a formless background—an originary world of bodies out of which medically revised bodies arise and into which they return. Beverly's attempt to leave his dead brother and their exhausted milieu at the end of the film is one of the few exterior shots, and even here there is no possibility of moving outside of the world of the medicalized body as nature. Beverly must return, impelled by impulse, to the originary world, the primeval ooze, the swamp of medicines and bodies. Technically altered bodies are displayed in the image of the trash heap to which Beverly returns in the closing scenes. The room, in the end has become a wasteland of medical apparatus, junk food remains and body parts. The bodies of the twins are displayed as mere fragments of this primordial dump; they are presented as body parts only partially differentiated from the other remnants. Here the twins are finally reunited in death amid the remains of the drugs and medical instruments. Here an originary world ". . . unites everything, not in an organization, but making all the parts converge in an immense rubbish-dump or swamp, and all the impulses in a great death-impulse."9

Derived milieux, in which decisive actions can no longer make real changes, are stitched together metastable and irreal mimics of determinate situations. Derived milieu are transient only partially contextualized fragments, marked as fetishes, which can only manifest truncated actions and illusory disclosures. For a short time they may cover over a deeper fragmentation and decontextualization, which undermines the effects of action and the sense of disclosure, with an apparently ordinary scene of action. But such a scene lasts only until the next impulse shatters the illusory determinacy of the sham situation.

The world of medical technology never forms a determinate scene of action, rather it is the scene out of which the impulses toward the refashioning of bodies are extracted. This is the derived milieu of *Dead Ringers*. It is derived from the determinate context of medicine by the interruptive force of impulses slicing off fragments and twisting actions into perverse modes of behavior. *Dead Ringers* is not a medical drama and its crises are not primarily medical emergencies, nor is the film to be interpreted as a psycho-pathological drama of mental breakdown, despite the psychological degeneration of the Mantle twins. The world of medical technology serves as the medium for a static violence—a violence in which the twins turn medical technology back on themselves—which never reaches any decisive action. This violence, of the impulse to revise bodies, springs from the twins at the outset. The childhood scenes with which the film begins establish this impulse. The twins operate on the technical body of the visible woman toy, and, of course, their division as twins, physical and psychological, is already a manifestation of the altered multiplicity of bodies. As a medium, medical technology makes possible the display of these impulses as symptoms which shatter bodies and the world of modified bodies into fragments leaving only the fetishes of medicine as signs of a primordial emergence.

An impulse is "an impression in the strongest sense and not an expression."[10] So impulses do not arise out of any form of consciousness. They are psychological only in their reception as effects not in their production. While they are extracted from real passions, feelings and emotions, impulses are not equivalent to any of these. Impulses take on forms waiting for them in the seemingly real environment of a derived milieu, but these forms are only the symptoms of the impulses that possess them and allow them to be manifested in an image. Acts of impulses appear symptomatically as images which break up the coherence of situations and the self-reference of affects.

Symptoms of the impulse appear in *Dead Ringers* as a technical impetus toward the refashioning of bodies. These technical impulses are embodied in the Mantle Clinic which specializes in making women fertile. The film is pervaded by revision—the impulse to alter the way bodies appear and function. So much so that only the constantly manipulated body has a place within this technoscape. As Beverly says when he tries to use a surgical retractor on an office patient, hurting her, "We have the technology! It couldn't possibly hurt." When Elliot points out his error Beverly replies, "There is nothing wrong with the instrument. It's the body. The woman's body was all wrong." Bodies are all wrong throughout the film and new technologies are applied to restructure these wrong bodies. Yet all that comes from these techniques are more wrong bodies. The impulse to revision arises out of the mire of medicalized bodies and returns to it. The twins are themselves wrong bodies in their fractured individuation. When the sculptor says that one responds to a body of sculpture according to one's individual nervous system, Beverly points out that that presupposes that one has an individual nervous system. Elliot and Beverly only have fragmentary, linked nervous systems and blood streams. They do not share a single body with one another: their bodies are fragments interconnected and absorbed into the medical apparatus (machines, syringes, drugs) that bring them together as ruptured cyborg bodies. Their nervous systems are likewise linked in the division of intellectual labor that connects their research, clinical work and medical politics, and yet which opens up into the sculptors studio and their sexual system. The increasing use of drugs on bodies that won't wake or sleep at the right times, Elliot's hope that by synchronizing the drugs in the twin's bloodstreams that everything will become "easy," and Beverly's invention of gynecological instruments for mutant women which also turn out to be sculptural forms and finally instruments for separating Siamese twins—instruments which almost kill one patient and are eventually used to kill Elliot (death as the ultimate alteration of bodies), all manifest the impulse to alter bodies and correct their flaws. Beverly says that he takes drugs for pain, since pain creates character distortion and is "simply not necessary." But the drugs soon bring about even more character distortion and wasteful pain. The corrected body is more fragmented with every attempt at its restoration to perfection, culminating in inevitable death and the return of the fragments of bodies to the swamp of partial objects, the Empedoclean world of randomly entangled pieces of technology and body parts (alive or dead, it doesn't matter).

The originary world of *Dead Ringers* is the world of medically altered bodies, but bodies are not just nature as the site from which impulses emanate. They are also the site on which impulses act, the medium in which impulses have their effects; tearing off fragments and producing a new form of time. The twins are, of course, the primary case of the fragmented body. They are functionally differentiated, Elliot as public liaison and Beverly as inquirer, and they identify with the Siamese twins Chiang and Eng, as the co-ordinated parts of a connected though already dismembered organism.

The slope of their degeneration begins with their liaison with the actress Claire Niveau. When Beverly wants to keep his experience with Claire for himself, Elliot says that Beverly hasn't had any experience until he, Elliot, has had it too. Claire herself is a fragmented body, an infertile mutant woman with three cervices. Her desire for a baby is to leave a part of her body, so she won't be just dead when she dies. Elliot tells Beverly, "She's an actress. She's a flake—plays games all the time. You never know who she really is." Nor do the twins ever know who they really are; they routinely pretend to be each other for functional reasons, even to gain leverage on their own behavior. When Elliot advises Beverly that he will be all right in his first sexual encounter with Claire, he says not to worry "Just do me."

There are no whole bodies only partial bodies as fetishes in the medical milieux.[11] Even body parts are not clearly functionally defined; a vein can be used as a fallopian tube. Nor do any of the three characters have more than partial gender identities: Claire says she will never really be a woman, she taunts Beverly for his woman's name and suggests that he needs to have his brother watching before he can get it up. Even Elliot, who would seem to behave more clearly in the male role, turns out in the end to be the weaker, more passive and dependent of the twins. When he is dying, Beverly calls him "Chiang," the weaker of the two original Siamese twins. Beverly's dream of he and Elliot as Siamese twins separated by Claire biting through the bridge tissue both fetishizes the psychological link as a biological link and displays Claire's role, as symptom, in the fragmentation and degeneration of the twins. She separates them through acts of perverse behavior that stimulate the refashioning of their illusory self-contained mutually reflecting duopoly. The incompleteness of the twins both separately and as a co-ordinated pair is progressively destabilized as Beverly slowly degenerates. Elliot attempts to save him, but their linkage soon traps Elliot, the weaker one, in an even swifter corruption, truly down a line of the steepest slope.

The impulse-image degenerates through perverse modes of behavior in the derived milieu for two reasons. First, because it cannot attain an encompassing real situation, it annihilates the possibility of norms. Second, because the fragmentation of bodies prevents true affects, since there is no single unified self for affective intensities to reflect back on. Behavior becomes perverse because it is set adrift in an originary world. Its perversion is felt only as symptoms of naturalistic impulses arising in the depths of that originary world and never returning to itself, assuring the continuation and eventual triumph of the world of naturalism.

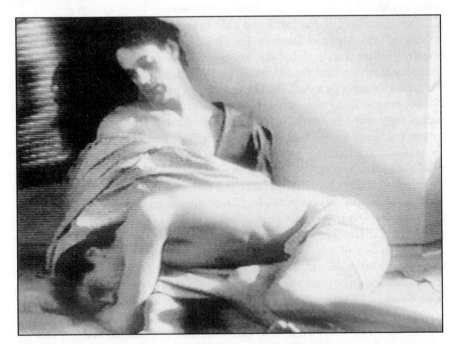

Pieta as detritus: the body as originary world in David Cronenberg's *Dead Ringers* (1988). Morgan Creek Productions. Still photograph by Christopher Sharrett.

In *Dead Ringers* sexual roles are confused and splintered; perverse modes of behavior take over. Despite Claire's professed need for humiliation and the suggestions of other sexual permutations, perversion here is not primarily sexual perversion. Perverse modes of behavior are the dominant modes of behavior: the twins' shameless use of each other's identities and abilities, the perversion of professional position, the perversion of medical oaths and violation of criminal law, and the perverse modes of medical practice—radical techniques eventually taken to the extreme of surgical instruments for mutant women. These perversions are inseparable from and symptoms of the impulses of altered bodies: the fragmented body and the technologies that refashion bodies.

Thus the impulse-image is constituted within the co-ordinates of naturalism: originary worlds, derived milieux, images and acts of impulses, and perverse actions in the derived milieu. While these co-ordinates compose the positive content of the image, they don't show its negative moment—what cannot appear in the image, what it consigns to nothingness. Here we must back off from the impulse-image and compare it to action-images and affection-images and see how impulse is an inchoate form of action and a degenerate form of affect.

Neither affect nor actions are able to survive for long in the derived milieu of refashioned bodies in *Dead Ringers*.[12] An action-image requires either that a global situation give rise to an action that modifies that situation or that an action forces a situation to disclose itself. The various attempts to avert the degeneration of the Mantle brothers fail. No action modifies the problematic situation. Applications of medical technology only exacerbate the situation until the fragments return to the primordial mire of naturalism. Elliot tries to put Beverly on a detoxification program. Soon he is drawn into taking an upper so Beverly won't take a downer, and then to the attempt to synchronize their blood streams. Nor does any action force the situation to disclose itself so that a different action is then possible. Claire questions, "how it really works" between the brothers, but this is never disclosed to her or to them by any action. Effective action leading to a resolution of a situation or to a modification of the type of action undertaken is impossible within the co-ordinates of naturalism, since everything must always return to and cannot go beyond the swamp of an originary world. Actions always falls short of their goals and only further the "diabolical intelligence" of the impulse.

As we have already noted, affect is also impossible within the co-ordinates of naturalism. The primordial world of nature is pre-conscious in so far as it is a *physis* out of which impulses arise but to which they never return as a quality of a possible object. What returns are shards of uncompleted feelings and unfulfilled emotions. The potential intensities of twins never return to just one of them: Beverly's desire to keep his feelings and experiences of his relationship with Claire cannot succeed, the energies of their intimacy return to Elliot in a perversion of surgical tubing, Claire's desire for a child is terminated by her mutant body, Elliot's pride in receiving professional adulation was never rooted in genuine strength. Elliot's emotions are cynical facades except when they turn on Beverly. It is only Beverly's comparative strength that allows him to even try for an integrity of feeling. Yet it is this very attempt that starts him on the path of decay.

The law of the impulse is that of the line of the steepest slope from the originary world as absolute beginning and source of the impulse to that same world as absolute end and rubbish heap of remains. Naturalism can "only grasp the negative effects of time: attrition, degradation, wastage, destruction or simply oblivion."[13] The world of naturalism is governed by the impulse whose destiny is the exhaustion of the milieu and ultimately the merger of impulses in a single death impulse. The impulse to refashion bodies takes charge of every aspect of the film and exhausts it. It is itself an impulse that tries to use every resource to leap into a completely new situation. Elliot uses every resource to re-establish the functional equilibrium of the twins. His deterioration comes swiftly once his social and manipulative resources are exhausted. Beverly atrophies more slowly, since his strength is in the technology as a symptom of the impulse to alter bodies. But this impulse exhausts the technical and medical resources in the marathon of drug taking and surgery in which Elliot dies and to which Beverly must return, now driven only by the death impulse. The violence of the impulse to refashion bodies is a static violence, since, in the end, the twins turn it only on themselves.

> The impulse scours the milieu, knowing no satisfaction other than that of taking possession of that which seems to be closed to it, to belong by rights to another milieu, to a higher level."[14]

The impulse to alter bodies originates in the splintered bodies of the twins and ends in waste dump of medicalized death. The conditions surrounding technological medicine are saturated with death. The Mantle Clinic is dedicated to altering infertility, a kind of death in which, as Claire says, no part of one's body lives on. Death is the final alteration of bodies: the twins death, but even more, under the regime of technology, the final disposal of bodies as pure partial objects, as absorbed into the apparatus of technical manipulation.

3. Television: The Televisual Body and the Impulse-Image

I never really done much with my life, I suppose. I never had a television.[15]

—Louise Erdich, *Love Medicine*

Television is also an apparatus which technically manipulates bodies. The manipulation of thought, if this means habituating viewers to think specific thoughts, is not nearly so important in comparison. It is more interesting to consider the habituation to a certain style of having thoughts. This is a style at one with the form of production of images on the screen made possible by a certain disposition of bodies. It is a style of having thoughts rather than of thinking, since its only operators are appearance and oblivion. In contrast, discursive thought requires negation and possibility to produce the coherence and consistency required by dialectical understanding. The only connective that operates in television is conjunction. Other connectives particularly conditionals can only appear as moments within the sound images, where their conditional force is quashed by the visual images. Language is either supported and surpassed by the specificity of images or overwhelmed by competing images. The latter is not a form of negation, since the image merely needs to present a positive content that has nothing to do with what is said for language to be engulfed. In either case the grammar of language, negation and conditionals, are effaced by the relentless positivity and conjunction of television images. But, then, television must no longer be concerned with thought at all, either logically or psychologically. What is habituated is neither primarily a select content nor an underlying structure of categories or preconceptions. Instead bodies are infused with impulses and television appears as an impulse-image.

However, in focusing on television we ought not give a privileged position to the content of the shows, the images on screen, the television apparatus, or bodies and the structures of lifeworld. Television is a technology of power that constitutes a spatio-temporal order which brings all of these together in a single complex but heterogeneous machine. The heterogeneous elements of this complex need to be considered as contributing parts of a single image: an impulse-image. Each element would be a complete object only in the context of a real situation in which specific use values could be assigned, and decisive actions and genuine affects could arise. Instead, these elements must be seen as partial objects, as fragments, which are reconstituted as the Empedoclean body of a televisual machine. The images on the screen are essential, but they are still only one element in this more inclusive image.

However, even calling the heterogeneous complex of televisual space-time a machine is misleading. This implies a functional unity, which is lacking here. There is no use or need that counts as the fulfillment of a specific function which the televisual complex produces. The only events that issue from this complex are the expulsion of impulses, and these are too violent and uncontrolable to serve any function: even capitalist consumption requires more restraint and direction. While the elements of the complex are distributed in a definite arrangement and each element imparts something specific to the whole complex, what each contributes are constituents of the impulse-image. Phenomenal images, organic bodies, electronic signals, electrochemical processes and physical objects all coalesce to form an emergent ontology: the ontology of naturalism under a regime of the negative effects of time. Naturalism is oblivious to the distinction between Nature and human constructs: it dumps bodies and devices together in a heap. The televisual complex, with its heterogeneity recapitulates the co-ordinates of naturalism: originary world, derived milieux and their exhaustion, impulses, perverse modes of behavior and the repetition and degeneration of time.

The absorption of the world into television is a phenomenon repeated in every room in which a television appears. The images on the screen skin the surface off of every material event and object. They dissolve the material ontology of things into a pure luminescent surface, not merely a second nature but nature taken to the nth degree. What Oliver Wendell Holmes predicted of photography has been perfected in television:

> Every conceivable object of Nature and Art will soon scale off its surface for us. Men will hunt all curious, beautiful, grand objects, as they hunt cattle in South America, for their skins and leave the carcasses as of little worth."[16]

The destruction of the Nature/Art distinction originates in the equiluminosity of the image on the screen. Here we have an originary world a source of emergence in which fragments of anything-in-the-world are dumped in a great rubbish heap of information without end. The content of worldly events and bodies is not obliterated by formal elements, rather it is splintered, decontextualized and finally released as a derived milieu; no longer situated in a system of relevances, no longer forming a scene of action, no longer capable of affective intensities. The screen is a pure physis: an arising out of itself. The emergence of one fragment after another on the screen forms a swamp of contingently conjoined fragments in a mire of images, of information; an originary world from which everything arises and to which everything returns;

a new nature under the sway of the violence of impulses.

This swamp of images, however is not limited to the boundaries of the image on the screen. Apparatus, bodies and their lifeworld are reoriented and become part of the image.

Light, luminescence, arises out of the apparatus, but at bottom information is always already there, even in the absence of light or in the variety of colors. Each dot is a site on which information must be specified. The photochemical processes stimulated by a scanning beam of electrons form an originary world in the static dance of light arising out of the screen. A totality, a primeval ooze, of all possible information is embodied in this static. A world of aimless jugglers, of informantic body parts, parades across the screen before any determinate image can arise and back into which every image must fall. This photoluminescent flashing of random alterations of light always lurks below the surface of every image on the screen and in the interstitial spaces between images. Images plunge into this originary world between channels, at the end of the broadcast day and when they collapse in technical breakdowns.

Television organizes bodies in space. A cartoon by Gary Larson shows a small group of viewers in the classic viewing postures clustered around and directed toward the blank space where the television should be. The explanatory title "In the days before television" is almost superfluous; the postures and orientation of the bodies before the absent icon are characteristic of the positioning of bodies within the televisual complex. The classic postures of the viewing body are exemplified in the humor which suggests that before television people were still viewers with bodies habitually disposed toward viewing. More humor, displaying the pervasiveness of this phenomenon of the orientation of bodies, is expressed in the addition to our everyday vocabulary of the term "couch potato." But the disposition and immobilization of bodies is not all there is to the place of bodies in the televisual complex. Bodies are joined together with the apparatus and surrounding objects to make each television room into a space capsule. The world outside the room becomes a great vacuum which can only be safely accessed through transmissions via the screen. "The simple presence of television changes the rest of the habitat into a kind of archaic envelope, a vestige of human relations."[17] Immobile bodies become modules in an enclosed habitat.

This habitat consolidates into an originary world. Viewing bodies become Empedoclean monsters cut off from social and functional contexts, conjoined with and absorbed into the originary world of the screen. "With the television image our own body and the whole of the surrounding universe become a screen."[18] The body is immobilized by the beam of light linking the eye to the screen. The body is oriented around this scintillating radiance. It remains oriented so long as the eye is locked onto the light beam. Like the medical apparatus in *Dead Ringers* , body and technology merge into a new sort of body. Here too the body is no longer individual and separated, rather it is a mere part of a larger conglomerate body which is at once organic, electronic, mechanical and luminous. This is the televisual body. The formation of the televisual body is the condition of the possibility of a volume in which an image can appear. In this volume only one sort of image, the impulse-image, is possible. An image is what appears and what appears within the volume of the televisual body are not just images on the screen, but an image formed from the entire organic, electronic and luminous amalgam: a new nature.[19]

When they become televisual, bodies cease to have a background in which action can occur and are dedicated to reception of images, bodies become information volumes, originary worlds of information, with impulses arising from and returning to them. The closure of the habitat around the television and the immobility of viewing bodies eliminate real situations which actions could modify or disclose. Instead space is warped and inundated with information.

Information, all possible information, whether on the screen, in the apparatus or arising from or decaying into bodies is the originary world of the televisual complex. Information is the mode of being of every message, of every image: it is nature taken to the nth degree. Information is a morass of every image linked at random with every other image. This morass is without context, without background; it obviates differences between public and private, form and content, bodies and apparatus.

The images that arise out of and fall back into this originary world do not form the coherent context of a determinate situation. Rather what appears are temporary metastable fragments. These fragments are derived milieux: they are torn off the surface of the world and displayed piecemeal. Situation comedies, sports, drama, news, games, variety shows, all the genres of television fare are partial, fragmented by cutting, commercials and station breaks. Image follows image and for a while a single situation may prevail, but it is soon shattered by an image with no connection to it. The interval may be longer or shorter (public television and pay per view), but the necessity of replacing one image by something completely different eventually succeeds. Since each fragment has an internal coherence and the appearance of a determinate situation, images on the screen seldom become any-space-whatevers which would nullify context. They stand in some relation to a determinate milieu, without themselves becoming encompassing situations.

Bodies and the television apparatus also form derived milieux. Viewing bodies respond to the images on the screen with truncated feeling and vicarious action. Since the images on the screen must fluctuate, fully developed feelings and actions which require determinate contexts cannot arise; the sheer speed of fluctuation undermines any real response. Bodies are not given sufficient time or context to incorporate the content of images as anything but fragments, bits of information. Responses, too, are limited by the switches, dials and buttons provided on the apparatus. No change of channel, tuning or volume can affect or disclose a real situation; it can only produce the simulation of operativity.

Arising from the originary world of information and preventing the formation of contexts sufficiently determinate to issue in action or affect are impulses. Impulses are generated first in the digital light deep within the originary world of the image on the screen. Each dot in the static randomly alternates between light and dark; each change is a micro-shock where the pure pressure of change appears as a diminutive impulsion. The early advocates of the social power of cinema recognized the shock of change in the cinematic image as the core of the power of moving images. Though they conceived of the shock effect in psycho-logical terms, they recognized that it was the interruption of constant sudden change that constituted the shock itself.[20] The television image multiplies, digitalizes and miniaturizes shocks. It makes these shocks the very basis of the image itself not just the vehicle of change. Walter Benjamin argued that "By means of its technical structure, the film has taken the physical shock effect out of the wrappers in which Dadaism had, as it were, kept it inside the moral shock effect."[21] The technical structure of the television image takes this much farther by transmuting the physical shock effect into pure impulses; a plethora of continuous and simultaneous microshocks, whose effect is to fragment images and produce images out of this fragmentation. The images produced by the combination of micro-shocks themselves are symptoms of these impulses: just as the change in light and dark of the dots are only a symptom of micro-impulses, and the change in content of the images are, themselves, symptoms of the impulse images on the screen. The commercial, the station break and the news flash interrupt the coherence of images that constitute the shows. But the differences between these are minimal compared to their status as symptoms of impulses. Impulses, blind interruptions destroying coherence of context, can only appear via such symptoms.

Micro-impulses across the digital screen are, however, only the first layer of impulses. Made manifest in symptoms, images, themselves, become fetishes. Changing images are fragmented and deprived of encompassing context. Among images, then, there is a further stratum of symptoms of impulses. The rapid fire concatenation of images in commercials, rock videos and in some shows also emerge as impulses breaking up any coherence of content and situation.

While subjection to this glut of impulses for six to seven and a half hours each day cannot help but force impulses into bodies in the televisual complex, those bodies have become more actively habituated to impulses with recent additions to television apparatus. Commercial and station breaks have always been the occasion for consumptive and eliminatory impulses, and interactive relations of the life world are dissevered by the pull and fascination of the screen. But with remote controls, cable television and video recorders, bodies have come to be actively accustomed to rituals of selection. Interactive controls encourage stops, replays, editing and constant change initiated on impulses arising out of televisual bodies. Proliferation of "choices" due to cable channels and video tape are symptomatic of increased propagation of impulses. The main effect is to elicit impulses for change, any change. Practically every viewer spends some time, even long periods of time, impelled to flip through the channels unable to settle on any one for long. Channel-switching at the press of a remote control button has become so prevalent among children in the United States that they seldom watch a program in its entirety.[22]

Benjamin thought that the revolutionary potential in the cinema lay in the habituation of a mass audience to collective behavior under conditions of distraction. He said that,

> The distracted person, too, can form habits. More, the ability to master certain tasks in a state of distraction proves that their solution has become a matter of habit."[23]

Benjamin's hopes for the mobilization of the masses through cinema have not come to pass. Moreover television, which individualizes and separates the masses in separate space capsule rooms, habituates televisual bodies not to coherent mass action but rather to impulses. Impulses do not arise out of any form of consciousness and they require no attention. The dialogic connections of the lifeworld are interfered with as the impulses to more and ever more information insert themselves within the interactions of viewing bodies, the tug of their fascination pressing on and often rupturing conversation, attention and practices. Habituation of bodies occurs in a state of distraction that meets the shock effect much more than half-way[24]; bodies, themselves become sites out of which impulses arise and to which they return.

No more information is gained by the active selection of images than is found in the raw static out of which every image arises. All possible images are always already there in the televisual complex. Once all possible information is intermingled in a single morass, its value as information is degraded without its character as information dissolving. The presumption of new information presupposes that the televisual complex is part of a determinate scene of action; it fails to understand the televisual complex as an originary world of information. It fails to grasp the reduction of selection and choice to aimless impulses, arising without concern for form or content but generating changes in images as symptoms and seizing their content as fetishes, fragments of a derived milieu. The multiplying of simulations of selection and choice functions primarily as an induction impelling bodies to more and more selection, dissipating the content of choice in favor of impulses, "a choice which chooses itself and ceaselessly begins itself again."[25] The act of choosing is deprived of any determinate context and is reduced to mere impulse; or rather in the televisual complex no real acts of choice occur, but distracted by symptoms and seduced by fragments bodies are disciplined as generators of impulses.

This indicates that behavior in the televisual complex is perverse. Behavior is perverse because the fragments that make up the derived milieux of shows, commercials, announcements and station breaks only promise decisive action and real affect which never arrive. The intensity of affective states is defeated by constant interruption. Many shows are scripted so that affective intensity is highest before commercial breaks. This is necessary for there to be any hope of bridging a gap filled with so many impulses. Yet in the end it fails, since even this, relatively prolonged, affective intensity only occurs within a derived milieu. Still, images are not sufficiently separated from their spatio-temporal co-ordinates to count as any-space-whatevers in which genuine affect could occur.[26] Impulses always appear as symptoms, perverse behaviors, that seem for the moment to give rise to determinate contexts. However, they eventually rip through the affective texture and reduce it to a shimmer, on a par with every other fragmented affect, dissolving their intensity. Likewise no action can be decisive when the situation that gives it meaning is fragmented and displaced by a completely different situation.[27] Because of this degradation of action and affect, perversion is normal in the derived milieu.[28] When images are subjected to perverse behavior, they become fetishes; not only the fetishism of commodities evident in advertisements, but also the fetishism of images themselves: the look of designer bodies, the circulation of the catch phrase or jingle. Impulses also appear in perversions of selective processes, since they arise from bodies grounded only in an abstract habit of choosing for its own sake. They are directed only to seizing fetishes, bypassing consciousness and rational calculation in favor of indiscriminate reflex. Bodies, in the televisual complex, display only perverse behavior, since they are cut off from any situation that could be determined by action. Immobilized, bodily activity is reduced to the absorption of images; without work, bodies are stored and oriented to the absorption of information. Viewing bodies become parasitic, monsters and invalids, as they feed off of images.[29]

This feeding frenzy consumes a enormous amount of time. While the co-ordinates of naturalism map out the territory of the televisual complex, the negative effects of time, temporal consumption as the repetition and degradation inherent in naturalism, constitute its most important effects. The time consumed should not be calculated primarily in terms of the almost one third of measurable life time spent with television; it must be grasped as the temporality of naturalism. "TV is not only the *real* time; it is the *only* time."[30] This remark is put forward as the climax of a meditation on tracking polls. The connection between television and polling has often been noted along with its deleterious effect on history. Trow calls polling "the history of no-history" and says that "television holds the archives of the history of no-history."[31] Polls have a special connection to the televisual complex since it is an originary world of information, and it is out of this originary world that the derived milieux receive "a temporality as destiny."[32] Time occurs in naturalism as repetition and degradation.

We have already noted the overabundance of repetition in the televisual complex; foremost as excess of information, but also in commercials, breaks, shows, replays, channels, etc.; and these heterodyne with the repetition of acts of viewing, channel switching, recording etc. Repetition, here, is always repetition of information, a repetition which, therefore, must eternally return to the originary world of the televisual complex. With television mired in a naturalism of information, every image arises out of bits and disappears back into them. This is the closed or bad repetition "the eternal return as reproduction of something always already-accomplished."[33] Since every image is a repetition of and return to the aggregate of all possible information, it subordinates time to the coordinates of naturalism and makes it dependent on the impulse.[34] The time of television is always the same time. Genres return whether in new incarnations or as nostalgia; syndication and cable have made the history of television into an ideal simultaneity. Viewing bodies, as a consequence, have only a degenerate temporality, destined to return again and again to exactly the same space, time and the accelerated oscillation of images.

Degradation is an inevitable consequence of the closed repetition. Impulses toward the new find their destiny in more information, resulting in an acceleration that changes images faster and faster threatening to dissolve them all in the originary static of all possible information. The average time between cuts (most noticeably in commercials and in music videos) has steadily decreased over the tenure of television. More than that, the rate of change increases within images; hence the proliferation of images of speed and violence. This bombardment of images generates more and faster impulses in absorbing bodies. Bodies accustomed to a swifter rate of impulses tolerate the duration of images less and less. They respond by actively changing the images by remote control and other devices.

The destiny of all images is to descend into the mire of information; all information reduced to just one bit following another, intensifying the indifference of one bit with another. This is the inevitable exhaustion of images as derived milieu. The shrewdness and joy of impulses lies in their impetus to change milieu. Impulses seek to absorb every milieu and, exhausting it, to move on to a different milieu until every possible derived milieu is exhausted and is returned to the originary world.

> The impulse must be exhaustive. It is not even sufficient to say that the impulse contents itself with what a milieu gives it or leaves to it. This contentment is not resignation, but a great joy in which the impulse rediscovers its power of choice, since it is, at the deepest level, the desire to change milieu, to seek a new milieu to explore, to dislocate, enjoying all the more what this milieu offers, no matter how low, repulsive or disgusting it may be."[35]

In the televisual complex, the multiplication of channels and peripheral devices, as well as of products, events, shows and personalities, apparatus and images decompose in the exhaustion of every image that arises. Desire and selection are exhausted so that "The space is so saturated, I no longer know what I want." Communication, content and messages reach saturation and are exhausted, wasting away into the primordial detritus of information.

> Information devours its own contents; it devours communication and the social, and for two reasons: Instead of causing communication, it exhausts itself in the act of staging the communication; instead of producing meaning, it exhausts itself in the process of simulation with which we are very familiar."[36]

Repetition was the only hope for a return to the real in the naturalistic world of television, and it does not succeed because it always ends in the swamp of fragments and never arrives at real situations or genuine value.[37]

Ultimately what is degraded is duration, the world of time and consciousness; faster and faster changes in images destined for an ideal simultaneity. Lifetime is destroyed in an orgy of impulses, a proliferation of microsacrifices: lived time sacrificed to the moment, impulses marked by changes of images, bodies seeking a televisual immortality in the moment. However, there is never really a sacrifice of duration. Viewing bodies are never dissolved in the moment: instead time is suspended in a simulation of the moment. It is true that television is entertainment in the archaic sense; it occupies and maintains time. The signs of information always inhabit televisual duration. It is sacrificed but only to the repetition of duration itself filled only with the pure signs of information, not to a true timelessness but to fragments of time. Impulses aspire to the destruction of time, but duration is never really destroyed although it is, perhaps, wasted or rather leveled and occupied. Micro-sacrifices don't reveal time. Instead information as a thing returns in its own duration. Information is confirmed in its reality by its own destruction. Yet, even this sacrifice is never complete. The naturalistic world of information and impulse oscillates between the poles of the boredom of ever more information and of the violence of impulses. The stakes degenerate into a morass of equivalence, rather than, as with a sacrifice of real stakes, in the return to intimacy. Information is only authenticated as its own image and sign not as a useful thing; only the signs of information are confirmed, the originary world of all possible information.

Factitious sacrifices are instances of the static violence of the impulse-image, a violence without a return to the real. The violence with which impulses take possession of every image is ultimately static, since it is incapable of transgressing the law of information. Impulses take possession of every image, striving for more and more information they turn on themselves and plunge back into the swamp out of which arise more impulses. Violence on the screen is spectacular and charming[38], yet it merely repeats the static violence of the underlying informational static and the violent paralysis of bodies. The fascination of even the blank screen produces a violent immobilization of the whole televisual complex.

The exhaustion of derived milieu, the desperation for ever more images, is the symptom of a hope for survival that drives the image into the hands of death.

> ... impulses have the same goal and the same destiny: to smash into fragments, to tear off fragments, gather up the scraps, form the great rubbish dump and bring everything together in a single

and identical death impulse. Death, the death impulse—naturalism is saturated with it."[39]

The televisual complex is permeated with death. On prime time network television alone there are three violent deaths every hour, and that only counts entertainment shows. Add to that the thousands of deaths reported on the news, the peculiar regeneration of deaths in cartoons, and non-violent deaths, factor in non-network channels and time outside prime time; the television image is saturated with death. By now this observation is a platitude. More interesting is the habituation of bodies to accelerated and empty selection. Bodies generate increasing doses of impulses until they all merge in one great death impulse. Duration is not sacrificed, but it is dead: empty rituals of selection—the death of concern in fascination; fetishism of information, images, and the images of products—the death of production in the signs of consumption; the reduction of bodies to the absorption of images—the death of activity and affect in impulses engrossing life time. The apparatus inures bodies to give themselves increasing doses of impulses unto death like a suicide machine (push three buttons and you're dead). But in the televisual complex death takes a lifetime; absorption into the screen, televisual immortality, exterminates space and time in a durable void pulsing with all possible information.

4. Televisual Bodies

He doesn't know the sentence that has been passed on him? No . . . There would be no point in telling him. He'll learn it on his body."[40]

Franz Kafka, "In the Penal Colony"

Dead Ringers fashions an impulse-image out of the continual medicalization of wrong bodies, while the televisual complex constitutes an impulse-image out of the death of space and time in the mutual absorption of images, bodies and apparatus. The televisual complex is a malignancy, an Empedoclean world of invalids and monsters. The televisual body is a wrong body; like the medicalized bodies of *Dead Ringers* it is the site of continual refashioning. The impulse alters the way bodies appear and function. But this refashioning is purified since it seeks, without goal or content, only the impulse to more, newer, faster impulses in a world always already containing all possible information. This purity of the impulse-image is unattained in the cinema because the impulse-image is only one image among many on the screen. It is not so essentially a part of the material aggregate of images, bodies and apparatus. The televisual complex is affixed in the order of the sensory-motor connection, differentiated within the movement-image, but unable to achieve a direct time-image. Therefore, it fails to achieve transgression and the sublime; it is mired in fragments of real situations, in fetishes, which do not become pure optical signs which could open onto time. Instead, it putrefies in the endless closed repetition of impulses and information. If all images on the television screen are dominated by the impulse-image, it is because the impulse-image arises out of a technology of power in which the televisual complex, as impulse-image, gives rise to an acceleration of images, immobilizing space and rupturing time in a destiny of decay into a morass of all possible information, bound to an endless oscillation between boredom and violence incapable of issuing in affect or action.

Notes

I would like to thank William Bogard, Ron G. Williams, Garrett Thomson, Iain Boal and the Retort group for stimulating my thinking on these matters. My presentation and discussion of some of this material at the Retort group was partially funded by Eastern Oregon State College.
 1. George Trow, "Within The Context of No-Context," *The New Yorker*, Nov. 17, 1980. P. 63.
 2. Gilles Deleuze, *Cinema I: The Movement Image.* (Minneapolis: University of Minnesota Press, 1986).
 3. Trow, "Television has a scale. It has other properties but what television has to a dominant degree is scale and the ability to enforce it" (63).
 4. Cf. Peter Sloterdijk, *Critique of Cynical Reason* (Minneapolis: University of Minnesota Press, 1988), p. 312-314
 5. Therese Bertherat and Carol Benstein, *The Body Has Its Reasons* (New York, 1979), p. 50. Quotation taken from Stuart Ewen, *All Consuming Images: The Politics of Style in Contemporary Culture* (New York: Basic Books, 1988).
 6. Deleuze, p. 134
 7. Deleuze, p. 124
 8. Deleuze, p. 139.
 9. Deleuze, p. 124.
 10. Deleuze, p. 123.
 11. "The invalid and the monster gain such presence in naturalism because they are both the deformed object of which the act of the impulse takes possession and the ill-formed sketch, which serves as the subject of this act," Deleuze, p. 128.
 12. "What makes the impulse-image so difficult to reach and even to define or identify, is that it is somehow 'stuck' between the affection-image

and the action-image." Deleuze, p. 134.

13. Deleuze, p. 127.

14. Deleuze, p. 136.

15. Louise Erdich, *Love Medicine* (New York: Holt, Rinehard, and Winston, 1984), p. 189

16. Oliver Wendell Holmes, "The Stereoscope and the Stereograph." *The Atlantic Monthly* 3, June 1859, reprinted in Beaumont Newhall, ed., *Photography: Essays and Images* (Boston: Museum of Modern Art; Bullfinch Press, 1981), pp. 53-54.

17. Jean Baudrillard and Sylvere Lotringer, "Forget Baudrillard," *Forget Foucault/Forget Baudrillard* (New York: Semiotext(e), 1983), p. 140.

18. Baudrillard and Lotringer.

19. Deleuze's classification of images is conceived in Bergsonian terms, where an image is not merely an unreal world but the world which itself becomes an unreal image. Cf. Deleuze, pp. 57-61.

20. "The spectator's process of association in view of these images is indeed interrupted by their constant, sudden change. This constitutes the shock effect of the film. . . ." Walter Benjamin, "The Work of Art in the Age of Mechanical Reproduction," *Illuminations*, ed. Hannah Arendt, trans. Harry Zohn (New York: Schocken Books, 1969).

21. Benjamin.

22. This point is made by Richard Kearney, *The Wake of Imagination* (Minneapolis: University of Minnesota Press, 1988), p. 321.

23. Kearney

24. "The film with its shock effect meets this mode of reception [habituation in a state of distraction] halfway," Kearney.

25. Deleuze, p.136.

26. "An originary world is not an any-space-whatever (although it may resemble one), because it only appears in the depths of determined milieux; but neither is it a determined milieux, which only derives from the originary world," Deleuze, p. 123.

27. John Cleese has said that Monty Python's Flying Circus demonstrated that transitions were unnecessary. This is summed up in their trademark announcement "And now for something completely different." However, the Python's just took advantage of and made obvious the existing state of the televisual complex.

28. "The impulse is an act which tears away, ruptures, dislocates. Perversion is therefore not its deviation, but its derivation, that is, its normal expression in the derived milieu," Deleuze, p. 128.

29. "TV also produces, then a whole rhetorical theatre of predators and parasites, each signified with either sunshine or dark charm, to momentarily disturb the media field, and to incite flagging interest in that postmodern fiction called the audience." Arthur Kroker, Marilouise Kroker, and David Cook, *Panic Encyclopedia: The Definitive Guide to the Postmodern Scene* (New York: St. Martin's Press, 1989), pp. 221-222. Also "It [the perversion of the impulse] is a constant predator-prey relationship," Deleuze.

30. Kroker, Kroker, and Cook.

31. Trow.

32. Deleuze, p. 125

33. Deleuze, p. 131

34. Deleuze, p. 127

35. Deleuze, p. 129

36. Jean Baudrillard, "Implosion of Meaning in the Media" in *In the Shadow of the Silent Majorities* (New York: Semiotext(e), 1983), pp. 97-98.

37. "The good man, the saintly man, are imprisoned in the cycle, no less than the thug and the evildoer." Deleuze, p. 131.

38. "In a TV mediascape which always verges on the immobility of stasis, the production of charm, positive and negative, and its assignation to a floating scene of political images is an absolute survival technique," Kroker, Kroker, and Cook.

39. Deleuze, p. 130.

40. Franz Kafka, "In the Penal Colony" in *The Penal Colony: Stories and Short Pieces*, trans. Willa and Edwin Muir (New York: Schocken Books, 1961).

At the end of romance, Mickey Rourke as Motorcycle Boy in Francis Ford
Coppola's *Rumble Fish* (1983). Universal. Still courtesy of Jerry Ohlinger's
Movie Materials.

Jon Lewis

The Road to Romance and Ruin: The Crisis of Authority in Francis Ford Coppola's Rumble Fish

In his 1926 poem, "The End of the World," Archibald MacLeish closes things out with the following chilling (and prescient, pre-nuclear) image:

> . . . there, there overhead, there, there, hung over those
> thousands of white faces, those dazed eyes,
> there in the starless dark the poise, the hover,
> there with vast wings across the cancelled skies,
> there in the sudden blackness the black pall
> of nothing, nothing, nothing—nothing at all.[1]

MacLeish's poem begins with a series of paradoxical images; an "armless ambidextrian," for example, striking a match as the circus big top "quite suddenly blows off." But the poem ends rather unambiguously; the apocalypse fulfilling its narrative and cultural function as the quintessence of closure.

Updating such a formal and ideological tack, contemporary novelist Don DeLillo reinscribes such a narrative trajectory into this, the post-nuclear, postmodern age. In his 1978 novel *Players*, for example, DeLillo opens the narrative aboard a commercial aircraft. Dinner has just been served and the in-flight movie has begun. On screen there are golfers, golfing. For some reason, there is no soundtrack. Instead, there's this strange woman sitting in at the piano bar who is either not watching or doesn't quite understand the film. Before long—and such is the logic of contemporary narrative—the tranquil play on the links is curtailed. Terrorists armed with machetes emerge from behind the trees that line the fairway. In short order, the golfers stop golfing and start dying.

The film-scene is ironically (but predictably) depicted in slow motion; the camera betraying a fascination with the lush slaughter. (Such choreographed violence relates our attraction and fear of the genocidal scale of things these days.) The onboard piano music that sort of accompanies the film provides, as DeLillo puts it, "a gruesomely humorous ambiguity," revealing "a spectacle of ridiculous people doing awful things to total fools."[2] "The simple innocence of the music," DeLillo continues, "undermines the photogenic terror, reducing it to an empty swirl."[3]

It is a scene common to DeLillo's "fiction"—a little apocalypse that is emblematic of something potentially far more global, far less amusing. The passage closes with an elegant and ambiguous twist: "History this weightless has an easy time of it, contending with the burdens of the everyday."[4] But for DeLillo, whose *White Noise*, *Great Jones Street* and *End Zone* all present timely, paranoid visions of Armageddon in the everyday (airborne toxic events, rock fans gone terrorist, college classes on football and nuclear war strategy), the apocalypse is a joke in very bad taste; a crisis he finds funny because if he didn't he'd never make it through the day.

In "The Time Disease," a short story by Martin Amis, the earth is beset by a peculiar, apocalyptic virus; a disease characterized first by a return to youthful energy and sexual desire and then by sudden death. While in part the story lampoons the cult of youth by having fitness and health signal the end, Amis, like DeLillo uses humor to correspond a hardly amusing scenario. For example, the story's variation on the classic love/death finale plays out as follows:

> Yes, and time often takes them this way, I thought, in my slow and stately terror. You've come this far: go further, I told myself. Go closer, nearer, closer. Do it for her and for old time's sake. I stirred, ready to let her have all that head and hand could give, until I too felt the fever in my lines of heat, the swell and smell of youth and death. This is suicide, I thought, and I don't care. . . . At one point during the last hours, just before dawn, I got to my feet and crept to the window and looked up at the aching, hurting sky, like a coathanger left to shimmer on the pole, with Happy there beside me, alone in her bed and her hot death. 'Honey,' I said out loud, and went to join her. I like it, I thought and gave a sudden nod. What do I like? I like the love. This is suicide and I don't care.[5]

Like DeLillo, Amis is fixated with the imagery, the narrative trajectory of apocalypse. In one of the many forays into self-reflexivity in his most recent novel, *London Fields*, Amis (the writer/narrator) ruminates on the task of writing fiction in this perilous age:

> Even the Old Testament expected the Apocalypse 'shortly.' In times of mass disorientation and anxiety. . . . But I am trying to ignore the world situation. I am hoping it will go away. Not the world. The situation. I want time to get on with this little piece of harmless escapism. I want time to get on to London Fields.
>
> Sometimes I wonder whether I can keep the world situation out of the novel: the crisis, now sometimes called the Crisis (they can't be *serious*). Maybe it's like the weather. Maybe you can't keep it out.
>
> Will it reach the conclusion it appears to crave—will the Crisis reach the Conclusion? Is it the nature of the beast? We'll see. I certainly hope not. I would lose many potential readers, and all my work would have been in vain. And that would be a real bitch.[6]

In these our times, the apocalypse is the degree zero of all human endeavor; the conclusion that indeed has proven to be "a real bitch."

In the rapidly assembling postmodern canon, the apocalypse (as a purgative climactic act) coordinates an aesthetic and political philosophy of anything goes (for the time being, since that's all there is). Critics of postmodernism, as opposed to the army of postmodern critics, view this attraction to the end as yet another affectation, yet another easy way out of facing things in an age dominated by narcissism, life-style, conspicuous consumption and avarice.

In "Of an Apocalyptic Tone Adopted in Recent Philosophy," Jacques Derrida offers the following exasperated appraisal of what he derisively terms "the fantasy apocalypse" alternatingly celebrated and reviled in the ever mounting critical literature on postmodernism:

> It is not only the end of this here but also and first the end of that there, the end of class struggle, the end of philosophy, the death of God, the end of religions, the end of Christianity and morals . . . the end of man, the end of the West, the end of Oedipus, the end of the earth . . . also the end of literature, the end of painting, art as a thing of the past, the end of psychoanalysis, the end of the university, the end of phallocentrism and I don't know what else.[7]

In defense of Derrida, even a cursory survey of the critical literature on the subject provides the following obituaries: the death of the subject,[8] the end of master narratives,[9] the critical deconstruction of tradition,[10] the loss of stable linguistic models,[11] the irrelevance of distinctions between high and low art,[12] the end of metaphysics[13] and the absolute failure of theory.[14] It seems hardly worth arguing that from the very start postmodernism has positioned itself at the end: of modernism, the modern era, the fascism of elite/high art, Marxism, the avant garde, the dialectic of the spirit—take your choice. But is postmodernism the end of something old and thus the beginning of something else different and new, or just the end (the exhaustion of inspiration, critique and intervention)? Is postmodernism a *critical* discourse or (just) a discourse of acquiescence?

Whatever our answers are to such questions, indeed, whatever we make of this evident crisis in theory and culture, the critical literature continues to mount touting works that coincide and resonate with the insanity of American culture here now in these last days before the apocalypse.

In *The Post-Modern Aura*, a vitriolic attack on postmodern fiction, Charles Newman quips that contemporary art "goes up like a rocket and comes down like a stick."[15] Newman, like John Gardner and more recently Edward Hoagland[16] chastises his fellow writers' and artists' refusal or inability to respond productively and morally to current crises in our culture. Art these days, Newman laments, uncritically defers to (rather than challenges) the dominant thematic of the age: the end as boring, as anti-climax, as euthanasia, as "nothing, nothing, nothing— nothing at all."

Newman's project is basically a call for standards, a nostalgia for high modernism. Indeed, for Newman the temporary contemporary exhibits little more than a whiney narcissism, evasion instead of confrontation. In such a scenario, postmodernism seems little more than a retreat into self-actualization, an acquiescence to a kind of Gresham's Law in cultural practice.

Fredric Jameson, who outlines postmodernism in two pivotal essays on the subject ("Postmodernism and Consumer Society" and "Postmodernism, Or the Cultural Logic of Late Capitalism"),[17] points to an emerging relationship between certain works of art and post-industrial society. The organic principals of Jameson's postmodernism can be summarized as follows: (1) postmodernism is misunderstood, (2) its tenuous unity is evident only in its opposition to high modernism, (3) it designates an erosion of distinctions between high and low art, (4) it effaces genre conventions, (5) it is ahistorical, (6) it models the multitude of intersections between art and the cultural conditions of late capitalism and (7) in its seeming randomness, it simulates an undifferentiated (schizophrenic) world vision. Additionally, postmodernism characteristically involves: historical eclecticism, replication/simulation, pastiche (rather than parody), bootlegging/recycling/plundering the art of the past, nostalgia and a (seeming) apoliticism.

Given these criteria, the text of primary interest to this essay, Francis

Coppola's photogenic, apocalyptic teen movie *Rumble Fish*, seems programmatically postmodern (hardly an end in itself, but significant nonetheless). From its premier at the New York Film Festival, *Rumble Fish* was widely misread and mishandled. The executives at Universal Pictures viewed *Rumble Fish* as hopelessly esoteric. Despite its teen heart-throb cast, the executives soon realized the film hadn't a passing chance at the lucrative teen market (especially since the genre was then dominated by ex-advertising executive John Hughes's *16 Candles, Pretty in Pink, The Breakfast Club, Some Kind of Wonderful* and *Ferris Bueller's Day Off*).

The reviews nationwide ran the gamut from goofy adulation to equally unreasoned hate. In *Newsweek*, for example, Jack Kroll described *Rumble Fish* as "a brilliant tone poem of inner exile. . . . Rusty James and his girlfriend are like mirror images, beautiful inheritors of a tainted legacy." He credits Mickey Rourke's eccentric performance with "a fierce delicacy" and concludes that, *Rumble Fish* is a welcome reach for beauty by an artist who won't surrender."[18]

In the *New Yorker*, Pauline Kael was far less flattering. "It's all a ridiculously trite configuration of adolescent heroics," she writes, "and to make it worse, Coppola tricks it up with arty trimmings." Her final blow is savage indeed: "I suppose there's a moral in all this, but it's not about those poor fish, it's about Coppola."[19]

On several other counts, *Rumble Fish* satisfies Jameson's checklist. For example, the film displays a narrative and thematic multiplicity. While at times hopelessly nostalgic, it is contemporary in its self-conscious and ambiguous relationship to the technology and capital that produced it. The multitude of film and literary references outline an allusory complexity; an ahistorical, seemingly random plagiarism. The teen culture depicted in *Rumble Fish* is hardly the stuff of gritty realist teen melodrama. Instead, Coppola re-presents shared ideas and stereotypes from past teen films, as if history were a series of reference points in a movie.

Coppola's pastiche supports Jameson's argument that contemporary cinema has gravitated towards a visceral but apolitical nostalgia. "The increasing number of films about the past are no longer historical," Jameson concludes, "they are images, simulacra and pastiches of the past."[20] But in its undermining of the conventions (pop music, method acting, ritual male gang violence, broken families and sibling rivalry) of a central post-war valorizing fiction (the teen film), *Rumble Fish* betrays a paradoxical and postmodern political agenda. By effacing and multiplying genre so deftly, it challenges the Hollywood (and very infantile) ritual of repetition and gratification typical of genre fiction.

In "Blissing Out: The Politics of Reaganite Entertainment," Andrew Britton cites the tendency of mainstream films in the 1980's to offer conservative reassurance through pure or mixed genre fare. In such films, Britton argues, the "high concept" of "entertainment" is an end in and of itself. "Reaganite entertainment," Britton posits, "refers to itself in order to persuade us that it doesn't refer outwards at all. It is purely and simply entertainment—and we all know what that is."[21]

"Entertainment tells us to forget our troubles and get happy," Britton continues, "but it also tells us that in order to do so we must agree deliberately to switch life off. The feeling that reality is intolerable is rapturously invoked."[22] Citing the irrationality or at least complexity of the pre-apocalypse mind-set, Britton concludes with the following deceptively complex sentence: "We are not told not to think, but we are told, over and over again, that there is nothing to think about."[23]

Given its opposition to the very trends Britton laments, *Rumble Fish* can be seen as a politically revisionist, anti- or non-genre film. Its subtle allusions to *West Side Story, Rebel Without a Cause, The Wild One, The Oresteia, Oedipus the King* and *The Iliad* are rendered in overt stylistic allusions to expressionism and film noir (two cinematic traditions that examined and epitomized the mind-set of wartime annihilation and genocide). The film's use of style as *the* defining principal of narrative models the apocalyptic mindset of today's post-punk, pre-apocalypse youth, a generation reared in the shadow of the big nuclear bang. Such a youth is glibly characterized by Gavin Smith as follows:

> Absurdist nihilism is the prevailing eighties style, an inverted grammar adopted by kids as they indulge in the peculiarly narcissistic masochism of adolescent self-martyrdom. Teen suicide is only the tragic *reductio ad absurdum* of this impulse. Ask any teenager.[24]

In *Rumble Fish*, valorizing and apocalyptic myths regarding the story of Christ (suicide), Oedipus (fratricide) and the Pied Piper (genocide) are appropriated, effectively stripping away the social imperative of these influential narratives. As Craig Owens argues, postmodern fiction indicates "a crisis of cultural authority."[25] In the absence of stable linguistic models and socially operative and relevant narratives (and this despite the argument regarding narrative and pleasure—that if you destroy the former, you destroy the latter), the disarray of contemporary culture finds a model in the seeming disarray of postmodern art.

It is *Rumble Fish*'s seeming allusory incoherence that makes it so timely; so political. But what is the film's (or the genre it so tenuously fits) relationship to the social conditions, the actuality, of contemporary youth culture? If postmodernism does effect a series of intersections between the presentations on screen and the everyday, how does *Rumble Fish* fit in the overall scheme of things?

In *Subculture: The Meaning of Style*, Dick Hebdige contends that youth's recourse to the material and materiality of style—its spectacularization of everyday objects, speech, fashion and music—evinces an act of cultural refusal. Youth's style, Hebdige argues, its expression of opposition in and through material culture, offers a symbolic violation of the social order, a serious challenge to cultural hegemony (what Antonio Gramsci described as the moving equilibrium of culture).[26]

Despite stylistic, tonal, industrial and by now even generational differences within the genre (and a dizzying array of seemingly autonomous youth subcultures with which these films resonate and respond), teen films all seem to focus on the apparent breakdown of (traditional forms) of authority (patriarchy, law and order and institutions like: the school, the church and the family). While a rapid succession of youth subcultures appear to have rejected the conventions of authority *tout court*, the teen film has rather enthusiastically negotiated the reverse. By and large, the teen film presides over the eventual discovery of viable and often traditional forms of authority (for example, the re-affirmation of: patriarchy in *Rebel Without* a Cause, law and order in *The Wild One* or the charismatic elite in *Heathers*); in effect, restoring the official culture, informed rather than radicalized by youth.

Teen films mitigate against the stylized rebellion of youth. What at first appears to be counter-hegemonic is in the end just deviant and transient, chronicling the end of a search for and delineating the eventual re-insertion of authority. We are forced then to re-read the narrative of youth (on and off screen) as hardly antisocial, as a ritual (an acting out) of impatience and need in the absence of functional and deeply desired authority.

Teen films provide youth with a wealth of substantive images, a picture of their own lives that to a great extent originates from outside their own experience. These films provide at best the principal artifacts of youth culture; at worst, they offer proof positive of the hegemonic effect of "the culture industry." The teen movie has proven to be one of the most profitable and proliferated film genres of the post-war period. But like virtually all media enterprises targeted at a mass audience, these films have, as Stuart Hall argues, "progressively colonized the cultural and ideological sphere."[27] they have appropriated the discourse of youth into the discourse of Hollywood and Madison Avenue. The net result is that neither youth culture nor the teen film can boast any real autonomy, any discernible origin; a phenomenon highlighting the layers of intersection between social representation and the media representation of the social (the paradox of youth as both mass movement and mass market).

In *Rumble Fish*, the culturally significant teen film narrative—one that re-writes the history of youth subcultures into the conservative and reassuring formula of Hollywood melodrama, musical comedy, horror and adventure—is dismantled, analyzed and ultimately rendered moot. The postmodern effect in *Rumble Fish* is that in the end, there is nothing save the failure of virtually every narrative and motion picture style (since they are, almost all of them, used at one point or another) to explain away the hopelessness and bankruptcy of post-war America here epitomized by bored and aimless youth. If there is a rapture (a denouement), it is evident only in the perversity of (in Jean Baudrillard's terms) "the obscene ecstasy of alienation,"[28] a dubious revelation indeed at the tail end of this apocalyptic scene.

When Warren Montag characterizes Baudrillard as "the veritable coroner of contemporary thought,"[29] he too speaks to the "apocalyptic fantasies" that proliferate much of the discussion of postmodernism. Citing a fundamental distinction between high and post- modernism, Montag offers the following elitist words of wisdom:

> The work of art, once full of meaning and affect and possessed of a depth that seemed infinite has become empty, alien and cold, no longer a representation of reality but a simulacrum of a simulacrum, a false representation of what is itself false.[30]

Such a shift portends the end of mimesis and the emergence of pastiche (exit Jim Stark, enter the Motorcycle Boy).

The seemingly depthless and cold world of Coppola's *Rumble Fish* is presented (mostly) in black and white—the "color" of realism—but it is hardly realistic. The film was shot on location in Tulsa, Oklahoma in 1982 where the S. E. Hinton novel (upon which it is based) takes place some 25 years earlier. While this could suggest realism, nostalgia, even urban history in a more conventional movie, Coppola's interests lay in the creation of a pointedly anti-realist, ethereal, ahistorical space, frantically allusory to expressionism and film noir while at the same time chronicling a familiar wild teen romance. The score, composed and performed by ex-Police percussionist Stewart Copeland, bears a distinct reggae beat, hardly a reference to Tulsa, circa 1960 (or 1982).

In the rumble that basically opens the action in *Rumble Fish*, we find a model of the film's deconstructive thrust. Two tough boys, Rusty James and Biff Wilcox, face off down by the tracks, but Coppola foregoes an establishing shot, visual continuity or theatrical blocking and staging to open up and delineate the scene. Instead, what we see is complex, visceral and formally decentering. Frenetic cuts on form, skewed camera angles and low key lighting (accompanying the pre-requisite steam rising from the overheated city streets) highlight style as content, as an end in itself.

During the carefully choreographed and expressive fight scene (not unlike the rumble as dance in *West Side Story* or *Absolute Beginners*), the Motorcycle Boy (played by Mickey Rourke) arrives. He is introduced framed in a choker close-up, his head tilted to the side, looking just like Marlon Brando in the publicity stills for *The Wild One*. And while Rourke apes Brando's quintessential anomic, rebellious youth, his performance (especially his body language and carriage) also refers back to his own breakthrough character performance as the truth-telling arsonist in *Body Heat*.

The Motorcycle Boy's first speech, which like everything he says is couched in metaphor and allusion, refers to the inconclusive struggle for authority that began with his departure from Tulsa. "What is this," he asks with irony, "another glorious fight for the kingdom?" His brother, Rusty James, who at this point has trounced Biff, looks up at his brother and away from his opponent. While he contemplates his brother's speech, Biff rises and guts Rusty James with a jagged piece of glass. The Motorcycle Boy's apparent ability to seize authority any time he feels like it paradoxically commences as his brother lies bleeding on the street and is dramatically staged as Biff is vanquished in an expressive *danse macabre* with the Motorcycle Boy's Harley Davidson.

The Motorcycle Boy's absence and then his presence on the scene at first appears to be an issue of some real importance to the story. But with the Motorcycle Boy (as a kind of postmodern teen anti-hero), the binary opposition of presence and absence is effaced. When he is present, he's not all there; he's hard of hearing and he can't see colors. When he's gone, his legend remains significantly behind. After the rumble scene, Rusty James and the Motorcycle Boy share a brotherly moment together. It is, for anyone who has taken an acting class, a familiar "method" exercise. It informs us in no uncertain terms that these actors (not characters) are doing "the method." As pure stylized performance, this scene tells us nothing about the characters though it tells us everything we need to know about the actors, leaving us, to defer again to Jameson, "awash in a sea of private languages."[31] Rather than use an acting style to prompt a narrative effect, Coppola reduces style to a code which is at once familiar (as a code), just as it is boring and meaningless.

The scene showcases and deconstructs the cold, anomic acting style and also chronicles, in the monosyllabic argot of "the method," the emptiness of the brothers' relationship. It plays out as follows:

Motorcycle Boy (MB):   Poor kid, looks like you're messed up all
                    the time.
Rusty James (RJ):   I'm OK . . . Let's go out and get a bite to eat.
MB: Hey.
RJ: What?
MB: Hey. (*pause*) Hey.
RJ: What?
MB: Hey.
RJ: I'm all right man.
MB: Why?
RJ: Why what?
MB: Why?
RJ: Fuck.
MB: Hey, hey.
RJ: What?
MB: Why? Why? —No, no, no—Don't tell me fuck fuck—Why?
      Why?—Huh?
RJ: Let's go get something to eat.
MB: You talk to me—why?
RJ: Why what? (*exasperated*) What?
MB: Why are you fucked up all the time one way or another, huh?
RJ: I don't know.

Early on in the film, a similarly earnest effort at "the method"
attends to the banality (rather than the more conventional desperation)
of teen romance. The scene begins as Patty and Rusty James settle down
to make out on her living room couch. Time passes (expressed in cliche
fast-motion photography). Rusty James falls asleep. Eventually Patty
wakes him. When he finally gathers his thoughts, he announces: "I gotta
fight Biff Wilcox at 10." Though he's lousy company, Patty begs him
to stay. But Rusty James poses and grunts and looks away. "You're
better than your brother," she says, cutting to the heart of the matter.
He laughs and replies: "He's cool." "You're better," she replies earnestly,
"you're warm."

But her payoff line falls flat—not because of her performance but
because of what (her) performance means in this film. We are meant
to understand that she is just acting, saying lines we've heard before.
The net effect is a kind of ennui—a boredom that characterizes this
generation born in the age of immanent catastrophe. The scene ends
as they exchange listless "I love you's"—undercut soon enough as Patty
dumps Rusty James for his rival, Smokey.

Much of what's left of narrative (in the face of so much style) is
undercut by the inability of either potential hero (the Motorcycle Boy
or Rusty James) to seize the day. In the absence of a functional hero
(the dominant structure of authority in narrative in general) or the gangs

(the organizing principle of teen street life) drugs take hold of the leaderless teen world. When Rusty James gets set to fight Biff, for example, his nostalgic euphoria at the prospect of a rumble is tempered when he discovers that Biff is high on pills. Throughout the film, Rusty James laments how drugs ruined the gangs, how drugs supplanted an authority he now yearns for.

Late in the film, as Rusty James recovers from yet another brutal beating, the Motorcycle Boy suggests that gangs and rumbles ended because they got boring. In a rueful, ambiguous speech set under a bridge and blocked as if it were on stage (as if it were a payoff scene in a film), the Motorcycle Boy looks to the future. "The gangs will come back," he says, "people will persist at joining things. . . . Once they get the dope off the streets, you'll see the gangs come back—if you live that long."

The Motorcycle Boy's glib analysis of a generation born to follow underscores his refusal to be a hero. While so many teen films portray an unlikely youth who through fate or chance or just desserts becomes a hero, the Motorcycle Boy seems a likely candidate who just wants to rest in peace. While the Motorcycle Boy eschews the mantle of authority, his power over the teen world remains unquestioned. Cassandra, his substitute-teacher ex-girlfriend, for example, descends into heroin addiction in his absence, and fails to rekindle their romance when he returns. She, like her namesake—the ill-fated soothsayer who foretold the carnage at Troy—is forced to stand idly by as the heroes of her generation totter off to their doom. This allusion to the mythic Cassandra reinforces the film's apocalypse theme. It also highlights both Cassandras' essentially romantic significance.

In his poem, "Cassandra to Helen," Andrew Harvey closes with the following image: "As was foretold—river to blood—sky to fire,"[32] linking the tragic heroine to an at once contemporary and Biblical apocalyptic scene. In a second poem, this time titled simply "Cassandra," Harvey again concludes with an image of Armageddon. This time around, Cassandra is unmasked in the image of an axe murderer:

> Between birdcries one
> hears an axe sharpening in the house . . .
>   How much blood did you
> need to get the walls that color?[33]

The significance of Cassandra as an allusion (perhaps to his own violent end) is not lost on the ethereal Motorcycle Boy nor his (and Rusty James') alcoholic father. "You know what happened to the people who didn't listen to Cassandra," the Motorcycle Boy muses. "The Greeks got 'em," his father replies. (But, as usual, Rusty James doesn't get it and asks them both to "speak English.")

In the novel, Rusty James introduces Cassandra as follows:

> There she was, college educated and from a good family and from
> a nice home on the other side of town, and she moves here into
> an old apartment and follows the Motorcycle Boy around. She
> wasn't even pretty. Steve said she was, but I didn't think so. She'd
> walk around barefoot like a hick and didn't wear any makeup.
> Almost every time I'd see her she'd be carrying a cat. I don't like
> cats. I didn't go as far as Biff Wilcox did, use them for target practice
> with a twenty-two pistol, but I didn't like them. And she'd try to
> talk like the Motorcycle Boy, try to say things that meant
> something. She didn't fool me.[34]

In the film, as we join their ill-fated romance, Cassandra is already
much in need of redemption from the Motorcycle Boy. But she is
frustrated at every turn by his impassivity, his cool. Like her, he is the
victim of the characters he finds himself alluding to; the characters he
simulates. As part Robin Hood, Pied Piper, Christ, Oedipus, James Dean
and Marlon Brando, the Motorcycle Boy is of no use to anyone, including,
eventually, "himself."

"If my girlfriend ever did dope," Rusty James tells Cassandra, "I'd
break her arm." "Just her arm," she replies, "I wish he'd show me that
much mercy." Later on in the film, the Motorcycle Boy leads Rusty James
and his nerd sidekick Steve to a seedy bar in a hostile, black
neighborhood. It is yet another scene in which the Motorcycle Boy
ventures on the road to ruin and his brother blindly follows. (In this
scene Rusty James and Steve drink too much, get left behind and get
mugged in an alley on the way home.)

But on the way to the bar, they stop at a carnival under a bridge.
Cassandra is there dancing dreamily by herself. Just as she spies the
Motorcycle Boy, we hear Queen Ida begin a contemporary New Orleans
Zydeco number. Cassandra dances alluringly up to her ex-boyfriend and
lip-synchs the words to the song: "You're the man of my dreams . . .
the sweetest man I've ever seen." But she is just mouthing the words.
And he has no way or intention of telling her how he feels (if indeed
he feels anything at all).

In the film, the point is not that the Motorcycle Boy can't live up
to his reputation; in fact it is suggested that he could if he wanted to.
Rather, it is that he is unwilling to fulfill his role in the myths he alludes
to. He won't be Christ or James Dean for Cassandra. And he does not
want to be the Pied Piper for anyone (though Rusty James sort of follows
him to the river but hasn't the slightest idea what to do when he gets
there).

Though "the river" as an image in literature and film often carries with it a baptismal significance, referring to re-birth or an awakening of sorts, this is hardly the case here. The reference seems more akin to Neil Young's anthem of teen alienation: "Down by the river / I shot my baby." A similar inversion of the significance of the river can be found in another recent teen film, *River's Edge*, which re-tells the true story of a young man who murders his girlfriend (down by the river) and then invites his friends to come on down and view the body. In the true story, the friends stand by their man; in the film, a lone hero's crisis of conscience offers a ray of hope.[35] In *River's Edge*, the failure of the adult world to instill any acceptable or consistent model of authority (the parents are doped-out ex-hippies or idiot rednecks or overly self-centered single guardians; the cops are mean and stupid; the teachers are bullies and phoney idealists) leads at least two youths to seize the day, re-establishing family ties and reinforcing more conventional hetero-sexual relations.

Structurally, *Rumble Fish* is set up for Rusty James to seize the day, but he's just not up to the task. Throughout, he remarks that when he gets older he believes he will be just like his brother. Steve rejects the idea with the following perceptive remark: "I never know what (the Motorcycle Boy) is thinking but I always know what you're thinking." In a later scene, when Rusty James loses Patty to his rival, Smokey tells him that had the gangs persisted, unlike the Motorcycle Boy (who was the president) Rusty James would be a lieutenant—a soldier, not a leader. When Rusty James tells his father his wish to be like his brother, his father reacts violently; he grabs Rusty James's hands, looks into his son's eyes, and says, "God forbid."

After the mugging, Rusty James has a rapturous out of body experience. Floating above the city, he envisions his own wake. There his friends offer a toast sadly but clearly more suited to his brother: "To Rusty James, a real cool dude." But it is a point well worth making that Rusty James doesn't die (like his brother) and in the end he is neither leader nor legend.

When the Motorcycle Boy goes to California to find his mother, he finds her in the arms of a Hollywood producer. "California," he tells Rusty James, "is like a beautiful, wild girl on heroin, high as a kite, thinking she's on top of the world, not knowing she's dying even if you show her the marks." In most teen films, the reunion of mother and son would lead to some kind of reconciliation or revelation. In *Rumble Fish*, their meeting precedes the film and despite the Oedipal overtones, in retrospect it turns out to be an unremarkable event. In the film, the family and the characters in the family don't change: the father remains a hopeless alcoholic, the mother is unrepentant despite abandoning her children, Rusty James is lost and the Motorcycle Boy is from the start suicidal, and in the end gets his wish.

What little institutional authority there is in the film is personified by Officer Patterson, the rigid and dispassionate cop who openly hates the Motorcycle Boy because Tulsa youths "think he's something that he's not." While Patterson is the film's truth-teller, and he frees Rusty James of the burden of his brother (it's not what he wants, but it is what he needs), we never actually see his eyes. His dark shades, like so much in the film, reflect only outward.

Patterson's solution to the problem of authority in the film is pretty simple. But it is also without adequate motivation or narrative explanation. In the end, Patterson guns down the Motorcycle Boy in cold blood, delivering the bullet his mysterious nemesis apparently craves. Here, as in so many teen movies, the climax is of the authoritarian kind. But unlike most other teen films, while the scene offers a catharsis of sorts, the death of the hero seems arbitrary and anti-climactic.

Near the end of the film, in a vain attempt to rescue the Motorcycle Boy from what he sees as an unreasoned death wish, Rusty James tracks his brother to a magazine store in downtown Tulsa. On the way, he passes graffiti scrawled on a street sign that reads: "The Motorcycle Boy Reigns"— an image we see in the opening pan and at the very end of the film. (In all three cases, the graffiti is written on an arrow pointing in the opposite direction from the movement of the camera).

Inside the store, we see the Motorcycle Boy perusing a magazine in which there is a photograph of him with the caption: "today's youth." In the face of such (increased) notoriety, the Motorcycle Boy wants the story kept quiet. But Rusty James doesn't get why. The conversation that follows articulates the distance between them and characterizes the Motorcycle Boy's peculiar brand of anomie:

> MB: I'd just as soon stay a neighborhood novelty if it's all the same to you—I'm tired of all this Pied Piper bullshit.
> RJ: The Pied Piper man—the guy with the flute—the guy in the movie.
> MB: (*sarcastic*) They'd all follow me to the river and jump in.
> RJ: (*misreading the Motorcycle Boy's tone—in earnest and with pride*) They probably would.
> MB: If you're going to lead people, you have to have someplace to go.

Unlike Jim Stark (in *Rebel Without a Cause* who is so conflicted he just wants someone to tell him what to do), the Motorcycle Boy is so bored he just wants someone to take him out. He is Tulsa's best fighter, lover, pool player and gang leader. He's a poet, and now I'm quoting from the film: "a prince in exile," "a hero miscast in a play," but it isn't close to being enough. In the novel, Rusty James describes his brother as follows:

> He had an expressionless face . . . he saw things other people couldn't see, and laughed when nothing was funny. He had strange eyes—they made me think of a two-way mirror. Like you could feel somebody on the other side watching you, but the only reflection you saw was your own.[36]

Though Rusty James's description suggests an instinctive, even profound understanding, it rather benefits from 20-20 hindsight. As the narrative in the novel closes out, Steve remarks to Rusty James: "You know who you look just like?" It's a rhetorical question—it is clear Steve is referring to the by then deceased Motorcycle Boy—but Rusty James has finally stopped seeing himself in his brother's vacant stare. To the realization of his boyhood dreams, his stomach clenches into a fist and he discovers, at that very moment, that he has rid himself of the burden of his past.

The end of the film is far more romantic. Rusty James is shot in silhouette, seated on his brother's motorcycle, peering out over the ocean at sunset. But it is also a far emptier scene; the end of the road in all kinds of ways.

The fundamental structural difference between the novel and the film is that the novel is told by Rusty James and is framed by two scenes on the beach in California sometime in the future after the Motorcycle Boy's death. In doing so, the novel—like Anthony Burgess's twenty-one chapter version of *A Clockwork Orange* in which Alex gets bored with all the ultraviolence and opts instead for adulthood (a wife, kids and a little house someplace)—subscribes to the condescending scenario that youth culture is transitional and thus involves a drama one either survives (to look back on in amusement or amazement) or not. The novel rather conventionally attends to Rusty James's transition into adulthood after his brother's death. Since what we see is his rejection of his brother's seductive authority, his growth as a character centers us as readers.

No such frame, and no such point of view strategy, is present in the film. Rusty James is not only not the narrator, he is little more than a sidekick, a buffoon, Little John to the Motorcycle Boy's Robin Hood, a dutiful rodent to his brother's Pied Piper. The film is primarily about the Motorcycle Boy, a character about whom, in a classic narrative sense, there is very little to say. To an extent, closure concerns Rusty James's embrace of the lesson his brother's death has taught him. But what is that lesson? Rusty James never understood anything the Motorcycle Boy said when he was alive and he certainly never understood what his brother signified.

In the end of the film, Rusty James exits to nowhere on his brother's (we gather stolen) motorcycle (the phallic symbol of power and authority in how many teen movies?). When he returns—if he returns—he has no message, no boon, no lesson, nothing.

Craig Owens argues that the postmodern aesthetic prompts a sort of anti-closure of longing and loss,[37] an appropriately incomplete effect given society such as it is these days. Building on Derrida's argument that the postmodern sign engenders an infinity of new contexts, Owens posits that "postmodernism neither brackets nor surrounds the referent but works instead to problematize the activity of reference."[38] Indeed, *Rumble Fish* so deeply problematizes the semiotic chain that the familiar codes of the teen film (and of youth culture as we have come to know it through the teen film) reveals a world in which no institutional or cultural authority can convince, can close off the narrative.

In *Rumble Fish*, the strong and silent, anomic hero not only *appears* to be suicidal, he accomplishes his goal (pointedly, and anti-climactically off screen). The benevolent cop of *Rebel Without a Cause* is transformed into the imposing, authoritarian Officer Patterson, whose role it seems is to help the Motorcycle Boy realize his death wish. One of the two female leads is a drug addict and while she seems at first to be a central character as well as metaphor, by the mid-point of the narrative she vanishes altogether. Patty, Rusty James' girlfriend, dumps him and takes up with Smokey, then remarks (to Rusty James) that "it's no big deal." The father doesn't quit drinking. The mother never returns. In the end, Rusty James is still a teenager, lost in a world he may never adequately understand. Though the film presents the decadence of institutional authority and the subsequent search for a viable and traditional alternative (that typifies the genre), such a search is thwarted at every turn. The film ends unambiguously in boredom, suicide and hopelessness.

If the heart of *Rumble Fish*'s peculiar postmodernism is a (however unintentional) undermining of narrative pleasure, then is such an obstruction of pleasure (of repetition, of genre conventions, of binary oppositions, of the sublime) somehow progressive? nihilist? experimental? avant garde? Is the rejection of the conformity of adulthood (and of teen life as well) somehow hopeful?

I think the answer to all of the above is no. Questions regarding whether or not narrative pleasure is "good" or "bad" are subsumed by the apocalyptic mindset, positing that on the one hand anything goes, on the other, that pleasure isn't real, that pleasure isn't attainable anyway. If all narrative attends to a struggle for control (and I think it does) and the sublime is that moment when all the pain and confusion is resolved, *Rumble Fish* depicts how (especially genre) narratives (these days) fail to adequately resolve the ideological contradictions inherent to contemporary society.

While most teen films are restorative and offer a rather complete closure, *Rumble Fish* coolly testifies to the ways in which such narratives are false and neat. While cultural historians like Hebdige and Hall maintain youth culture's progressive role in the drama of hegemony in the post-war period, *Rumble Fish* blankly rejects such lofty, optimistic notions. The depthless and cool world of Coppola's *Rumble Fish* is revealed in the shift from parody to pastiche; in the anti-ideology of boredom; in the calm before the storm.[39]

Notes

1. Archibald MacLeish, "The End of the World," in *American Poetry*, edited by Gay Wilson Allen, Walter B. Rideout and James K. Robinson (New York: Harper and Row, 1964), p. 874.

2. Don DeLillo, *Players* (New York: Vintage, 1977), p. 9.

3. DeLillo, p. 8.

4. DeLillo, p. 9.

5. Martin Amis, "The Time Disease," in *Einstein's Monsters* (New York: Harmony, 1987), p. 96.

6. Martin Amis, *London Fields* (New York: Harmony, 1989), p. 64.

7. Jacques Derrida, "Of An Apocalyptic Tone Adopted in Recent Philosophy," *Oxford Literary Review*, 6.2 (1984): 20-21.

8. Jean Baudrillard, "The Ecstasy of Communication," in *The Anti-Aesthetic*, edited by Hal Foster (Port Townsend, WA: Bay Press, 1983), pp. 126-134.

9. Craig Owens, "The Discourse of Others," in *The Anti-Aesthetic*, pp. 57-82.

10. Hal Foster, "Postmodernism: A Preface," in *The Anti-Aesthetic*, pp. ix-xvi.

11. Jean Francois Lyotard, "What is Postmodernism?" in *The Postmodern Condition: A Report on Knowledge* (Minneapolis: University of Minnesota, 1984), pp. 71-84.

12. Fredric Jameson, "Postmodernism and Consumer Society," in *Postmodernism and Its Discontents* (London: Verso, 1988), pp. 13-29.

13. Baudrillard, pp. 126-134.

14. Lyotard, pp. 71-84.

15. Charles Newman, *The Post-Modern Aura: The Act of Fiction in an Age of Inflation* (Evanston, IL: Northwestern, 1985), p. 30.

16. John Gardner, *On Moral Fiction* (New York: 1978); Edward Hoagland, "Shhh! Our Writers Are Sleeping," *Esquire*, 114.1 (1990): 57-63.

17. "Postmodernism and Consumer Society" was first anthologized in

The Anti-Aesthetic in 1983. It was based on a lecture Jameson gave at the Whitney Museum in the Fall, 1982. In the July-August 1984 issue of the *New Left Review*, Jameson published "Postmodernism, Or the Cultural Logic of Late Capitalism," a far longer but quite similar essay.

18. Jack Kroll, "Coppola's Teen-Age Inferno," *Newsweek*, November 7, 1983, p. 128

19. Pauline Kael, "The Current Cinema," the *New Yorker*, November, 1983.

20. Jameson, p. 20.

21. Andrew Britton, "Blissing Out: The Politics of Reaganite Entertainment," *Movie*, 31/32 (1986): 4.

22. Britton, p. 4.

23. Britton, p. 5.

24. Gavin Smith, "Pretty Vacant in Pink," *Film Comment*, 23.4 (1987): 71.

25. Owens, p. 57.

26. Dick Hebdige, *Subculture: The Meaning of Style* (London: Metheun, 1979).

27. Hall as cited by Hebdige, p. 85.

28. Baudrillard, p. 130.

29. Warren Montag, "The Debate on Postmodernism," in *Postmodernism and its Discontents*, p. 100.

30. Montag, p. 98.

31. Jameson as cited by Foster, p. xiv.

32. Andrew Harvey, Evidence (Oxford: Mid-day, 1979), p. 10.

33. Harvey, p. 14.

34. S. E. Hinton, *Rumble Fish* (New York: Dell, 1975).

35. In Milpitas, California in 1981, Jacques Broussard, a 16 year old black youth strangled his white, 14 year old girlfriend, Marcy Conrad, to death. Afterwards, he boasted openly about the killing and over the next two days he invited his friends to view the body. One spectator dropped a rock on her face; others poked her with sticks. None of them reported the murder to their parents or to the police. In 1982, Broussard pleaded guilty and he is now serving 25 to life. He will be eligible for parole in 1998.

In the film, all the teens are older and white. One of the youths who treks up to view the body goes to the police. But before the police get to the killer, he is murdered by a deeply paranoid ex-biker.

36. Hinton, p. 30.

37. Owens, p. 67.

38. Owens as cited by Gregory L. Ulmer in "The Object of Post-Criticism," in *The Anti-Aesthetic*, p. 95.

39. A far shorter version of this essay was presented at the Society for Cinema Studies Conference in Washington, DC in May, 1990.

Frank Burke

Fellini's Casanova: Male Hystrionics and Phallackcentrism

Fellini's recent films clearly exemplify the crisis of individualism/ /humanism/subjectivity that has marked postwar Western culture. More precisely, the crisis of subjectivity tends to be the principal avenue through which Fellini's films explore a contemporary sense of apocalypse.[1] This essay will attempt to situate *Fellini's Casanova* within that crisis, with specific reference to Fellini's career and cultural environment. Moreover, it will suggest that male hysteria is the operative mode in which crisis subjectivity exposes itself in *Fellini's Casanova*.[2] Finally, it will offer *Fellini's Casanova* as a model of signification in an age of hysterical (male) subjects adrift in the simulacrum.

1. Fellini and Individualism

Fellini's career en route to *Fellini's Casanova* (1976) seems to offer a classic model of the history and demise of postwar individualism. His major work in film began with Roberto Rossellini, as he helped script two of Rossellini's best-known neorealist films, *Rome, Open City* (1945) and *Paisan* (1946), and did a bit of directing on the latter. While neorealism was championed by Marxist Italian critics because of its orientation toward the social, many of the most notable neorealist films (e.g., *Shoeshine* and *Bicycle Thieves*—in addition to *Open City*) represented social ills principally from the point of view of individual victimization. These films were humanist more than Marxist, consistent with Rossellini's own statement: "Neorealism involves a greater interest in individuals."[3]

Fellini's own early films—especially *I Vitelloni* (1953), *La Strada* (1954), and *Il Bidone* (1955)—were also individualist and humanist, informed by a viewpoint articulated by Fellini at the time of *La Strada*:

> Our trouble, as modern men, is loneliness. . . . Only between man and man, I think, can this solitude be broken, only through individual people can a kind of message be passed, making them understand—almost discover—the profound link between one person and the next.[4]

Fellini's individualism has at least three sources:

—the Christian humanism of his Italian upbringing (Fellini never embraced Italian socialism or communism, finding them too prescriptive and rhetorical),

—the American ideology so prominent in the Hollywood films Fellini loved as a youth—and reinserted into Italian culture as a result of the Allied liberation of Italy in 1945,

—the postwar anti-collectivism that marked capitalist European and American reaction to Nazism, Fascism, and Stalinism. (Fellini's fear of collectivity is a principal theme in his interviews well into the 1960s.)

Individualism was, of course, fueled by American capitalism in the late 1940s and 1950s, especially as it manifested itself in the Truman doctrine and the Marshall Plan—the latter of which was instrumental in the political formation and economic recovery of postwar Italy.

By the end of the 1950s, with a host of international awards in hand, Fellini had been swept up by the *auteurist* movement, cinema's contribution to high modernism vis à vis the *grand artiste*. By the early sixties, he had become an international culture hero: "il maestro, il poetà"—the artist-guru par excellence. All this seemed rather stunning validation for an ideology of self-determination, self-realization.

This put Fellini right in tune with much of the sixties: an era of the "great individual" in world affairs (John F. Kennedy, Khrushchev, Pope John XXIII, Martin Luther King, Mao, Castro, Che Guevera)[5] and, equally important, an era of do-your-own-thing anti-institutionalism, propelled by the baby-boomer explosion of (late) adolescent self-assertiveness. Fellini's stated beliefs seemed most consistent with the least politicized and characteristically American version of 1960s ideology—as well as the "self"-centered psychology of people such as Carl Jung (a major influence on Fellini) and Abraham Maslow. In Fellini's words:

> self-acceptance can occur only when you've grasped one funda-mental fact of life: that the only thing which exists is yourself,

your true individual self in depth, which wants to grow spontaneously, but which is fettered by inoperative lies, myths and fantasies proposing an unattainable morality or sanctity or perfection. . . .[6]

During this period, Fellini films such as *8½* (1963) and *Juliet of the Spirits* (1965) were modelled on Jungian notions of individuation, favoring fantasy and imagination over engagement with a social real. By the end of the 1960s and beginning of the 1970s, escalating individualism seems reflected when Fellini's name becomes inserted into the titles of his films (*Fellini: A Director's Notebook* (1969), *Fellini-Satyricon* (1969)) and he becomes the protagonist in several (*Fellini: A Director's Notebook*, *The Clowns* (1970), and *Roma* (1972)).

However, as I have argued at length elsewhere,[7] the issue of individualism becomes highly conflicted in Fellini's films at precisely the moment the films appear to be most individualist. *8½* ends not with the triumph of the hero Guido who, as a filmmaker in his early forties, is in many ways a Fellini surrogate. Rather, it ends with his disappearance—and with the dissolution of all individual identity. The two principal films in which Fellini functions as protagonist—*The Clowns* and *Roma*—also conclude with the disappearance of the hero. Moreover, the "Fellini" they present is not the conventional artist/God who stands outside and controls the work, but a product of the work itself. In the case of *Roma*, the various figures—child, youth, adult—that we may choose to designate "Fellini" (the film does not identify the first two as Fellini), is a product, not just of the filmmaking process itself, but of the multiple conflicting discourses—historical, religious, political, aesthetic, and so on—that Rome is seen to comprise. As Fellini himself has said: "Rome *created* me in so far as I am an artist."[8]

In effect, in the decade between *8½* and *Roma*, Fellini's films foreground both Fellini and individual identity only to deconstruct them. Accordingly, his 1974 film *Amarcord* dispenses with a main character altogether. The closest we get is Titta, who does not serve as a consistent center of consciousness. He is missing from several episodes and narrates only a couple himself—sharing storytelling responsibilities with a variety of other narrators. Despite the fact that "amarcord" means "I remember,"[9] there *is* no I who remembers.

The increasing anti-individualism of Fellini's later films can be linked to a number of things, both autobiographical and sociohistorical. Most obviously, there is the matter of age. It is reasonable to assume that Fellini's faith in individual possibility and self-determination began to undergo revaluation as he began to experience the physical and emotional changes of growing older. More concretely, in 1967, he suffered through a mysterious illness which he feared to be terminal. At the same time, he experienced an artistic crisis that was never resolved: the failed attempt to film a project entitled "The Voyage of G. Mastorna." During this period of physical and intellectual crisis, he made a consummate film of dead identity, "Toby Dammit." Here the main character is not only resurrected from a story by Edgar Allan Poe, he speaks within Fellini's film from beyond the grave. Moreover his entire story focuses on the conditions which led to his demise.[10]

Fellini's personal experience aside, there is Fellini as economic entity. Working within a collaborative medium that makes the notion of the free creative artist difficult to sustain at the best of times, he has enjoyed little if any financial autonomy. His relationship with producers has been notoriously catastrophic. He received little financial benefit even from the enormously successful *La Strada* and *La Dolce Vita*, having given up his share of the profits in exchange for greater artistic autonomy (a real paradox of self-determination!). Though *8½* brought him momentary economic stability, by the end of 1966 he was heavily in debt to Dino De Laurentiis because of the aborted Mastorna project. The late 1960s saw a major crisis in the Italian film industry, which made Fellini reliant on American financing for the first time, and the international financial exigencies of the 1970s meant that his projects reached completion only as the result of 1) American money, 2) fragmented packaging (*The Clowns* and *Roma* each had four funding sources), 3) acrimonious turnover of producers (*Fellini's Casanova*), and 4) extensive interruptions in production (*Casanova* again). The success of *Amarcord* midway through the 1970s did little if anything to ease Fellini's task in getting his post-*Amarcord* films made.

There is also Fellini as media subject: Fellini in quotation marks, the international image, buzzword, and marketing inspiration for, among other things, a line of clothing. "Fellini" is product rather than producer, a thoroughly (re)constructed subject—and it is interesting to note that the moment Fellini becomes "Fellini" (following the enormous *cause célèbre* of *La Dolce Vita*), the subject begins to dissolve in his work.

Fellini's Casanova provides an instructive example of Fellini's highly determined representation of the artist as produced rather than producer, artifice rather than artificer. Though Fellini has been inclined to explain the surficiality of Casanova in terms of the latter's *History of My Life* ("It's the horrifying proof of a life lived for appearance's sake"[11]) and to attribute Casanova's dependency and sycophancy to his Italo-Catholic heritage ("He is a super *vitellone*, a do-nothing who avoids responsibility and lives in the comfortable conviction that everything is supposed to come from on high")[12] the artist as hollow showman and pliant hack is consistent with Fellini's experience in making *Fellini's Casanova*. Originally, Dino De Laurentiis signed on as producer, but only on the condition that the film be made in English. Then, De Laurentiis backed out, and Andrea Rizzoli came and went. Enter Alberto Grimaldi with Universal Studios—the latter only on condition that 1) Fellini use Donald Sutherland, 2) Sutherland's part be spoken with his own voice and recorded in direct sound (Fellini has always dubbed after shooting), and 3) the film be written by Gore Vidal. At a certain point, then, Fellini had little or no control over language, star, sound, or script. Though Fellini ultimately proved amenable to Sutherland (often talking as though the choice were entirely his), managed to avoid Vidal's script, and dubbed the film (albeit still with Sutherland's voice), the film's image of the artist as compliant lackey ever trying to please seems as much a reflection of the conditions of production as of Fellini's attitudes toward his protagonist. More important, Fellini has come to seem quite accepting of such conditions. At the time of *Casanova*, he claimed:

> A contract with an advance is one of the most valid things for me today. I'd even be in favor of a situation similar to what existed in the 1400s, when a Pope or a grand duke commissioned a work from a painter or a poet. . . . I've discovered that at one time I had to like a film to do it; now I like a film because I make it.[13]

These remarks suggest not only a certain kinship with Casanova as artist ("I see him as a sort of shadow of myself")[14] but a clear rejection of romantic and *auteurist* notions of the artist as free creative spirit. Under these circumstances, Fellini renounces the role of high modernist rebel/genius in favor of postmodernist *bricoleur*.[15]

Fellini's turn away from romantic individualism is of course consistent with major cultural shifts in the late 1960s and 1970s. To the extent that 1960s political dissent placed the individual against the system (clearly the case in the United States), the failure of the 1960s and the crushing reassertion of institutional power struck a mortal blow to the rhetoric and ideology of self-actualization. The international economic crises of the 1970s—the worst since World War II—not only impacted Fellini through the Italian film industry, it further eroded the sense of individual possibility in Western society. (The upsurge of romantic individualism in the 1960s was largely enabled by middle class economic ease.) One reaction was consumer fetishism and the culture of narcissism—a kind of hysterical and pseudo individualism strongly reflected in *Fellini's Casanova*. The other was a growing sense of political disempowerment and futility, also central to the film. In Italy, the latter became reflected in widespread terrorism, both from the right and the left, which fragmented the potential revolutionary collectivity of the late 1960s and early 1970s into a seemingly irrational (though actually quite calculated) denial of political process. Although terrorism was to peak in March 1978 with the kidnapping of Aldo Moro—an event which informs Fellini's *Orchestra Rehearsal* (1979)—it was a frightening fact of Italian life throughout the 1970s.

On the intellectual scene, the 1950s, 1960s, and 1970s saw the gathering momentum of structuralist and poststructuralist attacks on the subject, accompanied by ideological critiques of Western individualism and any privileged status for art or the artist—much of which became reflected in film theory and criticism. Though Fellini, unlike so many younger filmmakers, is no student of contemporary theory, it is impossible not to see his later films as made within the broad intellectual context of recent theorizations. Moreover, scriptwriters such as Bernardino Zapponi provide a dense intellectual dimension to Fellini's films which is fully consistent with recent theory.

On the cultural scene, the explosion of consumerism, media, and new information technologies in the 1960s and 1970s began to generate such externalization of the senses and internalization of mass produced environments that all the conventional notions associated with individualism—autonomy, creativity, originality, subject-object relations—have been eroded. Following McLuhan, Jean Baudrillard has become the prophet extraordinaire of this culture shift, emphatically proclaiming the reduction of the subject in postmodernity to "a pure screen, a switching center for all the networks of influence."[16]

As much of the above implies, by the mid 1970s, as Fellini was engaged in *Fellini's Casanova*, the cultural, political, and economic climate—especially in comparison with the euphoric 1960s—was dismal, particularly with regard to conventional humanist notions of self-determination. The 1970s, in fact, gave rise to an apocalyptic *fin de millenium* pessimism that is still with us in the 1990s. Given Fellini's stake in the creative individual earlier in his career, it is no surprise that the version of apocalypse that comes to dominate his work is the death of the individual—and, more specifically, the individual-as-artist. (Three of the four films following *Fellini's Casanova*—*Orchestra Rehearsal*, *And the Ship Sails On*, and *Ginger and Fred*—focus on either elite or popular art: the symphony, the opera, and the Italian variety theatre-become-television.) This is compounded by Fellini's intellectual formation in an era of high modernism, which privileged the rarefied, separate realm of art, over the decadent world of institutions and mass culture. As a high priest of high modernism, Fellini had become quite accustomed, by the mid 1970s, to that world apart, reflected not only in his numerous films about art but also in his repudiation of location shooting in favor of total simulation on the sets of Cinécittà.[17] (What little we see of a reality outside art or television in films such as *The Orchestra Rehearsal, City of Women,* and *Ginger and Fred* bespeaks strong paranoia about a world "outside.")

In short, it seems that for a high modernist who has staked everything on the individual and on art, the 1970s gave Fellini little choice but to proclaim their death—and no better place to do it than in the fully simulated environment, the deconstruction chamber, of Cinécittà. Enter *Fellini's Casanova* which, for all Fellini's proclaimed hatred of his subject matter, seems the perfect story at the perfect time: an emblematic moment of high modernism turning on itself in narcissistic self-negation.

2. Male Hysteria and Fellini

It is no surprise that, as Arthur and Marilouise Kroker (among others) have noted,[18] the contemporary crisis of subjectivity becomes manifest in a kind of male hysteria—an excessive, often violent, reaction to the

Enlightenment hysteria: Donald Sutherland in Federico Fellini's *Fellini's Casanova* (1976). Alberto Grimaldi. Still courtesy of Jerry Ohlinger's Movie Materials.

loss of privilege. After all, the autonomous self-determining subject/ego has been the prized figure of empowerment in modern patriarchal philosophy and psychology. Its demise is nothing less than the demise of masculinity.

Coupled with this is the rise of feminism and the refusal of women to reflect back to men their own desire and power. The power/sex nexus which has grounded patriarchy is dissolving, and hysteria—thought in the middle ages to result from a floating womb—now symptomatizes the floating Phallus: the once Transcendental Signifier wandering the simulacrum.

In Italy, feminism proved to be the most influential of the collective movements to develop in the 1970s.[19] It created a powerful public forum in helping defeat the referendum on divorce in 1974 (an attempt to repeal the divorce law of 1970) and promoting abortion rights.[20] Fueled by organizations such as Rivolta Femminile, Lotta Femminista, and Movimento della Liberazione delle Donne Italiane, and marked by large demonstrations in Fellini's home city of Rome, the women's movement reached its peak the year *Fellini's Casanova* was released. One can speculate with some confidence that the visible power and independence of women would be problematic for a figure who has cultivated both directly and through his repeated casting of Marcello Mastroianni an international persona as a Latin lover. (It is no accident that Fellini interviews appear in *Playboy* and *Oui*, that Bob Guccioni and *Penthouse* were initially behind the "Mastorna" project, and that Fellini seemed the logical choice to film the memoirs of the quintessential Italian chauvinist Casanova.) Certainly, women's autonomy had to threaten someone who has claimed, among other things, that: "Woman [is] a series of projections invented by man"[21] and

> ... the problem for man is to reunite himself with the other half of his being, to find the woman who is right for him—right because she is simply a projection, a mirror of himself. A man can't become whole or free until he has set woman free—his woman.[22]

While *Fellini's Casanova* can be seen a critique as well as a reproduction of the attitudes reflected in these quotations, *City of Women* (1980) conveys a strong fear of women and feminism on the part of its protagonist Snaporaz. Though we can claim authorial distance for Fellini, Snaporaz is played by Fellini's recurrent alter ego Mastroianni, and there is reason to suspect that the latter is acting out quite substantial fears of the former. Moreover, the grotesque (mis)representation of women in both *Fellini's Casanova* and *City of Women* tempts one to apply to Fellini the same analysis he has applied to Snaporaz:

it is clear that he knows nothing about women, he isn't able to create in his imagination . . . a single outstanding, real person, which is why the[se films have] no real female protagonists.[23]

Suffice it to say that women and their representation seem most problematic for Fellini in the films he made or began to formulate in the mid to late 1970s. Moreover, Casanova seems an apt opportunity for Fellini to explore not only the demise of high modernist individualism but the intimately connected hysterical (e)masculinity of late, let's even say posthumous, patriarchy. I see this hysteria principally in the film's and protagonist's compulsion to transform everything (women, history, the real, and most of all Casanova himself) into a play of signs that accelerates to a state of exhaustion and collapses back to utter stasis—precisely the trajectory of Casanova's mechanical bird, the signifier of his (lacking) sexuality.

I see this hysterical sign production as postmodernity's denial of the dominant phallus, yet one more failed attempt to erect monuments to masculinity. Or better still, it's postmodernity's *celebration* of Lack to the extent that it becomes the New Plenitude: everywhere yet nowhere, totally explanatory, the new Transcendental Signifier. Casanova himself becomes the supreme representative of this postmodern Phallackcentrism. Having created himself solely through *The History of My Life*, he circulates through his text and Fellini's film as the always already discredited Masculine, never there and ever impotent, yet always (re)producing himself as simulated power through writing. And, in a postmodern climate of empowered lack where simulated power is the *only* power and "writing" the only "real," Casanova does indeed succeed in res-erecting himself through his text, even if only to deflate simultaneously. Moreover, Casanova's ability to dominate in and through lack highlights a crucial problem of postmodernity, especially in relation to feminism: even if the phallocentric subject is dead, its ghost still rules under the sign of Male Hysteria. Accordingly, though the following analysis will emphasize Casanova's status as dead subject in the multiplied fictions of *The History [His-teria] of My Life* and *Fellini's Casanova*, I would like to frame my analysis with the notion that in posthumous patriarchy, the only good subject is a dead subject—and that dead subject is (still) *male*.

3. The Thematics of Fellini's Casanova

Given the conventions of traditional narrative analysis, it is tempting to approach Casanova as though he were, if not a real historical figure,

at least a "real" fictional one: constructed in realistic terms and under-
going experiences of sufficient verisimilitude to enable us as spectators
to identify with him. It is tempting, in short, to emphasize the reality
of problems such as homelessness, powerlessness, and failed relations
with women—and to view Casanova as a psychologically consistent
character in relation to them. Indeed, such issues are crucial to the film's
its late modernist/postmodern landscape. Yet, the reality of these issues
and of any consistently psychologized relation to them is highly qualified
by the hypertextuality of *Fellini's Casanova*. For Casanova is not a person
or a representation of one. He, like everything else in the film, is a sliding
signifier produced by a (his? Fellini's?) text, with no existence outside
it. Moreover, his problems are, to a large extent, mere humanist *effects*
or posturings in what is principally a post- or dis-humanist discourse.
And, they are largely narrative effects in a text that defies narrativity.
I will return to all this later on as I address the textuality of the film
(as well as some evidence that Fellini *does* ultimately try to re-humanize
his subject). I make this disclaimer here to warn (myself more than the
reader) against any overinvestment in Casanova as a character in the
classic humanist-realist sense.

Having done so, I turn to the thematics of dead subjectivity and male
hysteria in *Fellini's Casanova* as they manifest themselves in Casanova's
relation to home and origins, power, women, and textuality.[24]

3a. Home and Origins

Fellini's Casanova is (un)grounded throughout by a condition of exile.
This begins on a relatively conventional "autobiographical" note but
builds into something far more complex in terms of his relation to women,
power, and narrative. Early in the film, Casanova escapes from his
birthplace Venice, and, despite a confessed longing to return, never does.
(Fellini here departs from history, for the "real" Casanova did.) A clear
link is established between Venice and Venus in the opening sequence:
a carnival celebrating the Venice's love-patron but marred by the failed
communal attempt to raise a bust of Venus from beneath the water.
This initiates both a link and a process of substitution as home becomes
woman becomes Casanova's seemingly endless pursuit and loss/aban-
donment of women. The link and loss of home are emphasized in
Casanova's London encounter with the giantess Angie, an expatriate
from the Venetian region who was sold by her husband "like a circus
animal" to a travelling carnival. Angie and her two dwarf companions
offer Casanova a vision of domestic harmony that he can only gaze upon,
fascinated, from without. Angie's itinerant existence and the misty,

decontextualized landscape in this sequence underscore Casanova's dissociation from anything resembling home. In the same sequence, a symbolic link between woman and home or origin is forged by another carnival attraction, "Mouna," a beached whale surrounded by images of displacement: a contortionist with her head beneath her crotch and her toes next to her ears, a man with a woman's face painted on his belly, etc.

Mouna, of course, comes from the sea, the primal origin, and as her male huckster and "interpreter" exclaims:

> out of Mouna has flowed the world with its trees and its clouds and one at a time all the races of man. . . . He who dares not into the whale's belly will not find his heart's desire. Go in and see for yourselves. Down through her throat then down deeper ever deeper into the warm welcoming womb. . . .

Mouna is, in fact, a purely male symbol of the "female principle"—a "womb" intended to recuperate the very origin that is impossible in Casanova's world. Her status as hysterical production becomes clear from the violence and terror with which she is invested. Inside the whale/womb, the images are not only vaginal, they are grotesque and threatening. Some present the vagina as trap and swirling vortex. The final images reveal a vagina cradling the face of a black woman with prominent teeth—aligning woman not only with the promise of fellatio but with the danger of castration. The image of racial alterity also makes the womb a place of exile rather than grounding (while again making the "other" pure threat). This pleasure/pain womb-home-emasculator accentuates the impossibility of male grounding and the desperate—and in fact self-annihilatory—discourse that displaces home as male hysteria turns misogynistic and quite possibly racist.

The impossibility of home/woman/origin is most clearly exemplified in Casanova's encounter with his mother. The meeting is pure coincidence. Though Casanova is visiting Dresden, where she lives, he has made no effort to look her up and appears to have difficulty recognizing her. She is as unpleasant as he is unfeeling, complaining repeatedly that he never sends money. Though he offers physical assistance, carrying her out to her carriage on his back, it is clear that he has little intention of renewing their relationship. She knowingly mocks him when he claims he will try to visit, and as she rides off, he notes without regret: "I forgot to ask her for her address." Reminded by this meeting of his origins, Casanova can only refer to them vaguely and incompletely: "Have you had any word of our relations in Venice? I have hopes of returning there, you know, as soon as. . . ." The notion of biological origin or "roots" is visually reversed by the image of Casanova's mother up off the ground, piggyback, "grounded" by her son.

In short, Casanova's own mother proves incapable of reconnecting him to a home/womb and remedying his chronic exile. This is largely because Casanova has so completely displaced Venice with Venus, origin with (self-displacing) sexual adventure.

3b. Power

Unable to locate himself vis a vis home/womb/mother/origin, Casanova has no better luck in relation to power or the traditional realm of the father. Appropriately, he has no real father or biologically grounded authority. (But then this is always the case according to much contemporary psychoanalytical discourse, which replaces the biological with the Oedipal, the Symbolic, and the Name of the Father). More important, Casanova's relation to political authority ranges from the highly problematic to the impossible. In his first appearance, he ends up having sex to amuse the French ambassador de Bernis, who has apparently had his mistress Maddalena arrange an assignation so he (de Bernis) can watch. Yet de Bernis only exists (if at all) as an eye peering out from behind the image of a fish on the wall. And when Casanova uses sex as a way to ingratiate himself (his sexual acrobatics are followed by a *curriculum vitae*: "I have studied engineering and literature, I am conversant in the art of politics"), the presumed de Bernis vanishes altogether, leaving the fish eye blank. In one sense, power is absent except as sign (the eye and Maddalena's claim that it belongs to de Bernis). In another, power exists only through its effects on Casanova. He becomes the objectification of the putative ambassador's putative (voyeuristic) sexual urges—not the Phallus (the signifier of male power and the Father) but the purely instrumental penis. He becomes to the ambassador what his own mechanical bird, on which he depends for simulated excitement, is to him. Moreover, ambassador and bird signify a double displacement on Casanova's part: onto the desire of the Father, on one hand, and the pure functionality of the machine/organ, on the other.

Following the de Bernis episode, Casanova's impossible relation to the Father is underscored when he is imprisoned by the Inquisition for crimes (heresy among them) which are merely asserted, never proven. Casanova seems to be a transgressor without having transgressed—an interesting reflection of the Counter-Reformation climate in which he lived,[25] the psychology of sin in Christianity, and the Fascist experience which remains so central to Fellini's work. Then Henriette, designated by Casanova as "the great love of my life," is whisked off by invisible authority—something Casanova only discovers through a third-person report following her disappearance: "a person of the utmost importance at a certain European court has full powers over her and D'Antoine is only the emissary sent here to bring her back to her rightful place."

By the end of the film, authority is either utterly irrational (the inebriated Duke in the militaristic madhouse of Württemberg) or missing (the Count who is away when the old and decrepit Casanova needs him at Dux). The absent leader or the vacant "Dux" becomes the film's definitive statement of Casanova's lack as an authority-identified parasite in a world where power remains unidentifiable.[26]

The irrationality and virtual absence of male, paternal, power does not just reflect cultural and historical factors (Counter-Reformation Catholicism, Fascism) familiar to Fellini. As my earlier remarks would suggest, it reflects his own relation as a filmmaker to those representatives of power most crucial to his work: movie producers. With financing continually appearing and disappearing along with ever-changing demands from backers, Fellini is documenting, not just imaginatively construing, the relationship of artist to authority and (potential) patronage in his portrayal of Casanova. Consistent with this, the vision of power in *Fellini's Casanova* reflects less the historical reality of an 18th-century Casanova than the abstract power of postmodernity as articulated by Arthur Kroker:

> [P]ostmodern power . . . owes its seduction to the 'imminence of the death of all the great referents' and to the violence which is exacerbated by their last, desperate attempts at representation. This is power, not on its expanding and symbolic side (the side of a *political and representational* theory of power), but on its reverse side: the side of symbolic reversal where power affirms itself as void, as having only a cynical existence.[27]

Fellini's experience with producers in a world of multinational, fragmented financing in which there is no relation between one source of funding and the next, authorial intent and economic interest, provides a perfect conjunction between contemporary filmmaking and cynical, empty power.

3c. Women

Just as Casanova seeks to employ women or "the feminine" as a way of recuperating origins, he relies on them to reinstitute his sense of power in a world in which authority and the "Father" fail to provide it. Perhaps the most disturbing example occurs as he languishes in the Piombi prison, having been jailed arbitrarily by the Inquisition. In apparent compensation for his helplessness, he narrates a story of

extreme self-aggrandizement in which he restores a sickly and weakened
young woman (Annamarie) to health by having sex with her. In effect
he rapes her—taking her while she is unconscious—and, at least from
his point of view, she both needs and enjoys it.[28] This need to empower
himself through conquest is repeated in the Roman sequence, where
his ego is goaded into a virility contest with a coachman—and he ends
up again having sex with a woman (Romana) without her full consent.
The most grotesque instance involves the mechanical doll, Rosalba, whom
Casanova "seduces" at Württemberg. Casanova's use of women for
macho validation becomes linked to an inevitable masculinization of
women. Not only does woman get turned into technology, Casanova
explicitly identifies technological reproduction as male: "What a genius
of an inventor your *father* must have been" (emphasis mine). Then, he
implicitly turns his own love-making into sexual competition with the
father/inventor by making the father's relation to Rosalba incestuous.
(He asks the doll "Did you lie with him?")

As the Rosalba incident suggests, woman, in her coerced role as
empowerer for Casanova, is reduced to a signifier in a male system of
symbolic exchange, with gender and otherness effectively erased.[29] This
becomes even more explicit when Casanova seeks empowerment not
only through the desire of other women but through women-as-the-desire-
of-other-men. This clearly occurs when Casanova performs for de Bernis
and in Casanova's sexual rivalry with Rosalba's imputed inventor. (It
is also an ingredient in Casanova's contest with the coachman, though
a woman's desire to have sex with the coachman precipitates the contest.)

Henriette proves to be the consummate woman-as-signifier-of-male-
desire. Henriette begins in hiding, in the care of a Hungarian officer.
She then dons a man's military outfit and, while wearing it, is handed
over by the officer to Casanova. She finally becomes fully visible as a
woman by donning an elegant white dress, but as the immediately
preceding close-up of a neuter tailor's dummy suggests, gender resides
solely in the sign systems of clothing. It also resides in (male) cultural
iconography. In her white dress, Henriette does not become herself, she
becomes woman as virgin bride and symbol of perfection, a role she plays
exquisitely throughout her brief appearance in the film. She also
represents woman as art object intended for the male gaze—forming
part of a continuum from Annamarie, whom Casanova compared to a
statue, to Rosalba.

By the end of the sequence, Henriette has changed male hands yet
again, from Casanova to D'Antoine, and is again "in hiding"—this time
irrevocably. Casanova's inability to hold on to Henriette has nothing
to do with love and everything to do with Henriette's nonexistence except

as a token for exchange in the ever circulating economy and semiotics of male power. Moreover, in the very act of figuring male power, Henriette—and for that matter all women in Casanova's world—confirm its absence except as projection and sign play.

The kind of gender slide in which women become male signifiers is matched and reversed by Casanova. His existence solely as the doubly constituted desire of the "other" (women and women-as-the-desire-of-other men) places him in the conventional position of women—themselves, as I have just indicated, already the desire of the other. This is most obvious in his vanity, his costuming and makeup, his posing, and his catering to the male gaze (de Bernis and everyone else for whom he performs—including himself as teller of his own tale).[30] But it is more profoundly evident in his perpetual economic dependency on male authority and his concomitant need to please. In fact, Casanova is positioned in a role that has always been quite dear to Fellini—the prostitute—without any of the dynamism or rebelliousness that Fellini's prostitutes normally possess.

As the paradoxes of Casanova's impossible relation to women accumulate, women increasingly become signifiers of masochism and self-destruction. This is obvious in the hysterical symbolization surrounding Mouna, but it is even true in the company of Henriette: "A man who never speaks ill of women does not love them. To understand them and to love them, one must suffer at their hands." This willingness to suffer becomes quite physical and direct in Casanova's encounter with Moebius' daughters. Science becomes sadism here, as the sisters take obvious relish in spearing their objects of classification—worms—with long needles. Their sadism, in turn, becomes Casanova's masochism when he passes out in their presence and then identifies the sisters' violence with his own body. Moreover, when he awakens, Casanova is thoroughly smitten with Isabella—making love identical with the experience of pain and, since the worms are clearly phallic, with his own symbolic castration. Casanova and Isabella then make explicit the link between love and self-destruction that was implied earlier with Mouna:

> Casanova: I want to annihilate myself in you my wise Minerva.
> Isabella: What a strange man you are Giacomo. You can't talk of love without using funereal images. . . . What you really want is not to love but to die.

As women increasing signify only Casanova's own pathological lack, their physical identifiability as women loses importance. Casanova seeks out giants (Angie) and hunchbacks (in Dresden) in a quest for novelty that makes size and shape far more important than biological sex.

In short, the relationship between signifier and signified (i.e., between the image of woman and the "reality" of gender or sexuality) breaks down. In the case of Casanova's mother, this relationship dissolves completely, amidst a welter of simultaneous associations. When Casanova hoists his mother onto his back, her identity is largely effaced as he becomes a hunchback. Moreover, because his mother looks birdlike, their joined image resembles Casanova's mechanical bird: symbol of Casanova's presumed masculinity. Their mechanization as "moving parts" in turn anticipates Rosalba, whom the mother resembles in size, coloring, and gender. This kind of sign play subverts any potential grounding offered by the final image of the mother: trapped behind the glass of her carriage windows like Venus beneath the waters of Venice. Without all the other complicating associations, this image might make the mother simply equal to Venus/Venice and the missing or submerged Origin, Feminine Principle, and Mother with a capital M. However, linked also with hunchback-lover and surrogate penis, mother-under-glass is only one in a chain of significations whose mutual incompatibility makes simple identification, much less interpretation, impossible.

Ultimately, women disappear altogether even as *potential* signifiers. At Dux, Casanova no longer has lovers, no longer relates to women at all. The only object of desire remaining is an image of himself, younger, pasted with excrement on a latrine wall (the prank, we are told, of one of his perpetual nemeses at the castle). This confirms that women have always only been reflections of a (missing) self for Casanova. It also makes clear that Casanova is now too old, feeble, and unattractive to participate in the symbolic exchange of gender(ed)/power—i.e., the power structure, based on sexual desirability and its multiple (mis)representations, within which Casanova sought to advance himself. Having lost his currency as a signifier of sexual difference, he is reduced to a kind of absolute sameness or self-duplication.

Yet this self-to-self relation has its own kind of difference. On the one hand, there is the aged Casanova, finally become himself in the absolute immobility and there-ness of old age. He is what he is, un(ex)changeable. Then there is the object of his gaze and desire: the younger Casanova, pure circulating signifier, viable because purely semiotic. What we have here, then, is a nostalgic reversal. Not the harkening back, from a postmodern moment of radical semiosis, to the good old days of stable identity. But a wistful look back from the moment of stable identity to the good old days of pure signification. Here we end up 180 degrees removed from the Casanova who sought grounding through a Venice/Venus/origin/woman/mother matrix. This aged Casanova is indeed hysterical: *desiring* to be the wandering phallus, ever signifying power/masculinity/fullness in their vertiginous lack.

Perhaps, also, this self-mirroring hints at something larger: an operational paradox that fuels the entire semiotic system of gender/power in *Fellini's Casanova*. On the one hand, the system promises a kind of perpetual alterity based on sexual difference. On the other hand, since everything is sign and everything is ex- and inter- changeable, alterity is an illusion. Difference may materialize as constructed positions within the system (male vs. female, power vs. lack), but anything can occupy any position, thus ontologically, difference implodes as the sheer iteration of sign(s).

3d. Textuality

As much of the above suggests, *Fellini's Casanova* is marked by a kind of textual excess. For one thing, it is a text constructed from another text. This is not uncommon for Fellini, who has redone Petronius (*Fellini-Satyricon*) and Poe ("Toby Dammit") and taken other art forms (*The Clowns*) as his point of departure. However, here he chooses a figure who, in effect, has no history or existence apart from his writing (the memoirs); whose compulsion to narrate produced anywhere from six to twelve volumes, depending on which edition we cite; and whose work, as Fellini has put it, is a "kind of telephone book . . . [a] boundless, paper-like ocean . . . [an] arid listing of . . . facts amassed without any selection, feeling, or amusement. . . ." In short, Fellini has chosen as his subject a figure who is nothing more nor less than the hysterical production of signs—a figure exiled in language which (since Casanova wrote in French and *Fellini's Casanova* was made in English) is not even his own.

Appropriately, Casanova begins the film as "text": dressed in the costume of Pedrolino (Pierrot in the French tradition), a stock character from the Italian commedia dell'arte.[31] In fact, he does not become identifiable until the following scene, when he takes off his hood to read another text: a letter claiming that a nun who has seen him in church wishes to meet him. The first words he speaks—even though he is presumed author/narrator of all we see—are not his own, but those of the letter.

Repeatedly, the act of narration or dramatization itself takes priority over any reality that Casanova might be narrating *about*—or dramatizing.[32] For instance, his escape from prison is a feat of story-telling, not physical activity. He *talks about* the brilliant and elaborate machinations that enable him to break out, but we never see them.[33]

His response to Henriette's disappearance is pure playacting. In a passionless tone of voice that undercuts his words, he asserts: "[Henriette's] rightful place is with me, and I will find her and bring her back even if I have to face all the armies of Europe." Then he does no such thing. Instead, he reverts to narration, moving on to recount another episode. Moreover, the link he makes has to do not with lost love, but with melodramatic posturing: "In a delirium of grief I considered taking my life or burying myself in a monastery and ending my days as a monk. But that time I chose neither grave nor cloister, death, beloved friend of noble unfortunate souls. Many years later in London, I nearly did indeed cross of my own volition the final threshold."

Even his "near suicide" is pure theatre, as he dresses up in his finest clothes, quotes Torquato Tasso, strides pompously into the Thames, and fixes to whack himself on the head with a rock. Suicide is just another text to be performed (in fact he refers to it as "the last and greatest *ceremony*"), and of course he fails to go through with it.

The dissociation of narration from reality also becomes clear in Casanova's increasing authorial unreliability. He claims that Württemberg "boast[s] the most brilliant court in Europe" while we see mindless mayhem on screen. At Dux, he claims "as librarian to the count, I hold a position of considerable importance, in keeping with the attainments and congruous with the temperament of a scholar and a man of letters"—while we see an old and decrepit figure, treated with no special respect and, in fact, contemned by his coworkers.

Consistent with his role as librarian, Casanova defines himself here entirely in terms of reproduction and signification. Speaking to some visitors to the castle about his portrait on the latrine wall, he rambles on solely about images, texts, copies, and writing:

> It's a striking likeness. It was printed as an illustration to my famous novel, *Icosameron*. Have any of you happened to have read it? Allow me to give each of you a copy. I believe after my death that I will be talked about for many long years to come as the author of that work.

As he stares at his own image, he says "I am a well known Italian writer." Then he exits the scene, leaving only his portrait framed within his shadow—which becomes larger and larger as he departs off-screen. His final words as we watch his shadow/portrait are: "You're surely acquainted with my name. Giacomo Casanova of Venice. Man of letters. Philosopher." Here, as we approach the end of the film, Casanova embraces himself purely as writing, purely as text.

Expelled from the womb/home of Venus/Venice, lacking biological paternity (Casanova is not linked to any progeny in the film), and now deprived by decrepitude of sexual identity, Casanova reconfigures birth, paternity, and sexuality as compulsive self-production through language. Yet self-production is not a recuperation of home or masculine power— either of which might provide some kind of grounding. It is yet another form of exile, as is suggested when narrative is born in the film as Casanova's means not only of escaping prison but abandoning Venice.

Accordingly, narration (i.e., voice-over) is sporadic, and narrative structure is arbitrary if not nonexistent[34]—grounding events neither in point of view nor coherent plot. We cannot attribute any consistent motivation to Casanova as author. As Fellini himself suggests, Casanova is nothing more than a "glassy eye which allows itself to slide over reality—and to pass through and to erase it—without intervening with a judgement, without interpreting it with a feeling."[35] He certainly is not seeking self-understanding: his tales are entirely lacking in introspection. He does not seem to be trying to impress us—he repeatedly shows himself in an extremely negative light. He does not employ any of the conventional lures for entertainment: plot, appealing charac-terization, closure. He clearly has no moral purpose such as education or edification. It appears that his narration—like his reported life—is just another pose, a literary conceit. Even his habitual *raison d'être*, sycophancy, is missing, since he feels no compulsion to please! His refusal to please or impress suggests that even the goals of self-aggrandizement and empowerment, so evident with de Bernis, Annamarie, and others, are not consistent story-telling motives.

As a result, no episode need relate to any other, nothing need build into something larger or more coherent. His tale comprises the kind of meaningless seriality that Fellini's early films critique in relation to Italian vaudeville or variety theatre and *Ginger and Fred* critiques in terms of television.

The end result of all this is a pervasive surficiality to the film. There is nothing beneath, behind, or outside the sheer accumulation of signs to serve as a cause, source, or context. Everything is collapsed onto a two dimensional plane which, in eliminating any relationship except seriality, (again) eliminates all difference.

4. Casanova's Dream

The final scene of *Fellini's Casanova* helps crystallize the principal issues of the film. As a humiliated and lonely Casanova ponders "Venice. Will I ever see Venice again?" he recalls a dream he had the night before. We see Venice again, but the canals are now frozen, the bridges are devoid of people, and the eyes of "Venus," trapped in ice, stare blankly at Casanova and at us. Casanova kneels, and the lower torso of a figure in pants and boots appears. Casanova turns toward this seemingly male figure and whispers "Isabella." The lower torso of a figure in a skirt appears, and we cut to several darkly clad women walking down stairs then dissolving away. Casanova walks toward a figure in white who laughs and keeps receding, and we cut to a group of women whispering and moving rapidly away. The women disappear, and a golden coach arrives. Suddenly Rosalba appears. We cut back to the coach and discover the Pope and Casanova's mother within. The Pope points Rosalba out to Casanova with a mixture of complicity, command, and amused approbation. We cut back to Rosalba. Casanova courts her, and they begin to dance. We cut to the eyes of the old Casanova, observing the scene he is recollecting, then we cut back to Rosalba and the younger Casanova dancing. They end the film turning in circles like a couple on a music box. Casanova too has become a mannequin, mechanized and without expression.

Casanova's dream underscores his unceasing exile. Venice is only an image from the unconscious, and frozen over at that. He remains surrounded by signs of absent love, but clearly desiring a grounding relation to mother and "father" and all they represent. His relationship to women continues to exist in the shadow of male power. The first figure to appear seems to be a male authority, perhaps even the shadowy, mysterious D'Antoine who spirited away Henriette. Casanova cannot or does not relate to him, and instead "substitutes" Isabella. Then, though Casanova can temporarily substitute women for male authority, the Pope must appear to author-ize his liaison with Rosalba. (His mother remains clearly subordinate, in the background.)

Because women exist only as reflections of Casanova's need—especially for (male) power—they remain intangible, inaccessible. The only "female" who is not a mere apparition is a product of technology.

Like every dream, Casanova's is a series of displacements. In some instances the displacement is single: e.g., the real Venice is now merely a dream image. Often, however, it is doubled. Casanova is both a dream image and, by the end, a mere mechanized simulation of his former self. Similarly, the doll is a dream image of an earlier displacement: robot for actual women, such as Annamarie and Henriette, whom the doll resembles. As displacement doubles, referents recede.

The representation of women contributes to the defeat of reference. Not only does Casanova misrecognize a male image as Isabella, but a figure in white who might be Henriette appears only from the back and only partially on-screen. All the women remain faceless—characterizable as females only in terms of dress. Significantly, the only woman Casanova seeks to name is the one woman who has stood him up (at Dresden) and failed to become his lover: a sign, in short, of absence and lack.

The foregrounding of signification is reflected in the fact that we are not confronted solely with a dream but with the *memory* of a *dream* within a *narrative* which has, for the most part, been pure posturing. Casanova's recollection, in turn, reinstitutes both spectacle and voyeurism, so crucial to the opening scenes of the film. However, there are differences which further accentuate the dominance of sign play. What was originally a public space (the bridges and walkways of Venice) is now private, lodged within Casanova's dreaming unconscious and narrating consciousness. And instead of someone watching Casanova perform, he is watching himself (we recall the portrait at Dux). In each case, he has managed to exclude anything outside his own signifying activity. His story has become entirely self-referential, narcissistic.

This movement to privacy and self might seem to signal the recovery of some interiority or depth. But Casanova's "inner life" just consists of superficial representations (most indicatively the twinned mannequins, Rosalba and himself) of depths that do not exist. The "inside" is only a mirror reflecting a surface. Concomitantly, even the dream imagery works to eliminate depth: freezing the formerly undulating waters of Venice and eliminating the former depth of Venus, whose eyes are no longer beneath the water but have, instead, become part of the ice surface.

Inevitably, this dream triggers no self-awareness. We just see Casanova looking, without apparent regret or acknowledgment of any kind. We do hear some sounds of breathing which might be construed as crying, but the brief shot of the old Casanova shows no tears. Moreover, Casanova devolves in the course of this recollection from narrator to mere spectator—and then from spectator to mannequin. The final simulation of Casanova can neither speak nor see; it can only move in circles, staring blankly.

In the final moments, then, Casanova has been projected entirely outward as pure sign, pure reproduction. The origin (this time Casanova himself) has been effaced, the voice of the author has been extinguished, and mute exteriority rules supreme. Dead unto himself, Casanova exists solely, in the terms of Baudrillard, as a "resurrection effect."

5. Conclusion

The killing off the subject, the real, and the referential in *Fellini's Casanova* is not without its problems and inconsistencies. First of all,

Casanova's lack of point of view as a narrator generates a largely amoral text. For instance, he can tell of exploiting women (Madame D'Urfé), taking sexual advantage of them (Annamarie), and degrading them (Romana), without any hint of regret or wrongdoing. Moreover, for the most part, the film merely adopts Casanova's "glassy eye." We see Annamarie as Casanova sees her: "needing" to be taken sexually and, in fact, appreciating it. There is no distancing of filmic point of view from Casanova's exploitation of Madame D'Urfé, his treatment of his mother, his grotesque passion for Rosalba.

We may assume that this amorality is purposeful: yet another way in which the film operates as pure surface and strips its signifiers of meaning. It could also constitute an act of self-effacement on Fellini's part—a dissolution of authorial point of view amidst the film's play of surfaces. In all this, the film would serve as a postmodern denial of totalizing moral systems, unified interpretation, and authorial control over the text. However, in so doing, the film would still fall liable to critique by those (and in the case of *Fellini's Casanova*, particularly feminists) who see in postmodernism's cultivated groundlessness a dangerous evasion of the political, social, and historical.

We could defend the film, pointing to those moments where the film does appear to adopt its own, critical, point of view. For instance, following Casanova's callous use of Romana, there is a brief close-up of her turning away from the camera in anger and humiliation. We also see her apparent lover del Brando prominently in the background, humiliated. The perspective offered here, and especially the close-up of Romana, are quite at odds with Casanova's insensitivity and can easily be taken as the film's point of view.

Yet the arbitrariness of moral stance here—the fact that it is not part of a consistent filmic vision—gives it the status of merely another literary convention: something that perhaps even Casanova threw in as an apt narrative gesture, a posture of self-critique.

We could also point to the final dance of the mannequins, which clearly seems to offer some sort of critical commentary on the culminative emptiness of Casanova's life. Here, however, the criticism seems to be outweighed by a strong sense of sympathy. The film seems to take a sudden shift in attitude consistent with Fellini's interview remarks:

> Who knows, perhaps as an old man when the servants of the Count of Waldenstein mocked him and played atrocious jokes on him, and he—bedecked with plumes and powdered like an old clown—continued to act as he had before the French Revolution . . . there, then, he might perhaps have aroused a little bit of sympathy, of empathy—who knows?[36]

This sudden emotional identification with Casanova seems to tacitly redeem a career and a narrative filled with crudeness, largely directed toward women.

We could see all these inconsistencies as a postmodern celebration of inconsistency itself, as well as the parodic recuperation of nostalgic humanism as another mere effect of signification (though this again invites critique on socio-political grounds). However, I am inclined to see the ruptures in the film's postmodern surface (the tears as it were in the glassy eye) as the assertions of a still-felt humanism—and a Fellini who cannot succumb entirely to the postmodern denial of subjectivity, coherence, and an accessible real.

In fact, I think *Casanova's* calculated avoidance of history, politics, and morality may be read as the strategy of a recalcitrant humanism intended to place the surficiality of postmodernity in a highly problematic light. To support this conclusion I go beyond the film, citing Fellini's comments at the time of *Fellini's Casanova*, on the current role of the artist:

> It is evident that unmasking the lie, identifying the inauthentic, and taking apart the indefinite of false absolutes continues to be, for now, the only corrective resource—a mocking inexhaustible safeguard—against our bankrupt history. . . .[37]

I also cite Fellini's next film, *The Orchestra Rehearsal*, which employs a kind of moral and socio-political critique that makes it anomalous within Fellini's canon—implying an equal and opposite reaction following his strategic repression of the artist-as-moralist in Casanova.

What all this may suggest is the extent to which *Fellini's Casanova* marks a moment of anxiety for Fellini. And it would be no accident if anxiety proved to be the determining characteristic of Fellini's most complete encounter with postmodernity—for postmodernity itself is nothing if not an anxiety site. With the death of romantic high modernism, there may be nowhere to go but the simulacrum—yet it hardly seems an enabling place to be. Accordingly, while Fellini can render in great complexity the death of the referent, the real, and the artist-subject, he cannot do so without retaining the kind of rhetoric ("unmasking the lie," "identifying the inauthentic," "*false* absolutes"), which still implies their possibility.

Read in this light, *Fellini's Casanova* may well deny its director status within the postmodern. Nonetheless, his resistance to the glassy eye of endless signification may confirm for us that it is precisely the refusal to relinquish all ties to reality, reference, and subjective intervention that distinguishes postmodernity in its politicized forms. And it is precisely in the space between the referent and its denial, between the signified and the signifier, between, in short, the increasingly reversible poles of political and aesthetic postmodernity, that postmodernism as a form of cultural resistance seems to derive its greatest dynamic. Yet because it resides always in between, deriving its energy from what it is not, its empowerment is ceaselessly conflicted. It is this fear of irresolution, this resistance of the simulacrum, this anxiety of exile in postmodernity, that now impels an old high modernist like Fellini to direct films which articulate the death of reference and subjectivity within the shadow of some impossible longed-for resurrection.

Notes

The author would like to acknowledge funding of the Social Sciences and Humanities Research Council of Canada and of the Advisory Research Council of Queen's University, which made research on this essay possible.

1. For an extensive discussion of subjectivity in Fellini's films, see Frank Burke, "Fellini: Changing the Subject," *Film Quarterly*, 43.1 (Fall 1989): 36-48.

2. Male hysteria is a guiding metaphor for the contemporary subject in crisis in *The Hysterical Male*, eds. Arthur and Marilouise Kroker (Montreal: New World Perspectives, 1991).

3. Quoted in Christopher Williams, ed. *Realism and Cinema* (London: Routledge and Kegan Paul, 1990), p. 31.

4. Federico Fellini, *Fellini on Fellini*, trans. Isabel Quigly (New York: Delacorte Press/Seymour Lawrence, 1976), p. 62.

5. The fact that some of these "great individuals" were radically opposed to capitalist individualism just serves to highlight the conflicted nature of individualism in the 1960s.

6. "*Playboy* Interview: Federico Fellini," *Playboy*, 13 (February 1966): 60.

7. "Fellini: Changing the Subject."

8. Hollis Alpert, *Fellini: A Life* (New York: Atheneum, 1986), p. 229.

9. Consistent with his problematizing of the subject in *Amarcord*, Fellini has on some occasions maintained that "amarcord" means "I remember" and, on other occasions, denied it.

10. For a more extensive discussion of "Toby Dammit" in the context of the death of the subject, see "Changing the Subject," pp. 42-43.

11. "Conversation with Federico Fellini," *Oui Magazine* (January 1972): 154.

12. Fellini, "Conversation with Federico Fellini," p. 154.

13. Fellini, "Conversation with Federico Fellini," p. 154.

14. Fellini, "Conversation with Federico Fellini," p. 154.

15. Another clearly disempowering dimension to Fellini's *Casanova* experience was the mysterious theft then return of several reels of film

as Fellini was trying to complete the project.

16. "The Ecstasy of Communication" in *The Anti-Aesthetic*, ed. Hal Foster (Port Townsend, WA: Bay Press, 1983), p. 133.

17. It is also reflected in his refusal to make films outside Italy— and for that matter Rome.

18. Kroker and Kroker, *The Hysterical Male*.

19. Paul Ginsborg, *A History of Contemporary Italy: Society and Politics, 1943-1988* (London and New York: Penguin, 1990), p. 366.

20. See Robert Lumley, *States of Emergency: Cultures of Revolt in Italy from 1968 to 1978* (London: Verso, 1990), pp. 313ff; Donald Sassoon, *Contemporary Italy: Politics, Economy and Society Since 1945* (New York: Longman, Inc., 1986), pp. 101ff; and Paul Ginsborg, *A History of Contemporary Italy: Society and Politics 1943-1988* (London and New York: Penguin, 1990), pp. 366ff.

21. Gideon Bachman, "Federico Fellini: 'The Cinema Seen as a Woman . . .'" *Film Quarterly*, 34.2 (1980-81): 8.

22. "*Playboy* Interview," p. 62.

23. Bachman, p. 8.

24. The link between Fellini's Casanova and male hysteria has already been made by Dale Bradley in an essay entitled: "From History to Hysteria: *Fellini's Casanova* Meets Baudrillard," *Canadian Journal of Political and Social Theory* 13.1 (1989): 129-139. However, as the title suggests, Bradley's essay is principally Baudrillardian in focus, covering much different ground from that of the following analysis.

25. Fellini has emphasized that Casanova is less a figure of the Enlightenment than of the Counter-Reformation—"Conversation with Federico Fellini," p. 154.

26. Dale Bradley notes the thematic significance of the absent Count at Dux ("From History to Hysteria," p. 138).

27. In Arthur Kroker and David Cook, *The Postmodern Scene: Excremental Culture and Hyper-Aesthetics* (New York: St. Martin's Press, 1986), pp. 116-117. The words are Kroker's and are a commentary on Jean Baudrillard's "Forgetting Foucault," *Humanities in Society* 3.1 (Winter 1980).

28. The Annmarie episode, in fact, illuminates an apparent blind spot on Fellini's part regarding Casanova and the *Memoirs*. In answer to an interview question, "Did Casanova ever rape anybody?" Fellini claims, "If there is anything that saves him from being too disgusting, it's that there isn't a single episode of violence in his memoirs" ("Conversation with Federico Fellini," p. 155). In fact, there *are* incidents in the *Memoirs* of Casanova's violence toward women, sexual and otherwise, and though Casanova's conquest of Annmarie is not particularly violent, it is certainly sex without consent.

29. Within this system it is not surprising that women end up desiring to be men. Madame D'Urfe wants Casanova to have sex with her so that she can perform "the great work of dying as a woman and being 'transformed into a man . . . who will live forever.'"

30. The elegant costuming, make-up, and so on are, of course, historically accurate, not just Fellini's idea!

31. Appropriately, given Casanova's relation to power, Pedrolino as stock character is a humble servant, and Casanova is first seen—through not yet indentifiable—assisting the Doge in the ceremonial attempts to raise Venus.

32. Something quite similar happens with Fellini's "garbage-bag" sea: a Cinécittà simulation made out of black plastic and undulated by wind machines. The signifier (plastic) is so dramatic and absurd that it dominates attention while the signified (sea) recedes into virtual nonexistence.

33. The narrative effacement here is all the more significant in that Casanova's escape may well be that only event in the film which can be historically verified. For the most part, the film recounts episodes from *The History of My Life* which remain uncorroborated by external evidence.

34. Fellini himself has claimed, somewhat hyperbolically, "there is no narrative either in the romantic or the psychological sense. There are no characters, there are no situations, there are neither premises nor developments, nor catharses. . . ." "*Casanova*: An Interview with Aldo Tassone" in Peter Bondanella, ed. *Federico Fellini: Essays in Criticism* (New York: Oxford University Press, 1978), p. 31.

35. "*Casanova*: An Interview with Aldo Tassone," p. 28.

36. "*Casanova*: An Interview with Aldo Tassone," p. 31. See also Millicent Marcus' observations on the concluding scene: "*Fellini's Casanova*: Portrait of the Artist," *Quarterly Review of Film Studies* 5.1 (Winter 1980): 33.

37. "*Casanova*: Portrait of an Artist," p. 35.

Catherine Russell

Decadence, Violence and the Decay of History: Notes on the Spectacular Representation of Death in Narrative Film, 1965 to 1990

In David Lynch's 1990 film *Wild at Heart*, Sailor and Lulu come across a wounded girl in a still-smouldering car accident who is more concerned about her lost pocketbook and credit cards than her dead boyfriend and bloody head. In Godard's 1967 film *Weekend*, Corinne emerges from a car wreck screaming "Help! My Hermes bag!" Perhaps this intertextual motif is an incidental point of contact between two films that might seem to have very little in common. Where Godard's film ends with the titles "End of Story/End of Cinema," Lynch's ends with a *deus ex machina* of redemption. And yet both are road movies featuring lots of fire and car accidents, both are about a couple, a dead father and a bad mother, and both narratives are constantly interrupted by stories and corpses.

A comparison of *Weekend* with not only *Wild at Heart* but a contemporary European film, *The Cook, the Thief, his Wife and her Lover* (Greenaway, 1989), and a discussion of two American films of the late 60s—*Bonnie and Clyde* (Penn, 1967) and The Wild Bunch (Peckinpah, 1968)—alongside *Pierrot le fou* (Godard 1965), is a means of addressing several issues of crisis cinema and apocalyptic culture. It should indicate the kind of shift that has taken place since the late 60s both in Hollywood and non-Hollywood narrative cinema, and it should suggest something about the role of vision in apocalyptic cinema. If biblical apocalypse is about catastrophe and revelation couched in the terms of vision, it is very difficult to articulate in a medium in which vision is inevitably limited to the image. Because the image always belongs ontologically to the past, and narrative realism involves a disavowal of this historical difference, cinematic apocalypticism has displaced the revelation of historical difference with the visual excess of catastrophe. In the cinema, spectacular violence has become the sign of a crisis of vision, seducing the spectator into a belief in the unrepresentable—the death of an actor. Moreover, spectacular violence stakes its apocalyptic vision in narrative cinema upon the conjunction of belief in the image and belief in mythic historiography. What is most radical about *Weekend* is the suggestion that it is the cinematic image itself which has to be sacrificed for historical vision.

The analyses of *Wild at Heart* and *The Cook, the Thief, his Wife and her Lover*, made more than 20 years after the bloody ballets and tableaux of Vietnam-era cinema should also suggest something about the nature of the crisis in late 1980s cinema. Their redemptive thrust will be analyzed as a mythic enterprise strongly tied to aesthetic values, authorship and patriarchy, whereas the crises of the earlier films are more properly historical. History in postmodern crisis cinema has become a discourse of decay and decadence which the aesthetic practice of auteurs such as Greenaway and Lynch is designed to purify. And yet analysis of Godard's films—in light of Walter Benjamin's theory of allegory and "dialectics of seeing"[1]—should demonstrate that once the ruins of affirmative culture are perceived as the decay of representation, the radical secret of crisis cinema might be glimpsed. Less important than which of the following films are "modernist" and which "postmodern" is the identification of different discourses of historical vision and representation that inform their imagery and narrative forms.

Lynch's reference to Godard points to a lingering residue of late 1960s radicalism in a postmodern aesthetic of excess. Godard's last narrative films before his so-called Maoist period may in fact be regarded as a threshold of the postmodern, articulating the potential of a cinema of crisis that may never have been completely realized. The excessive blood and violence of films such as *Pierrot le fou* and *Weekend* delineate a regime of artifice that mark the very limits of representation. The narrative teleology insists on going beyond the end of the film and the end of history towards historical transformation. Crucial to this temporality is the articulation of the unknown and the unrepresentable of which the film and the images that we do see are only the threshold. Like *Pierrot le fou*, *Wild at Heart* involves a redemption of popular culture romance and utopianism, but the 1990 film is so obsessed with its affirmative project that it is unable to articulate a future free of the trappings of American bourgeois nationalist ideology, despite its surreal discourse of transgression, deformation and corporeality.

1. Apocalyptic Closure

In *Pierrot le fou* the political optimism of the 1960s is precariously mingled with a renunciation of aesthetic and subjective mastery and autonomy. Unlike later theoretical and cinematic manifestations of teleological crisis, the apocalypse of *Pierrot le fou* retains a utopian dimension, involving a notion of historical difference articulated through an allegory of transcendence. One of the most sensational aspects of the film upon its release was its casual attitude toward violence and its histrionic representation.[2] "Not blood. Red," as Godard puts it.[3] By exploiting the discursive potential of fictional death, Godard's film may be aligned with some of the central tenets of poststructuralist apocalypticism. Blanchot's *Writing of the Disaster* and Derrida's "No Apocalypse, Not Now" both situate literature on the limits of the annihilated referent.[4] The impossibility of envisioning a post-nuclear future subverts teleology at the same time as "presence" is deconstructed in the mortifying effect of representation.

Pierrot le fou may be plotted on two crucial grids of Andreas Huyssen's "map" of the post-modern. On one hand, it demonstrates the "temporal imagination" of the historical avant garde that resurfaces with the 1960s exhaustion of modernism. And it also indulges in that sense of loss which characterizes the post-structuralist recognition of "modernism's limitations and failed political ambitions."[5] It is a film, viewed from a 25-year distance, in which discursive heterogeneity becomes an historical and cultural threshold of postmodernity.

Ferdinand's (Jean-Paul Belmondo) final gesture in the film's last scene is to paint his face blue, wrap his head with yellow and red dynamite and blow himself up. In his adventures with Marianne (Anna Karina) bloody corpses are discovered littering apartments and landscape, and as the pathos conventionally associated with images of death is consistently subverted, so also is its narrative function of binding and totalizing. The adventures of Marianne and Ferdinand are built upon an archeology of modern art and literature, with visual and verbal quotations from a gamut of sources, including Joyce, Baudelaire, Celine,

Picasso, Faulkner, and especially Rimbaud. At the same time, there are multiple allusions to Hollywood gangster and noir films, as well as the ostensible source novel, Lionel White's *Obsession*.

Godard claims that the film, especially the second half, was invented on the spot, "a kind of happening."[6] The Vietnam war references not only anchor that happening historically, but do so within the terms of the representation of death. Godard is fully aware that film is a mechanism of "death at work," but unlike Bazin, he exploits its historical, rather than transcendental, properties. The representation of death and the references to historical death (e.g. body counts from Vietnam, newsreel images of marines) are instrumental to the film's quest for "poetry," which is to be found beyond pathos and the myths of harmonious mimeticism and romance, and must be dialectically wrenched from the continuum of images and history.

The apocalyptic dimension of Ferdinand's death recalls Benjamin's advocacy of a "blasting out of the historical continuum." This is the secret promise of dialectical images and the passage through time of the *mémoire involontaire*. If historical hope is grounded in the image of the past, rather than the teleology of progress, "the utilization of dream elements upon waking is the canon of dialectics."[7] Moreover, the "freedom" which the narrative is concerned with involves a specific collusion of "documentary" and "fictional" realities, a phenomenological desire to locate representation somewhere between and beyond them. Frank Kermode (whose *The Sense of an Ending* was published one year after *Pierrot*), describes the depiction of time in Sartre's *La Nausée* as a "redemption of contingency. The freedom from novelistic structure is only manageable, or communicable, through a discovery of form latent in contingent or 'found' reality."[8] Here we may think of Godard's use of actors as "documentary subjects,"[9] of Raymond Devos' absurd and lengthy monologue inserted at a very critical point in Ferdinand's adventure, but more specifically, it may offer a clue to the abrupt recovery of closure in a film which takes place in a world "without beginning or end."

Marianne and Ferdinand's voices are finally conjoined after their deaths in a whispered poem over a shot of the Mediterranean sea and sky. Speaking alternate lines of the last stanza of Rimbaud's poem "L'Éternité":

> Elle est retrouvée!
> Quoi? L'Éternité.
> C'est la mer mêlée
> Au soleil.

The "romance" of *Pierrot* derives in part from the repeated coincidental

Blasting out of the continuum of history. Jean-Paul Belmondo as Ferdinand in Jean-Luc Godard's *Pierrot le fou* (1968). Films Copernic, Lira Films, Comacico, Ascot Cineraid. Still photographs by Christopher Sharrett.

reunions of Marianne and Ferdinand and their reconciliation after death. But equally important is Thanatos, violence and death. In this respect, Sam Fuller, who appears in *Pierrot* as the director of a film of *Les Fleurs du mal* is not just any Hollywood filmmaker, but one whom the *Cahiers du Cinéma* critics appreciated especially for the excessive violence of his films.[10] Fuller describes cinema as a "battleground," and it is indeed through the representation of death that the film engages questions of phenomenology and spectacular representation in a way specific to the mid-sixties' intellectual climate. The existential "Freedom" of *Pierrot* is achieved through contingent violence, a violence of historical discontinuity, Benjamin's "shock" effect, as much as it is through the imaginary of eternity.

The absurdity of Ferdinand's suicide, followed by the resurrection of the self "outside of this world" is an allegory of transcendence, signifying its impossibly mythic dimension, but at the same time, it inscribes a desire to ironically remember a belief in the ability to go beyond the limits of history. Ferdinand blasts himself out of the momentum of narrative, the continuum of history and the finitude of existence, but he also blows himself out of representation. There is no corpse, no body at all to organically "reenter the world" because of course it would not be a dead body at all, but Belmondo acting dead. The "renewal" of this carnivalized death is not organic but spectacular. Throughout the film, death is at once ironic, spectacularly "fake," but instrumental to the film's momentum, driving the couple on to further adventures, reversing expectations, generating action: a crucial decoration of the underworld that Ferdinand traverses.[11]

In *Pierrot*, one finds the traces of modernism still potent, instilling a memory of materialism, the hint of an historical referent informing its apocalypse. But what is perhaps most intriguing about the threshold that is delineated in *Pierrot* is that it also anticipates the crisis of historical vision of the postmodern apocalyptic and allows us to situate that crisis within the philosophical, political and aesthetic framework of the French New Wave and the *Cahiers du Cinéma* critics' "necessity to be modern."[12] The spectacle of death and the poetry of eternity are finally separated from each other with the cut away from the protagonist's explosive body, and it is perhaps in that cut, in that which is not representable, that the future of the society of the spectacle might be hidden.

In American film of the same period an apocalyptic discourse can be identified in which the historical content of apocalypse is displaced onto spectacular violence. In Guy Debord's society of the spectacle "neither death nor procreation is grasped as a law of time. Time remains immobile, like an enclosed space,"[13] and indeed Hollywood's apocalyptic vision tends to turn in on itself, curtailing both the promise and the threat of apocalyptic historiography.

In the secular world of late capitalism, apocalyptic discourse points, in most cases, to a loss of social consensus, but the "loss of myth" that informs Godard's work is figured quite differently in American genre revisionism that fails to question the status of the image in its deconstruction of myth. Death and closure converge more teleologically in the American apocalypse, as crisis is institutionalized as commodified spectacle. *Bonnie and Clyde* (1967) and *The Wild Bunch* (1968) were particularly "shocking" to contemporary audiences. It is instructive to analyze the particular representations of death in these films because, taken together, they illustrate the tendency of the American mythos of "regeneration through violence," to disintegrate into an aesthetic discourse of excess. Stylization takes up where coherent belief systems dissipate, and death, likewise cut off from those metaphysical, religious and melodramatic discourses in which it was "tame," explodes in a violent destruction of the body.

Bonnie and Clyde includes scenes which were described at the time as "the most brutally violent ever filmed,"[14] mainly because of the amount of blood involved. The spectator knows the couple is doomed from the outset, and the narrative is, as Penn says, simply a matter of "waiting out history."[15] *Bonnie and Clyde* are finally machine-gunned to death in a complex montage of very short shots, cutting between the two bodies twisting, twitching, writhing and falling under the force of the bullets. Cross-cutting between Clyde (Warren Beatty) falling and rolling on the ground in front of the car and Bonnie (Faye Dunaway) hammered into the front seat with bullets and finally dropping head first onto the running board, to the accompaniment of a loud machine gun rattle, the scene consists of 30 shots in the space of one minute. The film ends immediately after the police emerge from the bushes and drop their guns to their sides.

This is an entirely different order of violence from *Pierrot*. Godard uses great amounts of red on static, motionless bodies to signify death, as well as the impossibility of signifying death. Penn uses motion, the movement that characterizes life in its last vestige of being, a violent movement through which the body is transformed from subject (facial expressions) to inert and lifeless object (the emphasis on the weight of the bodies, something that Hitchcock also does).[16] The sequence moves from four extreme close-ups alternating between Bonnie and Clyde's faces, realizing suddenly the gravity of the situation, to Bonnie's limp hand finally signifying death.

The stoppage of the film immediately after this stoppage of bodily
movement delimits representation to subjectivity, as the movement of
both subjectivity and film are abruptly curtailed in a dead car. Bonnie
and Clyde drive even more cars across this film than Ferdinand and
Marianne do in *Pierrot* and the distention of time in the representation
of their deaths is in contrast with the energetic pace of the film. The
spastic movement of their bodies in the hail of bullets is likewise at
odds with the momentum of the narrative, a momentum that has been
driven precisely by the desire for the couple's death. Far from being
an accident or a surprise, the scene fulfils the dictates of genre, myth
and fate.

If the final fragmentation of the film's spatial and temporal unities
through multiple speeds and focal lengths is a literal disintegration of
the image, the failure of subjectivity and desire is coextensive with the
failure of representation. If it can no longer signify *anything*, the film
signifies itself within the very code of excess (as Barthes has said of
Japanese melodrama),[17] but it does so only at the end. Violence here
does not become a form of "writing" because it says nothing, except
that this is the end. The desire repressed in the narrative (Clyde's

The Romance of History: Faye Dunnaway and Warren Beatty in Arthur Penn's
Bonnie and Clyde (1967). Warner Bros./Seven Arts. Still courtesy of Jerry
Ohlinger's Movie Materials.

impotence) is finally realized in the desire for closure, for these deaths that were anticipated all along. The telos of the myth of fate is celebrated in the excesses of representation, which give to the spectator precisely what was missing when Bonnie and Clyde went off screen, out of frame, to make love.

Moreover, the spectacle of violence in *Bonnie and Clyde*s situated within a closed historical discourse of nostalgia. Where *Pierrot*is set in a highly fragmented yet historically specific contemporary France, Penn's is set in the never-never land of the American 1930s. Depression America is represented as a timeless zone of poverty and social ills in which *Bonnie and Clyde* will die over and over again. That mythic time when gangsters were the heroes of the underclass, a New Deal America in which "the people" were a viable unified collective (however impoverished) is preserved as a fantasy outside the irreversibility and cruelty of history. In the displacement of the melodramatic excess of unfulfilled desire onto the bodies of the actors, onto the body of the film itself, with the violence of *Bonnie and Clyde*, desire is enunciated as such—as desire for the fantasy of coincidence, timelessness and return. Despite the emphasis on vision and catastrophe, this apocalyptic ending curtails the very possibility of historical anticipation, displacing teleology onto visual pleasure. The historical Others of future and past are thus transformed into the phenomenological Other of the screen.

If *Bonnie and Clyde* was the "first" film to represent death in anatomical detail, opening "the bloodgates" of American film, *The Wild Bunch* is the mythic initiator of a "celebration" of violence.[18] In the complexity of this film's historical setting, however, the romance of heroism encompasses a utopian vision of social transformation and the apocalyptic finale, with all its visual excess, does not completely overwhelm historical possibility. The exploding bloodbags and swooning bodies that represent death in *The Wild Bunch* constitute an iconography of death that is at once baroque and excessive.

Slow motion interrupts the narrative momentum for a veritable *danse macabre* in the final shoot-out, which lasts five minutes. It is the choreography of dying that has been charged against Peckinpah. In the sheer demonstration of cinematic representation, violent death is *attended* to by filmmaker and viewer (and in this respect it is much like *Bonnie and Clyde*). The heroes are each shot several times, falling back from the force of the bullets again and again, while the Mexicans fall mainly in slow motion waves of men. But the point at which stasis is finally reached is only a stoppage of Dutch's (Ernest Borgnine) body and an end to the sound of guns, and not a stoppage of the film. After the final close-up of Dutch's face, the scene then continues with the slow, silent resumption of movement as the scattered survivors emerge from the carnage.

A transcendent, regenerative function of the violence is suggested in *The Wild Bunch* through the conversion of Thornton (Robert Ryan) who witnesses the massacre, from vigilante back to outlaw. Moreover, after their deaths, a series of flashbacks of each of the five dead members of the gang is superimposed over Thornton's ride back into the wilderness. Insofar as their suicidal action results in the perpetuation of their values precisely through the staging of violence, the death of the wild bunch is sacrificial. Their values of fraternity and outlaw ethics survive in Thornton and his ragged bunch of outlaws despite the fact that the film has demonstrated the historical anachronism that those values embody.

And yet an important shift has taken place and "the work" that this group of survivors at the end of *The Wild Bunch* have to do is not simply to terrorize the landscape. Sykes, the old man who Thornton finally joins up with (an ex-cohort of the bunch) says, "It ain't like it used to be, but it'll do." The men with him are Mexicans whose outlaw status is that of revolutionary guerillas, so it is Ché Guevara, finally, on whom the heroism of the film is modeled. Or almost. The bunch die out of loyalty to their buddy Angel, not so much to his cause, and as Sykes' words suggest, the recourse to revolutionary action is a reluctant one. In this sense the "necessity of violence," implicit in the heroes' moral code, is ironically pushed to a limit at which it accommodates revolutionary violence. Capitalism is represented in *The Wild Bunch* as sheer greed which has totally corrupted the once-open frontier, and in order to preserve the frontier ideology of individualism, the narrative is literally forced into the defence of the oppressed and an embrace of history.

This ending is in fact neatly balanced on an historical threshold. The past is much more fully lost here than in *Bonnie and Clyde*, and the bodies that die over and over again in the "ballet" testify to the different historical time of representation. In the sheer length of the interruption that this massacre occupies, time is felt to be passing; narrative time and viewing time are radically collapsed into a present tense from which the mythic time of the American wilderness is absolutely excluded. The corpses of the aged heroes in their final dance are the very ruins of history. At the same time, there is the coda of regeneration, return and transcendence awkwardly tacked onto the bloodbath. In the spectacle of the dance itself, the pleasure in fantasy which was noted in *Bonnie and Clyde*, survives as desire. And yet any radical potential of this discourse is, like the suggestion of revolutionary activity, ultimately enfolded within the structure of myth: the regeneration of the buddy system and American patriarchal individualism. It *is* "Ché" and not Marx who lurks outside this Western.

Peckinpah leaves the viewer on the threshold of history as it escapes from myth, and of course the body counts and disabled men returning to the U.S. from Vietnam during this period rendered the myth of manifest destiny inadequate and dangerous. The depiction of death as a violation of the body was undoubtedly a response to the experiences and media imagery of the Vietnam war, and yet it is a mistake to label a film like *The Wild Bunch* as "an allegory of the My Lai Massacre."[19] The lingering faith in the image and its myths of pleasure, desire and closure is quite removed from the horrifying televisual imagery. In the very excess that verges on allegory, the possibility of regenerative violence remains in the desire to see, a desire encouraged by the careful choreography of cameras, bodies and blood. Moreover, this vision is linked to an apocalyptic historiography in which social change resides, however awkwardly, with repetition. The cataclysm of the massacre is off-set by the pressure of memory, visually represented in the final series of superimposed flashbacks.

René Girard's theory of sacrificial crisis has been invoked by several critics with respect to American film of this period.[20] Girard argues that in primitive societies, the ritual of sacrifice was a preventative mechanism *against* violence; it displaced the violence of revenge onto a victim with no social powers of vengeance and thus stemmed the tide of cyclical violence. "Sacrificial crisis" is, for Girard, the failure of ritual to organize difference in society. The unleashed violence of reciprocal killing is an infectious crisis of mimesis, into which sacrificial violence constitutes an inoculation of "difference." He offers the historical repressed of sacred violence as that which lies behind "the endless diversity of myths and rituals ... that ... all seek to recollect and reproduce something they never succeed in comprehending."[21] Certainly the Christian myth of the Crucifixion and its related ritual of Communion serves as an example of "good" violence that is all but lost in contemporary society. And while Girard can certainly be accused of an unacknowledged Christian orientation,[22] his notion of sacrificial crisis remains pertinent to the representation of death in contemporary American film. From *Birth of a Nation* to *Platoon* the Christian mythology of sacrifice has informed Hollywood melodrama.

Girard's conception of "equilibrium" derives from an analysis of the identity and doubling of the antagonists in Greek tragedy, and from the superstitions regarding twins and fraternal resemblance in primitive cultures. But it is equally true that the American myth of "regeneration through violence" is based in a structure of mimetic, reciprocal violence.

Beyond the end of history; violent closure in Sam Peckinpah's *The Wild Bunch*
(1968) Warner Bros. Stills courtesy of Jerry Ohlinger's Movie Materials.

Indeed, in *Bonnie and Clyde* and *The Wild Bunch*, the final eruption of violence is both a repetition of previous instantiations and motivated by revenge; the cop, Hamer, taking revenge against Bonnie and Clyde by assuming their violence for himself, and "the bunch" taking action against Mapache for his violence against Angel. Most of the violence in recent American film is grounded in a cyclical, repetitive schema of vengeance, epitomized in the *Dirty Harry, Cobra, Death Wish* and *Lethal Weapon* narratives in which the hero-killers aspire to the enemy's capacity for violence. The regeneration in sequels indicates their ritualistic impetus, and the failure of the ritual to stem the tide of violence.

2. The Consumption of Transgression

Sacrificial crisis is also the operative discourse linking the last films I want to discuss: *Weekend, Wild at Heart* and *The Cook, the Thief, his Wife and her Lover*. Apocalyptic narrative here is less teleological than above, and the crisis pertains more centrally to aesthetics than history. But, historical discourses figure quite critically in all three films, and violent excess and spectacular death is closely linked to a failure of narrative to redeem history. Where Lynch and Greenaway valiantly attempt to disavow this failure, in *Weekend* it is celebrated as a total failure of cinematic representation. While Penn and Peckinpah "celebrated" death with their spectacular imagery, twenty years later Lynch and Greenaway's excesses are more of ugliness, scatology and degradation of the body. However, the following analyses indicate that these transgressions of visual pleasure are still in the service of a closure of representation. The comparison with Godard indicates how historical vision is curtailed and limited by these strategies of transgression.

Greenaway's *The Cook, the Thief, his Wife and her Lover* (1989), is divided like *Weekend* into days of the week but, also like the 1967 film, shifts to the French Revolution for its codification of time. It also shares with *Weekend* a cannibalistic ending and an anti-Hollywood ambition. While the distanciation and theatricality of *The Cook, the Thief* may be reminiscent of Godard (and Greenaway sees himself within a Godardian tradition),[23] it is Lynch who is more often invoked by critics writing about Greenaway, as both directors come from an art-school background. Indeed, both *Wild at Heart* and *The Cook, the Thief* have been criticized as being pretty pictures with little narrative substance.[24] My object here is not to redeem these films; nor is it to wax nostalgic for the political intensity of 1967 and the genius of Godard. The category of authorship may, however, lie behind both Greenaway and Lynch's

references to Godard. Both have recently won the autuerist mantle from
the popular press, but their "visions of the world" turn Godard's historical
decay into decadent historiography.

Perhaps the most immediate difference between *Weekend* and the
two more recent films is that Godard's violence is directed at the viewer
as much as it is against his characters. The stylization of *Wild at Heart*
and *The Cook, the Thief* contain their cruelty as spectacles and the
aesthetic contract between audience and auteur is never seriously
jeopardized, despite the rampant scatology and violence. Godard's theatre
of cruelty, on the other hand, struggles to escape the circuit of
consumption to which its bourgeois protagonists eventually succumb.
Greenaway claims that *The Cook, the Thief* was a strategic attempt
to reach an audience on a passionate and emotional level, but his cool
British wittiness, taken to the extremes of Albert Spica's (Michael
Gambon) monologue, makes it a particularly chilling film. For his part,
David Lynch plays a particularly manipulative game of seduction with
his audience and with his heroine, which the scene between Laura Dern
and Willem Dafoe not only comments on, but codes as brilliant
filmmaking craftiness, a *tour de force* of threat and rescue, in the tradition
of D. W. Griffith.

Sexuality as allegory of good taste: *The Cook, the Thief, his Wife and her Lover*
(1989). Miramax Pictures. Still courtesy of Jerry Ohlinger's Movie Materials.

The respectively cold and hot performances of *The Cook, the Thief* and *Wild at Heart* are highly stylized. And yet both these films are centered around a core of believability, a sign of authenticity anchoring all of their respective excesses, in the discourse of romance and True Love. Both Greenaway and Lynch are engaged in a resanctification of decadent and debased worlds, Greenaway through the iconography of the Garden and the ritual of communion, Lynch resorting to a mélange of Elvis and the Wizard of Oz, an American iconography of pleasure and resurrection. In both cases, this truth-value is eroticized, its indubitability ironically guaranteed by its invisibility. The bodies of the lovers in both films are the harbors of goodness; and intercourse in secret secluded spaces is the only escape from the evil of unbearable, inhospitable worlds.

Unlike Almodovar's *Tie me up! Tie me down!*, the eroticism of these two films is not as graphic as one might be led to believe by reviews and publicity. In fact in both films, sexuality is displaced onto highly coded imagery. In *The Cook, the Thief* this includes the raw meat and vegetables that surround the lovers in their culinary rendezvous. In *Wild at Heart* sex is associated with fire, combustion and ultimately, the film's primal scene of Lulu's father's death which both Sailor and Lulu were witness to. Towards the end of *The Cook, the Thief* Georgina (Helen Mirren) asks Richard, the cook (Richard Bohringer), to describe her love-making with Michael (Alan Howard). Likewise, it is an erotic story that gets Lulu hotter than Georgia asphalt, as if in both films, sex talk and the naming of sex were a necessary supplement to the performance of sex in order to insure its authenticity.

In a very long scene near the beginning of *Weekend* Connie tells an erotic story to an unidentified friend about a *menage à trois* in a kitchen, which functions in the film as a symptom of bourgeois decadence, but also as an analysis of the spectacle of cinema. The scene is so underlit that we can barely make out the two actors, let alone the scene that is being described. In all three films, the invisibility of the erotic is compensated for by the excessive visibility of violence, but where Greenaway and Lynch valorize sexuality, Godard valorizes revolution and the third world, which also lie beyond the representations of *Weekend*. The displacement of the regime of truth from a political legitimation in 1967 to erotic sexuality in 1989, is symptomatic of postmodernism, but how has the discourse of violence shifted? If Godard's violence is of and against cinematic representation, how have Greenaway and Lynch deployed violence in their quite different projects of resacralization and redemption, which is also to investigate the means by which surrealist crisis has been appropriated for cultural consumption.

It is from the excessive imagery of death in 17th century German Tragic Drama (*Trauerspiel*) that Walter Benjamin develops his theory of allegory. While baroque aesthetics may seem somewhat remote from the late-20th century problematic at hand here, Benjamin himself had one eye on the German expressionism of his contemporary Weimar Germany, and his thoughts on representation and history are couched precisely in terms of the textuality of the mortal body. Like *Pierrot le fou*, these three films are allegorical in Benjamin's sense insofar as each is a "written" form of cinema: highly intertextual, codified, displaced from naturalistic, realistic or symbolic representation, but nevertheless "theological."[25] Their images are inevitably directed towards an invisible signified content beyond the scope of representation. For Benjamin, the latent promise of allegory is its structural representation of historical transformation and its failure is its capitulation to the romance of resurrection. While I will argue that in *Weekend* this "promise" is inscribed, if not fulfilled, and that allegory in both *The Cook, the Thief* and *Wild at Heart* loses "everything that was most peculiar to it: the secret, privileged knowledge, the arbitrary rule in the realm of the dead. . . ."[26] The point to be made is more precisely about the strategies of representation by which this occurs.

Benjamin describes the role of history in allegory as follows:

> When, as is the case in the *Trauerspiel*, history becomes part of the setting, it does so as script. The word 'history' stands written on the countenance of nature in the character of transience. The allegorical physiognomy of the nature-history, which is put on stage in the *Trauerspiel*, is present in reality in the form of the ruin. In the ruin history has physically merged into the setting. And in this guise history does not assume the form of the process of an eternal life so much as that of irresistible decay. Allegory thereby declares itself to be beyond beauty. Allegories are, in the realm of thoughts, what ruins are in the realm of things.[27]

The death's head, or skull, a prominent baroque motif, figures this process most perfectly for Benjamin as it denotes the ruin of the human subject and the subjection of history to nature. It is precisely the void signified by the death's head by which historical difference in the form of transience is registered as allegory, and it is insofar as the myth of resurrection "fills" this void that allegory loses its radical potential. Benjamin effectively adds to Brechtian aesthetics a conception of temporality so that historical time and historical *desire* might be redeemed from the ruins of realist and symbolic representation.

Aesthetic and visual excess is a symptom of social decadence in *Weekend* as well as in *The Cook, the Thief* and *Wild at Heart*, but while each film is set in a vaguely contemporary period, a constant slippage takes place by way of intertextual referents and costume to different historical periods. History is indeed less a question of "setting" than of script and *mise en scène*. Death, in each case, is linked to a discourse of bodily processes, sexuality and consumption, potentially "ruining" any transcendent ideology of mortality. The invocation of surrealism by critics of all three films suggests the means by which scatology is representative of transience,[28] but only in *Weekend* ("A film found on a scrap-heap")[29] do we find a surrealist discourse that links social transgression to historical transformation.

The political rhetoric of Black liberation and class society spoken over images of a black and an Arabic worker eating lunch, like the erotic story-telling of the earlier scene, is the domain of spoken language. Benjamin describes this as "the domain of the free, spontaneous utterance of the creature, whereas the written language of allegory enslaves objects in the eccentric embrace of meaning."[30] "Writing" in *Weekend* pertains to the discourse of the auteur, which is distinguished here and in the other films, from the spoken discourse of the characters.[31]

Allegory in Godard involves the recovery of "meaning" from the fall of cinematic transparency and the representation of death is the death of the cinematic sign. The corpses lying by the side of the road mark the limit of spectatorial belief in the image, and form a counterpoint with the documentary or verité aspects of Godard's filmmaking technique. The durational realism of the long tracks of the traffic jam in which the camera documents the tableaux of French leisure activities, ends with the discovery of the excessively fake accident. Likewise the sadistic burning of Emily Bronte is accompanied by a conversation between Corinne and Roland, the protagonists, about whether they are more or less "real" than the character they have just burned.

It is by way of the ontology of the photographic image that Godard's allegory is "an abstraction, a faculty of the spirit of language itself, [and] is at home in the Fall."[32] The scene in *Weekend* in which the ruin of the cinematic signifier is exposed is also an image of sacrifice. While Corinne and Roland kill Corinne's mother off-screen, waves of red liquid are thrown over the body of a skinned rabbit. The murder of the rabbit, unlike the murder of the mother, is not fictional but real. The addition of blood, however, marks its status as spectacle, and all of the very fake violence of the rest of the film attains the status of sacrificial ritual. The subsequent horrors performed by the hippie-revolutionaries, the confused action and unidentified characters, are not nearly as violent as the rabbit scene, but displaces that violence into a primitive framework. The "regression" of the end of the film into the pre-historic and the un-cinematic is perhaps a desperate narrative attempt to match the "regression" of representation beyond the artificial present tense to the profilmic, which always exists in the past. The ontological impossibility of filming spontaneity is the death of signification and the end of cinema.

Connie's pleasure in eating her husband in the final shots of *Weekend* suggests that the ritual of cannibalism has caused the film's violence to be re-appropriated by bourgeois culture and the aesthetics of "good taste." The film itself, however, remains a "bad" film, in bad taste, transgressing the conventions of visual consumption. Transgression of course often only confirms the social codes which are broken, and ritual sacrifice is the institutionalization of such transgression. But Bataille's transgression, or the properly surrealist dynamic,[33] involves the eroticization of death, the pleasure of murder, and it is this potential which is subversively linked with third world revolution in *Weekend*. The film itself is only an allegory of pleasure and desire, of which the conflagrations of smashed cars are the signifiers. The body of the film itself, signified by the rabbit, whose lifeless eye returns our gaze as fixedly as those of the immigrant laborers, is the auteur's sacrifice and signature of historical transformation.

In Peter Greenaway's *The Cook, the Thief, his Wife and her Lover* "taste" itself is the category of the ineffable, unknowable, that lies beyond representation. Greenaway is manifestly concerned about the decline of culture in the hands of the Thatcherist *nouveau riche* characterized in the film by the excessively vulgar Albert Spica. To some extent, Albert's non-stop monologue and violent acts constitute an assault upon the spectator, and yet this is a film more concerned with beauty than ugliness, a redemption of Art from the "free" market. Greenaway describes his style as metaphorical, but while the cook and the thief may well be metaphors for artistry and consumerism respectively, the rest of the characters are more allegorical. The wife and the lover are simply allegorical figures of gender, which the film produces without actually accommodating within its metaphorical strategies of scatology and purification.

Historical references in *The Cook, the Thief* operate on so many levels that they become allegorical by virtue of being reduced to an accumulation of signifiers. Insofar as the fluid tracking shots that link the green-lit kitchen to the red dining room to the white bathroom move from an 18th century still-life aesthetic to a 19th century textural richness to 20th century high tech, the restaurant itself covers three centuries.[34] Outside these highly aestheticized spaces is the violence of reality, no less allegorical, no less staged than the rooms of the restaurant. If the library contains the traces of the French revolution, the parking lot is Margaret Thatcher's England.

Complicating this schema, however, is the 17th century dutch painting of bourgeois mastery hanging over the dining room, and on yet another textual axis is a characterological figuration of the French Revolution. If Michael (the Lover) is the intellectual advocate of the Rights of Man, Richard (the Cook) is the cultural value liberated from aristocratic service and Albert is both Girondist thief and Jacobin terrorist. The history of the European bourgeoisie is thus alluded to in an almost random fashion. The dispossessed kitchen staff are certainly liberated from their feudal existence by the end of the film, and yet Albert's death is brought about not by revolution, but an act of vengeance drawn from 17th century English drama.

Greenaway's refusal to distinguish between bourgeois greed and the historical terror performed against it is symptomatic of his allegorical technique in which history becomes discursive style. If the evil of Thatcherism is, in Greenaway's words, "an incredible vulgarian hypocrisy which slams anyone who makes radical sexual movies,"[35] perhaps its devaluation of quality is Girondist and its censorship is Jacobin. But by emptying historical signifiers of their referents Greenaway's elitism is betrayed, because as sexuality becomes an allegory of good taste in *The Cook, the Thief*, the ideological significance of the Girondist and Jacobin periods of the French Revolution lose their impetus when they are collapsed into one character. Greenaway's purpose may be to re-invest the ruins of history with new meaning, which is indeed the potential of Benjaminian allegory, and yet the effect is a redemption of bourgeois cultural consumption and mastery.

Greenaway is, in Benjamin's words, "at home in the fall," insofar as the film avoids the existential anxiety and nostalgia of modernist art cinema and, despite the reflexivity, there is no crisis of representation. The crisis is, rather, one of aesthetics. The "hell" that is depicted in *The Cook, the Thief* is not the void that lies beyond representation, because this "void" is filled by the aesthetics of consumption; the signified "content" of romantic love and good taste is preserved in the fetish of the lover's corpse. Michael's body, as it is glazed and garnished by the cook, is revealed in a close-up lateral tracking shot, not unlike those that have displayed the laden tables of culinary materials and products throughout the film.

At this point, though, the lover's body is a metaphor for the body of the film; an *objet d'art* prepared by a master craftsman. It is also the body of the host and, as Kathy Acker has argued, transforms "violent political vengeance into the ritual of eating and drinking Christ. The transformation of death into life."[36] But in the process of remystifying a debased culture, Georgina's feminist vengeance is displaced onto Michael's prairie oysters: the male genitals perched cockily atop the corpse like a flag. The male body is finally raised to the status of those beautiful women's and children's bodies that Albert has so cruelly disfigured and symbolically castrated. Although the narrative structure of *The Cook, the Thief* takes the form of apocalypse, its alliance of purification and aestheticization redeems the transient body of history with the aura of art. The scatological is cleansed with the pleasures of the erotic body, the mortal flesh itself is redeemed as good taste, and the rights of Man are given visual and carnal representation.

The Cook, the Thief concludes with a theatrical act of vengeance on the parts of women, children, people of color and servants against the white patriarch. But Michael, like Oedipus, is merely a surrogate victim, symptomatic of sacrifical crisis, or a cultural misapprehension of religion and the function of violence. Insofar as Michael is also Albert's rival, his wife's lover, the film's tragic structure participates fully in the mimetic desire of sacrifical crisis. For Girard, "desire itself is essentially mimetic, directed toward an object desired by the model [the rival, the double]."[37] "*Mimetic desire* is simply a term more comprehensive than *violence* for religious pollution" because "violent opposition . . . is the signifier of ultimate desire, of divine self-sufficiency of that 'beautiful totality' whose beauty depends on its being inaccessible and impenetrable."[38] In *The Cook, the Thief,* the mimesis of tragic conflict between the thief and the lover is displaced onto the mimesis of representation and the salvation of the image.

The body of the film, like the body of the lover, is of course a "cooked" image, one prepared and served up for the purpose of visual consumption, a signifier of desire that is indeed inaccessible because it is only the look of death: like the black food that Richard serves, it is not death itself. And yet we are left again on the verge of allegory because this ironic consciousness is ultimately lost to the ritual of film narrative, the desired image of the desired end. For Bataille, the erotic importance of beauty is its befoulment, and the power of death is its ugliness, a power of which it is robbed in the final moments of *The Cook, the Thief.* Greenaway, like the cook, has made death safe for visual consumption by transforming mortal flesh into a sacrament of moral justice, and he has indeed charged a lot for it. The image of sacrifice in this film has the effect of closing history off from that which cannot be represented, which for Girard is the sacred, and for Benjamin the theological difference of historical change.

The closure of representation is also the theological force informing

Wild at Heart, although here it is American popular culture that is redeemed from a hell ruled by a monstrous mother. Death in *Wild at Heart* is not in itself allegorical, as it is inscribed quite securely within an ideology of failure. It only happens to other people, which in *Wild at Heart* includes a black man, a number of anonymous strangers, Johnnie the incompetent detective, Lulu's cuckolded father and the very bad Willem Dafoe character, Bobby Peru. Sailor's redemption at the end of the film by the good (white) witch is more fully allegorical, especially when he incarnates Elvis' immortality, singing "Love me Tender" on the hood of Lulu's car. The iconographic artifice of *Wild at Heart*, epitomized in Sailor's repeated comment about his snakeskin jacket and its representation of his identity, involves a redemption of signification and a recovery of meaning. Sailor's "identity" is finally secured through the mythology of family romance. The flashbacks of patricide, Marietta's attempted seduction of Sailor and Sailor's acquisition of fatherhood, are the tokens of an Oedipal trajectory of which Marietta, the wicked witch, is both mother and sphinx, brought down by ridicule and ugliness and replaced by Lulu.

Purification in *Wild at Heart* takes the form of fire and flame which link the primal scene of patricide to Lulu and Sailor's love-making. Both the plate-glass windows through which the fire is glimpsed in blazing flashbacks, and the extreme close-ups of matches lit by Sailor's thumbnail, emphasize the spectacular nature of this imagery. An obsession with point-of-view informs this film on a more subtle level than *Blue Velvet*, an obsession that is focused more centrally on death than sex, as the look at every death is tied to a character's gaze (Johnnie seems to die almost by virtue of being caught between two gazes).[39]

Lynch is also preoccupied with forcing the viewer to look at transgressive imagery of the body, from grotesque deformities and accident victims to vomit and disabilities, symptoms of the "hell" in which Sailor and Lulu find themselves. The discourse of the grotesque reaches its climax in *Wild at Heart* with the death of Bobby Peru, and yet the decapitation and amputation of this scene is contained within the generic conventions of the splatter film. Tania Modleski has argued that the violence of representation in the contemporary horror film confounds the critical distinction between modernist and mass culture insofar as visual pleasure is a terrifying, rather than gratifying, experience. In answer to Hal Foster's question, "How can we break with a program that makes a value of crisis . . . or progress beyond the era of Progress . . . or transgress the ideology of the transgressive?" Modleski suggests that "perhaps the contemporary artist continues to be subversive by being non-adversarial in the modernist sense, and has

Laura Dern as Lulu Pace Fortune and Willem Dafoe as Bobby Peru in David Lynch's *Wild at Heart* (1990). Polygram/Propaganda Films. Still photographs by Christopher Sharrett.

returned to our pop cultural past partly in order to explore the site where pleasure was last observed. . . ."[40] Certainly this return is accomplished in *Wild at Heart*, with the effect of transforming crisis into an aesthetic of excess, but is this recovery of pleasure really worth the price?

Both Foster and Modleski evoke the terms of Benjaminian allegory, and yet where these critics, like Benjamin, are concerned with historical difference and the potential of postmodernism to break quite radically with the cultural assumptions of modernism, *Wild at Heart* fails to realize this potential because of its cultural affirmation and closure of history. The work of the text blurs the distinction between "classic" American popular culture and the 1990s on all levels. From cars and costume to rock music, the difference between the 1950s and the 1990s is lost to the universalizing discourse of Americana. If the radical potential of allegory is the inscription of history in the ruins of signification, these ruins become the foundation in *Wild at Heart* for a mystification of American cultural history. The representation of death and violence does not open up representation onto the void of the future, or mark the limits of representation, but is the signifier of a weirdness that the film manages to bring under control through a discourse of belief.

The primary strategy of containment is Lulu's sexuality. The "other" series of flashbacks, of Lulu's weird male relatives and her abortion, illustrate a series of deviant desires. If fire links Sailor's memory to his sexuality, Lulu's discourse is one of flesh, and the sign of its bodily incarnation is the close-up of her flexing hand. The "wildness" lurking within the "weirdness" is channelled into sexual proficiency and, ultimately, reproduction through Lulu's body. The displacement of sexuality onto this hand during the love-making of the film's early scenes allegorizes desire as a discourse of interiority. In keeping with the melodramatic strategies described by Peter Brooks,[41] the limits of the visible are aligned with the limits of language, and visual excess becomes the signifier of the overcoming of social repression. Within *Wild at Heart*, the dialectic of interiority and exteriority is centered on the body itself, as a vessel containing moral goodness. The bodies of Sailor and Lulu are the only ones which are neither weird on the surface nor bad underneath, and the fact that we never see Lulu pregnant or Sailor dead indicates the value of these stars' bodies.

Moreover, the audacious over-the-top performances of Laura Dern and Nicolas Cage are precisely the means by which allegorical distanciation is preserved and contained through the immortalizing codes of the star system. The end of *Wild at Heart* waffles between reconciliation, a failed romance, and apocalyptic death, arbitrarily concluding with the former. Despite the non-necessity of this ending, it recalls the destined resurrection of the beautiful couple in *Bonnie and Clyde*. Alive or dead, the image of smooth (white) skinned youthful excess triumphs over history and its claim on the body.

The Cook, the Thief, on the other hand (like *The Wild Bunch*) does veer towards an allegorical representation of mortal history, only to transform its violent transgressions of mythic transcendence into symbolic representation in the end. Where *Weekend* constitutes a submission to death as a representation of historical difference, both *Wild at Heart* and *The Cook, the Thief* involve a struggle to contain and control death in the interests of cultural affirmation. While this affirmation pertains to popular culture and high art respectively, and the strategies of the two directors differ accordingly, there is a concern on the parts of both films to rescue culture from its historicization.

The failure of allegory in these two films is not simply due to their visual pleasure and aesthetic excess. Allegorical violence need not be against pleasure, but against representation and its claim on the eternal present tense, so Modleski is quite right to point to the terror of pleasure as a radical gesture. It is indeed a means of transgressing the ideology of the transgressive, and allegorical historiography also involves a memory of auratic experience for its inscription of temporal distanciation, a process exemplified in *Pierrot le fou*. Both Benjamin and Godard are fully cognizant of the role of narrativity and the spectacular for historical vision and utopian discourse.[42] Perhaps what neither Lynch nor Greenaway fully appreciate is the effect of narrativity and its powers of closure on their allegorical, painterly, imagery.

Although both Lynch and Greenaway employ reflexive and highly theatrical representational strategies, and both have a "theological" intention that has to be respected, on some level, despite their misogyny and auteurist pretensions, neither seem to be capable of cinematic mortification. Despite the historical regression and bodily transformation that takes place in their work, neither are able to reach back to the pre-historic of the profilmic material. Their refusal to violate representation to this extent constitutes a closure of history and cinema within the limits of the visible and knowable. Their allegorical stylistics inscribe a desire to transgress these limits, but the body of the film itself will not be sacrificed. In both the European and the American contexts, it may be authorship itself that is being preserved from the threat of history.[43] The discourse of gender in the two films also suggests that the crisis at hand is one of male mastery, and the abstraction of belief that the narratives strive to salvage from the ruins of representation is, on some level, a belief in patriarchy.

In the end, their transgressive imagery is not so different from the excessive violence of *Bonnie and Clyde* or *The Wild Bunch*, still contained within the limits of a spectacle which is now disguised as the aesthetic, auteurist production of images. For both directors the body is the site of transience, semiosis and transformation, and the most potent symptoms of decay are Lynch's flies on vomit and Greenaway's maggot-ridden meat. And yet the body is also eroticized, the decay corrected and historical temporality closed off in the symbolization of trans-cendence, resurrection and immortality. This is also true of Penn and Peckinpah's genre revisionism, in which myths of romance and nostalgia are inseparable from the spectacular bodies of actors and actresses: the repressed homoeroticism of *The Wild Bunch* and the destiny of the couple in *Bonnie and Clyde* are only realized in the fantastic and violent des-truction of those bodies. The discourses of historical utopia in the earlier films have, however, decayed into the ruins of theatrical settings for narratives of redemption in the late 1980s, and are thereby quite incapable of being themselves redeemed.

The sticky stuff in the girl's hair at the accident encountered by Sailor and Lulu, is not real blood any more than the red liquid is in Godard's films of the 1960s. And yet Lulu's disgust is quite different from Connie and Roland's nonchalance towards the accident victims that they discover. In *Weekend* car accidents and traffic jams are signifiers of the ruins of desire in commodity culture and the trajectory of the film is towards the pre-automotive realm of nature for a redemption of historical desire. The traffic jam at the end of *Wild at Heart* is a symbolic desire for progress in a stagnant culture and Sailor and Lulu fulfil this desire. Their romantic reunion is a transcendence of the stagnation. Insofar as the film's trajectory is towards L.A., it is a Western in which the morality of the wilderness has been fully eclipsed by the civilizing force of the nuclear family. Indeed the dying girl in *Wild at Heart* is more afraid of her mother finding out than of dying. While Lynch's mythology of pleasure may be more populist and even more democratic than Greenaway's elitism, his redemptive project involves a somewhat limited utopian vision, and it is precisely these limits that allegorical violence has the potential of articulating.

At the end of cinema Godard offers a demonstration that the historiographic potential of cinematic allegory depends on the temporal relation between the filmic discourse and that which was filmed. Of course cinema had to continue to be made, and while Godard has con-tinued to work more or less within this historical dialectic, as have other filmmakers, one finds in the films under discussion here a capitulation of transgression to transcendence. *Weekend* may be a dead film, insofar as its political rhetoric is a somewhat naive appreciation of post-colonial culture, and yet its use of violence is in the service of an historiography which in Benjamin's terms, is genuinely authentic.

The narrative forms of violence and eroticism, the pleasures of historical thought, are indeed necessary to a historiography of the future, which finds allegorical expression in the apocalypse of *Pierrot le fou*. The myth of total cinema, however, remains stronger than the representation of historical difference, repeatedly overwhelming the representation of violent death in so much narrative film. From *Bonnie and Clyde* and the *Wild Bunch* to *The Cook, the Thief* and *Wild at Heart*, the mythic forms on which historical temporality is potentially envisioned have retained their mythic content despite the extensive imagery of transgression.

Notes

1. Susan Buck-Morss, *The Dialectics of Seeing: Walter Benjamin and the Arcades Project* (Cambridge, MA: MIT Press, 1989).

2. Aragon, although hardly an impartial or representative critic (he recognizes himself as one of the many quotations in the film), has written most eloquently about this in "What is Art, Jean-Luc Godard?" in *Focus on Godard*, Royal S. Brown, ed. (Englewood Cliffs, NJ: Prentice-Hall, 1972), p. 139.

3. Jean-Luc Godard, *Godard on Godard*, Jean Narboni and Tom Milne, eds. Tom Milne, trans. (New York: Da Capo Press, 1972), p. 217.

4. Maurice Blanchot, *The Writing of Disaster*. Ann Smock, trans. (Lincoln, NE: University of Nebraska Press, 1976); Jacques Derrida, "No Apocalypse, Not Now (Full speed ahead, seven missiles, seven missives)," *Diacritics*, 14.2 (1986): 20-31.

5. Andreas Huyssen, *After the Great Divide: Modernism, Mass Culture, Postmodernism* (Bloomington: Indiana University Press, 1986), p. 209.

6. *Godard on Godard*, p. 218.

7. Benjamin, "N[Theoretics of Knowledge; Theory of Progress]," trans. of the *Passagen-Werk* by Leigh Hafrey and Richard Sieburth, *The Philosophical Forum*, 15.1-2 (Fall-Winter 1983-84): 10.

8. Frank Kermode, *The Sense of Ending: Studies in the Theory of Fiction* (New York: Oxford University Press, 1966), p. 145.

9. This is a theme that runs through all Godard's comments on his own films as well as others' films. Of Pierrot, he says, "The life itself which I wanted to capture by way of panoramic shots of nature . . . movements of Anna and Jean-Paul, actor and actress free and enslaved. . . ." *Godard on Godard*, p. 214.

10. Luc Moullet's "Sam Fuller: In Marlowe's Footsteps" (*Cahiers du Cinéma*, March 1959) is perhaps the seminal example of this appreciation of Fuller. Godard's own commentary on *Forty Guns* is basically a euphoric

description of the film's most violent scenes. See also James Hillier's introduction to Part Two of *Cahiers du Cinéma, The 1950s: Neo-Realism, Hollywood, New Wave* (Cambridge: Harvard University Press, 1985), p. 79.

11. The narrative form of Pierrot is in many ways an example of Mennipean satire, as Bakhtin defines it in *Rabelais and his World*, Helen Iswolsky, trans. (Bloomington: Indiana University Press, 1984). The attitude of laughing at death, and the function of death in historical renewal is central to Bakhtin's analysis of Rabelais).

12. This is a theme that runs throughout the essays that Hillier has collected in his volume of writing from the 1950s. See especially, Jacques Rivette, "Notes on a Revolution" (*Cahiers du Cinéma*, 54 (Christmas 1955)) and Godard, "Nothing but Cinema" (*Cahiers du Cinéma*, February 1957).

13. Guy Debord, *Society of the Spectacle* (Detroit: Black and Red, 1983), p. 126.

14. William J. Free, "Aesthetic and Moral Value in Bonnie and Clyde" in *Focus on Bonnie and Clyde* (Englewood Cliffs, NJ: Prentice Hall, 1973), p. 104

15. "Interview with Arthur Penn by Jean-Louis Comolli and Andre S. Labarthe," in *Focus on Bonnie and Clyde, op. cit.*, p. 18.

16. As Penn explained to an interviewer: "I wanted to get the spasm of death, and so I used four cameras, each one at a different speed, 24, 48, 72, and 96, I think, and different lenses, so that I could cut to get the shock and at the same time the ballet of death. . . . I wanted two kinds of death: Clyde's to be rather like a ballet and Bonnie's to have the physical shock. . . . We put on the bullet holes—and there's even a piece of Warren's head that comes off, like that famous photograph of Kennedy. . . . [I asked the actress] simply to enact death, to fall and follow the laws of gravity. Faye was trapped behind the wheel. We tied one leg to the gear shift so that she would feel free to fall. . . ." Comolli and Labarthe interview, p. 16.

17. Roland Barthes, *Empire of Signs*. Richard Howard, trans. (New York: Hill and Wang, 1982). p. 49.

18. Robert Philip Kolker, *A Cinema of Loneliness*, 2nd edition (New York: Oxford University Press, 1988), p. 52.

19. David A. Cook, *History of Narrative Film* (New York: Norton, 1981), p. 632.

20. See in particular Christopher Sharrett, "The American Apocalypse: Scorsese's *Taxi Driver*," *Persistence of Vision*, 1 (Summer 1984); Garrett Steward, "Coppola's Conrad: The Repetitions of Complicity," *Critical Inquiry* 7 (Spring 1983): 3; and Sharrett, "Apocalypticism in Contemporary Horror Film," Ph.D. dissertation, New York University, 1983.

21. René Girard, *Violence and the Sacred*. Patrick Gregory, trans. (Baltimore: Johns Hopkins University Press, 1977), p. 316.

22. This orientation is made more explicit in *Things Hidden Since the Foundation of the World*. Stephen Bann and Michael Metteer, trans. (London: Athlone, 1987).

23. Greenaway also appreciates Lynch as "the only decent American filmmaker." Peter Greenaway interviewed by Gavin Smith, "Food for

Thought," *Film Comment* (May June 1990): 58.

24. For reviews of *Wild at Heart* see: Jay Scott, "Over the Rainbow and Around the Bend," *The Globe and Mail* (Toronto) August 31, 1990; Stuart Klawans, "Review of *Wild at Heart*," *The Nation* September 17, 1990; Richard Combs, "Review of *Wild at Heart*," *Monthly Film Bulletin* 57 (September 1990): 680. For reviews of *The Cook, the Thief* see Stuart Klawans, *The Nation*, May 7, 1990; Georgia Brown, "Cuisine Art," *Village Voice* April 10, 1990; Richard Combs, *Monthly Film Bulletin* 56 (November 1989): 670.

25. This is one of the successive definitions Benjamin gives to allegory. Walter Benjamin, *The Origins of German Tragic Drama*. John Osborn, trans. (1928; London: New Left Books, 1977), p. 177.

26. Benjamin, p. 232.

27. Benjamin, p. 177-178.

28. Lynch, who says that "The American public is surreal and they understand it," (*MacLeans*, September 3, 1990) has been described by Jay Scott (*op. cit.*) as a "cub scout surrealist."

29. This intertitle appears several times over the course of the film.

30. Benjamin, p. 202.

31. Jean-Pierre Leaud, as St. Juste, says, "freedom, like crime, is born of violence," but the words only attain credibility once language itself has been emptied of its illusionist properties, after Leaud has returned as the stranded driver of the red sports car.

32. Benjamin, p. 234.

33. The political dynamics of transgression are developed by Bataille in his reading of de Sade whose language, he says, is the means by which violence is apprehended by the conscious mind. His description of de Sade's text is remarkably similar to the experience of watching *Weekend*: both are a means of changing violence into "something else, something necessarily its opposite: into a reflecting and rationalized will to violence," *Erotism: Death and Sensuality*. Mary Dalwood, trans. (San Francisco: City Lights Books, 1968), p. 192.

34. The historical allegory of the three spaces is suggested by Sean French in "Split Roast: *The Cook, the Thief, his Wife and her Lover*," *Sight and Sound*, Autumn 1989, p. 277.

35. Kathy Acker, "The Colour of Myth: the World According to Peter Greenaway," *The Village Voice* April 17, 1990. p. 61.

36. Acker, p. 67.

37. Girard, p. 146.

38. Girard, p. 148, italics in original.

39. The car accident that Lulu passes on her way to meet Sailor towards the end of the film is the exception in the destabilized, unsutured shots of an hysterical man at the scene who continues to wail over the dead man long after Lulu's car has passed. Point of view is, however, brought under control in the last shots of the child's gaze at his parents' embrace on the hood of the car.

40. Tania Modleski, "The Terror of Pleasure," in *Studies in Entertain-*

ment: *Critical Approaches to Mass Culture* (Bloomington: Indiana University Press, 1986), p. 164-165. She quotes Foster from the preface to *The Anti-Aesthetic: Essays on Postmodern Culture* (Port Townsend, WA: Bay Press, 1983), p. ix.

41. Peter Brooks, *The Melodramatic Imagination* (New York: Columbia University Press, 1976).

42. See Benjamin's "The Work of Art in the Age of Mechanical Reproduction" and Susan Buck-Morss, *The Dialectic of Seeing: Walter Benjamin and the Arcades Project* (Cambridge, MA: MIT Press, 1989) for an analysis of the place of the image in Benjamin's historiography. For a more detailed analysis of Godard, see my "Narrative Mortality: Death and Closure in International Postwar Cinema," Ph.D. dissertation, 1990.

43. Lynch's auteur status has somewhat ironically been guaranteed by TV, but even there, Agent Cooper is the agency of a belief structure that the disbelief in the image only serves to redeem. However, in "Twin Peaks" it is belief for belief's own sake, and is thus perhaps more properly allegorical. Greenaway's auteur status may be more conventional, but his anxiety is not of the existential variety of Truffaut, Antonioni, or Wim Wenders. Readings of his earlier pseudo-documentaries and some of his other features and TV work, in terms of Benjaminian allegory, may well be more successful, perhaps because Greenaway seldom has an ideological axe to grind as he does in *The Cook, the Thief.*

The hyperreal world of the imagination in Terry Gilliam's *Brazil* (1985). Universal Pictures. Still courtesy of Jerry Ohlinger's Movie Materials.

Tony Williams

Thatcher's Orwell: The Spectacle of Excess in Brazil

In 1979, Britain's Keynesian post World War II consensus concerning the welfare state came to an abrupt end with the electoral victory of Thatcherite conservatism. The next decade saw a consistent attack upon everything British society had taken for granted since 1945—full employment, adequate welfare provision, concern for the less well-off members of society, community spirit, and Keynesian economic preferences towards full employment rather than reducing inflation. This era's philosophy restored Victorian values of market economy social Darwinism under the clarion call of "individual freedom." At the same time a brutal assault upon human rights and welfare provisions began resulting in the victorious hegemony of Thatcherite conservatism. The old post-war conservatism tenets of "one nation" and consensus soon collapsed. With the successful state management of the Falklands War resulting in a Tory landslide in 1982, the introduction of Cruise missiles into England despite the active protests by Greenham Common feminists, the crushing of the 1984-1985 miner's strike, media support by Rupert Murdoch, and the cosmetic concealment of rising unemployment and urban deprivation, British society fell into the malaise of "dictatorship by consent." The third successful Thatcherite victory in 1987 made this clear. All the old radical English traditions of liberal opposition collapsed virtually overnight parodying the Cold War domino theory. From 1979 to the present day British society was an ugly one for the unemployed, senior citizen, racial and sexual minority to survive in. George Orwell's "Big Brother" was now reincarnated in the nanny figure of Margaret Thatcher, a woman who had made it to the highest office in British society but one who incarnated patriarchal values and rapacious capitalism with a vengeance.

Apart from early oppositional movements such as the 1981 People's
March for Jobs (recalling the 1930s Jarrow "hunger marches" of the
unemployed), attitudes soon collapsed into those characteristic British
masochistic capitulations towards authority. A collective psychic trauma
accompanied political collapse. If Thatcherism achieved a decisive
political victory over the post-war Welfare state consensus it similarly
achieved a victorious "soul murder" over those British principles of
decency and fair play analyzed in the writings of George Orwell. To
those living in the early 80s Margaret Thatcher appeared a brutal
reincarnation of those hostile nannys and castrating mothers seen in
the fiction of Charles Dickens. Ironically, 1987 saw not only Thatcher's
third electoral victory but also the release of Christine Ezard's *Little
Dorrit*. Whatever the director's intentions, the opening scenes of
castrating capitalist matriarch, Mrs. Clennam, victor of a triumphal
soul murder over her helpless son, had undeniable parallels with a
contemporary political figure who had achieved similar effects on the
British psyche. It is thus not accidental that characteristic examples
of 80s British cinema feature images of male subjective trauma and
dominant mothers.[1] *Brazil* is also a product of this historical movement
presenting an apocalyptic scenario of catastrophic proportions in which
the crisis situation is impossible to recuperate. With Thatcherite
ascendancy British society collapsed before all those dormant conservative forces Raymond Williams has documented in his work. Individual
and collective revolt seemed futile. Cynicism, self-interest, malaise and
depression reigned. Williams' "long revolution" appeared a distant
utopian dream.[2]

The political situation had its effects on the arts world. As Kenneth
O. Morgan has recently stated, "the new generation of novelists and
playwrights in the 1980s were somewhat more inward-looking in finding
their cultural stimulation than, say, their predecessors in the fifties
and sixties. They were increasingly prone to introspective analysis
without a social cutting edge . . . significant groups of intellectuals and
artists, often in a somewhat modish, self-conscious way which attracted
derision in the press, seemed to move away from identification with
their society, so alien to their instincts did what they saw as the
unacceptable, philistine face of Thatcherism appear to be."[3] The era
was one of loss of confidence both in political and artistic life. A tendency
emerged to look inwards, to refuse participation in an outside historical
world in which defeat appeared inevitable.

Terry Gilliam's *Brazil* (1985) is one example of such a retreat. It
is apocalyptic in the fatalistic sense. Within its fantastic parameters,
it reworks the premises of *1984* to affirm, even more, the futility of

individual revolt. It's subject, Sam Lowry, exists within a microscopic apocalyptic world. Indulging in masochistic romantic fantasies and desiring the unobtainable object, Sam exists within a hyperreal world of his own imagination. He retreats from his own fantastic environment that is also a recreated parallel world to that of the British viewer in Thatcher's England. Caught between the polarities of sadism and masochism Sam desires to obtain Jill Layton as object of his desire. It is a frenzied retreat from the brutal society of his day, a return to the womb, the realm of infantile power as well as guilt. We thus see in *Brazil*, a peculiarly British phenomenon whereby the mother figure occupies the powerful place of the father that Raymond Bellour finds characteristic of the Hollywood cinema.[4] Within its postmodernist parameters *Brazil* presents a crisis situation illustrating the catastrophic dilemma of contemporary British society. Witnessing the rise of capitalist greed and rapaciousness, assaults on the welfare state, the development of homelessness, increasing attacks on "permissiveness" and individual liberties, the British people suddenly found how fragile the humanitarian post-war consensus actually was. The characteristic tendency became retreat into apathy and solipsism. A new Right achieved hegemonic victories. In both style and theme *Brazil* represents a pessimistic crisis reaction to the mid-80s victory of Thatcherite hegemony, a postmodern collision between history and individual escapism. Within its formal mechanisms, it presents an allegorical fantasy of a contemporary situation suggesting the origins of the roots of defeat as lying in a masochistic capitulation to an authoritarian scenario. Although the maternal figures in *Brazil* bear no explicit relation to Thatcher herself, they nonetheless present a condensation and displacement of those psychic mechanisms stemming from early childhood which will result not in an authoritarian personality, but rather a passive one. Sam Lowry's Winston Smith figure is the contemporary result in a psychic landscape of catastrophic dimensions.

Recreating an Orwellian fantasy situation, *Brazil* is a visually spectacular film. This is no accident since cinematic spectacle may be understood as a social process inserting an aesthetic dimension into everyday life. Such a process may have the conservative functions of escapism and disavowal of historical reality. In referring to two Hollywood musicals Dana B. Polan defines spectacle in the following manner:

> What we find is an 'entertainment' in its virtually etymological sense—a holding-in-place, a containment, in which awareness of any realities other than the spectacular, give way to a pervading image of sense as something that simply happens, shows forth,

but that cannot be told. This is the fiction of spectacle, its Imaginary." (italics mine)[5]

Polan further defines the fictional spectacle as an aestheticizing activity operating to preempt the demands of other practices by banishment and transformation. The relevance to the Freudian mechanisms of condensation and displacement is obvious. Terry Gilliam's *Brazil* (1985) attempts spectacular mechanisms to disavow its symptomatic origins in the reactionary climate of Thatcher's Britain. This is after all the work of one of the Monty Python team which "we are not expected to take seriously" (!). Although operating at the manifest level of spectacle and excess it contains an important latent message which *can be told.* This message intertwines within the anti-realist discourse of British cinema and an ideological re-working of the premises of George Orwell's *1984* to display a pathological example of a contemporary British postmodernist crisis. It is an excessive crisis reaction to the conservative challenge of Thatcherism which still remains victorious. The fantastic and a-historical world of its hero is one of pessimism and alienation.

Brazil aptly illustrates René Girard's concept of triangular desire that oppressively affects human beings who believe themselves free agents.[6] Unlike Orwell's *1984*, the film reveals a crucial "connection between individual desire and the collective structure."[7] Thatcherism is displaced under the signifier of the maternal figure similar to the battle for Arthur Clennam's soul by both his mother and Amy Dorrit. Thus the psychic trauma of *Brazil* has historic as well as contemporary dimensions. *Brazil* also unveils Sam Lowry's masochistically destructive metaphysical desire he attempts to deny and displace. *Brazil's* world has two apocalyptic dimensions. We see an urban landscape finally triumph in an industrial wasteland of decay, bureaucratic inefficiency and totalitarian oppression. Also the redundant hero's personal odyssey ends in apocalyptic self-destruction. Orwell's master-narrative foreshadowing the film's pessimistic conclusions collapses beyond repair. *Brazil's* multi-colored world is surrealistic, spectacular and signifying. It is a parallel realm to contemporary British society. The formal organization is no accident. Its spectacular aura represents "the collapse of reality into hyperrealism, in the minute duplication of the real, preferably on the basis of another reproductive medium"[8]—in this case film. Many reviewers have noticed *Brazil's* surrealistic depiction. But it is more correct to term it "hyperreal" according to Baudrillard.

"Surrealism is still solidary with the realism it contests, but augments its intensity by setting it off against the imaginary. The hyperreal represents a much more advanced phase, in the sense that even this contradiction between the real and the imaginary is effaced.

The unreal is no longer that of dream or of fantasy, of a beyond or a within, it is that of a *hallucinatory resemblance of the real with itself.*"[9]

Despite the film's social and personal catastrophic conclusion, its hallucinatory hyperreal structure contains spectacular and excessive textual mechanisms that do not merely revel in a pessimistic conclusion. Although the spectacular may approach a postmodernist discrediting of previous explanatory narrative and mythic modes aiming at *signifiance*[10] (Kristeva) rather than significance, the text's repressed "other" may contain socially relevant elements. In this sense they act dialectically calling on the reader to take a critical distance from the filmic representation and aim at alternative oppositional strategies. Its pastiche representation of an influential Cold War "master narrative" can have this effect. Here, one may advance beyond the negative connotations of implosion. Socially relevant elements, while not being "necessarily or automatically subversive of or outside of historically sedimented ways of seeing," may actually condemn the text's basic intention of "revelling in the fictiveness of one's own fictive acts."[11]

In both style and content, *Brazil* presents the audience with a spectacular desire for illusion. The film attempts transcendence of the main narrative's pessimistic conclusion by offering dream as an escape from everyday realities. Its undefined geographical location is a quasi-futuristic parallel world to 80s Britain. In contrast to wallowing in past imperialistic glories (*Gandhi, The Jewel in the Crown, A Passage to India, Brideshead Revisited*, etc.)[12] *Brazil* offers its audience the nihilistic pessimism of *1984* in which Sam Lowry, if not loving Big Brother, revels in narcissistic fantasies. *Brazil* is supposedly remote from everyday reality. But its spectacular format does not entirely succeed in repressing underlying social and historical realities. Sam's Lowry's figure expresses an historically dangerous triangular desire whose masochistic associations actually parallel contemporary ideological victimization. History has become re-written in a new conservative fantasy. The film explores the underlying basis of this fantasy in connection with spectacular formal mechanisms.

Brazil's fantastic/surrealistic form has several affinities to Guy Debord's definition of the spectacle as the affirmation of appearance and all human, namely social life as mere appearance.[13] In a predominantly technological society, "everything that was directly lived has moved away into a representation."[14] Because the spectacle has created a representational world that can no longer be grasped directly "that exists only through specialized mediations" like television and drama, we are denied direct lived experience in our spectacular society.[15] If John M. Jakaitis sees Tim O'Brien's *Going After Cacciato* as a "complete denial of lived experience, a total immersion in a representational world which prevents unmediated confrontation with the horrors of Vietnam"[16] this is as much true of *Brazil's* form as it is of its hero's escapist fantasies.

If Sam Lowry attempts to escape the responsibilities of his involvement in a terrorist state bureaucracy by dream fantasies, *Brazil* offers its undiscriminating viewer a similar narcotic of immersion into the fantastic realm. Its spectacular mode offers an "absolute fulfillment in the spectacle, when the tangible world is replaced by a selection of images, which exist above it and which simultaneously impose themselves as the tangible par excellence."[17]

Although the fantastic mode has a relationship to a definable social context, the form itself does not make any work progressive. *Brazil's* immersion in the spectacular has that recuperative function Rosemary Jackson comments on in relation to particular works:

> A literature of the uncanny, by permitting an articulation of taboo subjects which are otherwise silenced, threatens to transgress social norms. Fantasies are not, however, countercultural merely through this thematic transgression. On the contrary, they frequently serve (as does Gothic fiction) to re-confirm institutional order by *supplying a vicarious fulfillment of desire and neutralizing an urge towards transgression.* A more subtle and subversive use of the fantastic appears with works which threaten to disrupt or eat away at the 'syntax' or structure by which order is made. (italics mine)[18]

Brazil certainly does not fall within the latter category. As in *1984*, the establishment neutralizes transgressive urges. Winston Smith finally loves Big Brother. Sam Lowry remains in a narcissistic escapist rural fantasy with dream girl, Jill Layton, the fetishistic object of his desire. The film thus functions as a *simulacrum* of an already well-known text.

Although directed by an American who has worked in the zany humor traditions of *Mad Magazine* and *Monty Python*, *Brazil* has undeniable links to contemporary British society.[19] These links occur by means of spectacular mechanisms. A discourse appears resembling media operations which ignore contemporary Thatcherite authoritarianism by producing a mystical ideological smoke-screen involving parallels to Churchill and World War II.[20]

Gilliam is not on the same level as Orwell. The latter wrote his book as a warning. The former belongs to the inane, comic tradition of the Python school which makes no attempt at social relevance. As a director who "does not pretend to have a fully developed adult attitude about the world in which he lives." existing in "a state of suspended adolescence"[21] his hero exists in a similar condition. Sam ignores the realities of his everyday world in which citizens are arrested by security forces (clearly modeled on the SAS recently responsible for the murder of IRA members in Gibraltar) and tortured by civil service bureaucrats. The film presents a similar monstrous scenario to that of contemporary Britain: alienating highrise apartment blocks; deteriorating facilities; ghetto wastelands for the working-class; facile televised entertainment; the pollution of the environment screened from public knowledge by advertising billboards glorifying the "healthy countryside."

Brazil has several links with British cinematic discourses. Although an opening caption, "Somewhere in the 20th Century" (with its *Star Wars* associations), locates it within the anti-realist strand of British cinema, the fantastic environment contains ideological nuances of the opposing realistic strata.[22] As Sam Lowry, Jonathan Pryce would have evoked a special British audience recognition in 1985. He had starred in the "realistic" narrative, *The Ploughman's Lunch* (1983). The film criticized British establishment manipulation and its Orwellian "Newspeak" media perversion of language—factors which also appear in *Brazil*. Critical of Thatcher's new "yuppie" class, *The Ploughman's Lunch* pastiched late 50s and early 60s "Angry Young Man" influenced "kitchen sink" realist British films[23] such as *Room At the Top, Saturday Night and Sunday Morning, A Taste of Honey, The Loneliness of the Long Distance Runner, This Sporting Life, Live Now—Pay Later, and A Kind of Loving*. They usually featured a working-class alienated hero or heroine powerless to change the social conformity and class system of a Conservative ruled Britain. Despite his different class background Sam Lowry belongs in this tradition.

If the "kitchen-sink" was blocked another route was possible: fantasy. Tom Courtney took this path in *Billy Liar*. Billy's self-deception and fantastic adventures uncannily anticipate Sam Lowry's later exploits. *Brazil* spectacularly reworks *Billy Liar*, a version of *Miracle in Milan's* escapist coda to the Italian neo-realist tradition.

Brazil's world is far removed from any realistic representation. For both ordinary audiences and Universal executives,[24] Sam's everyday life is fantastic. Sam's alternative dream world is even more fantastic than his ordinary life. The film's nine dream sequences present an excessive scenario. Ironically, they also lay bare the nature of Sam's desire by revealing the apex of its fundamental triangular nature. These sequences both complement Sam's everyday world of mundane reality as well as uncovering the repressed reasons for his complicity with a totalitarian society

The dreams are an excessive re-enactment of repressed conflicts existing within Sam's role in the society of the spectacle. They finally

move towards a position in which "reality" and illusion become inseparable. Ultimately, the viewer may mistake the final dream sequence
for the mainstream narrative. This resembles Baudrillard's *trompe-l'oeil*
enchanted simulation whereby "Release from the real is achieved *by*
the very excess of its appearances. Objects resemble too much what they
are, and this resemblance is like a second state, their true depth. It is
the irony of excess reality, through *allegorical* resemblance, and diagonal
lighting."[25] Like the excess elements noted by Kristin Thompson, they
"may delay the narrative flow through repetition (redundancy),
expansion (the insertion of repetitions or causally unnecessary events),
deflections, or deformations."[26] Most significantly, they explode the
main romantic narrative of *Brazil* laying bare the triangular device
underlying Sam's seemingly free individual pursuit of Jill—an incestuous
fixation.

The first dream sequence follows Kurtzmann's call for Sam. Like
minister Helpmann, Kurtzmann is an impotent father-figure. He signifies
the redundancy of Orwell's original patriarchal Big Brother in *Brazil's*
narrative structure.[27] Following his call we see "a thick wall of gray-
white clouds against a brilliant blue sky." As Steve Neale notes, clouds
have a particular association in the world of spectacle.[28] We then view
Sam as a winged armored knight flying in the air, a composite of one
of William Blake's angelic creations[29] and Stan Lee's *Marvel Comics*
warriors. He gazes at the idealized twin of Jill Layton, a white-gowned
blonde angel in an *amniotic membrane* (italics mine).[30] Once they kiss,
Sam flies into an acrobatic loop before the telephone interrupts his dream.

There are several significant features in this initial sequence. Sam
is in a fantastic illusion, inverting Debord's definition of spectacle as
"the material reconstruction of the religious illusion."[31] Jill is the
fetishistic object of his gaze returning the look within the scopic drive.[32]
It is not accidental that in Sam's room we see movie posters of Dietrich
and Garbo whose cinematic fetishistic associations need no further
comment. Dietrich, particularly has significant links with recent work
on cinematic spectatorship involving the mother figure and the
masochistic aesthetic.[33] In the dream Sam disavows his desire for the
mother by enclosing Jill (not himself) within the maternal amniotic
sac.[34] Both inside and outside the dream sequences Jill is the object
of his gaze. In terms of Jill's function within the mainstream spectacular
narrative, Neale's comments are important:

> What counts in spectacle is not the visible as guarantee of *veracity*
> (of truth, of reality) but rather the visible as mask, as lure. What
> counts is not the instance of looking as *observation*, but rather as
> fascinated gaze. It addresses the imbrication of looking and the

visible not as the prior condition to the construction of a form of knowledge about a particular subject or issue, but rather as that which hovers constantly across the gap between the eye and the object presented to it in the process of the scopic drive. . . . Spectacle . . . is essentially concerned . . . to institute an oscillating play between vision and the visible in order to address scopic drive exclusively, to lure the gaze of the spectator and fill that gaze with plenitude of the image itself.[35]

The mainstream spectacular narrative parallels the excessive dream elements: reunion with the heroine after separation. Both move towards a final reality/dream reunion in mother's bedroom. Jill eventually becomes a symbiotic version of mother in the final dream. The excessive nature of the dream narratives reveal that Sam's "individual" desire is actually a triangular masochistic infantile desire for reunion with mother. Sam's second dream follows an important dialogue interchange between Sam and Ida Lowry.

SAM   I don't want dessert. I don't want promotion.
       I don't want anything.
MOTHER   Of course you want something. You must
       have hopes, wishes, dreams.
SAM   No, nothing! Not even dreams!

The second dream reveals urban skyscrapers separating Sam from Jill. They blast the pastoral landscape.[36] These skyscrapers parallel William Blake's industrial blight preventing England from becoming once more a "green and pleasant land." Sam's denial (and repressed admittance) of his incestuous dreams leads to technological separation.

The third dream sequence follows Sam's desire to transfer to Information Retrieval to gain access to Jill's restricted file. Searching for his dream female, Sam flies down to a cage dragged by figures wearing baby masks. These figures depict the monstrous nature of Sam's incestuous desires. Jill calls to him inside the cage. Sam's dream again follows another aspect of denial in his "real" life. Pursuing Jill in the urban wasteland of Shangrila Towers, he encountered the orphaned Buttle girl "Waiting for My Daddy"—victim of an oppressive system Sam is part of. He refuses to help her. The fourth dream follows the vengeful destruction of Sam's flat by maintenance men, Spoor and Dowser in retaliation for the repair-work by Sam's heroic alter-ego figure, Tuttle. In this dream, an armored Samurai warrior (symbolizing the system's technological power) slices off the tips of Sam's wings. This action admirably depicts Sam's Oedipal fears of castration by the father for his incestuous desires.

Other dream sequences lead to the ultimate reunion of Sam and

Jill together in his mother's bedroom. The penultimate (eighth) dream sequence of Jill and Sam together in the clouds follows their successful sexual union. She finally becomes the object of Sam's desire appearing in mother's blonde wig and white nightgown. Sam has thus achieved his individualistic dream of male supremacy but it is one founded upon a guilty pleasure which both will pay for. By erasing Jill from the computer records he is free to recreate her in mother's image. But Sam's imaginary power-ideal is ultimately masochistic. Jill dies when the security forces invade the bedroom. Sam is taken off for interrogation by torture. He will pay painfully for his brief, individualistic, moment of pleasure. It will lead to an apocalyptic crisis of the imaginary.

As Girard states, "The truth of metaphysical desire is death. This is the inevitable end of the contradiction on which that desire is based."[37] Unconsciously aware of the triangular nature of his desire, Sam's odyssey leads to death for Jill and a destructive masochistic trajectory whereby the spectacular and excessive worlds collide in a self-destructive apocalypse. His dangerous journey into the deepest realms of desire is in reality, a search for self-annihilation. For Girard, "Once the stage of masochism has been reached it becomes very obvious that metaphysical desire tends toward the complete destruction of life and spirit."[38] Such is the nature of Sam's journey whereby he will face physical annihilation (torture) and eventual mental destruction in Jack Lint's torture chamber. Before Jack can begin his work, a shot rings out. Jack falls and Sam's alter-ego Tuttle arrives to his rescue.

In the ninth (and final) dream sequence spectacle and excess worlds of reality and fantasy finally intertwine, although they were never really separate. Retreating before history, social involvement and personal sanity, Sam falls into an excessive hyperreal domain of his self-created personal apocalypse. He escapes into a cathedral. At a funeral ceremony for Mrs. Terrain,[39] he sees Ida reincarnated in Jill's youthful form as object of male gigolo desire. In response to Sam's calling her "Mother," she replies "Stop Calling me that!" The final shot of "Mother" reveals not Jill but Ida. It lays bare the incestuous origins of Sam's romantic fantasies which lead not to freedom but death and enslavement. This scene is significant since it reveals the nature of a triangular desire structure whereby mother exists at the apex of the Sam-Jill relationship. Sam sees but does not recognize. This uncannily parallels Girard's concept of "blind lucidity" whereby a negation actually underlies a self-affirming act within a personal apocalypse.

> Ever since Hegel, the modern world has boldly and openly presented this same negation as the supreme affirmation of life. The exaltation of the negative is rooted in that *blind lucidity* which

characterizes the last stages of internal mediation. This negativity, which it is easy to see is woven all through contemporary reality, is never anything other than a reflection of human relationships at the level of double mediation. This superabundant 'annihilation' should be regarded not as the true substance of the spirit but as the noxious by-product of a fatal evolution. The massive and dumb *en-soi* which the *pour-soi* always denies, is actually the obstacle that the masochist avidly seeks and on which he remains fixed."[40]

Sam plunges into the womb-like interior of Mrs. Terrain's coffin. This figure has appeared at earlier points in the film. Her gradual physical deterioration (ostensibly at the hands of plastic surgeons) formed an inverse parallel to Sam's mother successfully reversing the rigors of age. Mrs. Terrain's increasingly damaged physical body represented the realistically impossible nature of Sam's desire. Ida's increasing cosmetic youthfulness parallels Sam's spectacularly fantastic metaphysical desire. As Sam increases his pursuit of Jill so mother becomes younger. Both women finally merge in *Brazil*'s spectacular and excessive narrative levels. Jill puts on Ida's nightgown and wig in the bedroom scene. Both women merge in the funeral scene. Thus, at this moment of blind lucidity Sam plunges into the dark coffin for his final excessive dream escape.

Sam finds Jill safe once more. He escapes with her into the countryside to "live happily ever after." This pastoral idyll parallels *1984*'s "golden country" where Winston and Julia briefly retreat from the city as well as George Bowling's lower Binfield boyhood haunts in *Coming Up for Air*. It also aptly signifies *Brazil*'s key structuring motif. "The Golden Country is the mother's body—partly the personal mother retained in the memory, but more importantly those traces of a once-intimate closeness to nature, to some primitive condition of vitality and serenity perhaps still hidden entirely somewhere in the mind—the possession of and by which is linked to the dreamer's present a sense of loss, isolation, and impotence."[41]

The heads of Helpmann and Jack erupt into the idyllic Blakean countryside scene in the final scene. We see that Sam has never really escaped from the torture chamber. It emphasizes once more the symbiotic nature of spectacular "reality" and fantastic "excess" that can not be totally separate. Both recognize Sam's mental escape into the fantastic realm. They depart and leave him to his incestuous fantasies, loving "Mother" as Winston Smith loves Big Brother in the final page of *1984*.

There are several interesting links in the narrative that illuminate *Brazil*'s triangular desire and personal apocalypse. Significant numerical associations exist in the names of the three major characters, Ida Lowry, Jill Layton and Sam Lowry. The initial letters of the surnames are identical. We see that repressed desire for the mother is the common denominator linking Sam and Jill—"Ida." "I" is the *ninth* letter in the alphabet. The gap between the initials, "J" and "S" is one of *nine* letters, thus "Ida" is the text's incestuous structured absence which can not be openly expressed. Only *Brazil's* spectacular mode can allow it veiled representation. There are thus significantly *nine* dream sequences.

Other numerical dualities also exist. The surnames of the arrested father, Archibald Buttle and Harry Tuttle have a rhythmic parallel. As opposed to the domesticated father, Tuttle is the unattached man of action. He flies through the air similar (but not identical to) Sam's dream warrior. The numerical division between "B" and "T" is 18 letters, a doubling of the significant numeral "9." Ida holds up Jack Lint as a model "son" to Sam, a man who unquestionably serves the system although his brains do not match his ambition as Ida points out. "You haven't got the ambition, but luckily you've got *me*." The gap between "Jack" and "Sam" is, again, one of nine letters. In the torture chamber Jack appears wearing one of the baby doll masks of the forces of darkness who are harnessed to Jill's cage in the dream sequences. The mask macabrely signifies Sam's infantile fixations. Also the torture chamber parallels Orwell's "Room 101," the area of punishment for attempted rebellion against authority.

Brazil's spectacle and excess modes are no mere formal mechanisms. Whereas *1984* presented its hero's capitulation to the authoritarian Law of the Father, *Brazil's* Sam Lowry suffers from a matriarchal mother fixation that symbolically echoes the British love-hate masochistic fixation for a female Prime Minister who has done her utmost to destroy the fabric of British society. Ida Lowry's figure is actually a displacement for 80s matriarchal authoritarianism. Despite her representation as a silly figure, Ida appears to have influence in *Brazil's* world. Sam's antipathy towards her is actually a displacement of unconscious desire. Sam is a victim of pre-Oedipal romantic fantasies, dominating and clothing Jill in the figure of the mother. He becomes the victim of his own unconscious desires for infantile unity with an authoritarian symbol. This parallels the British electorate voting for a strong leader, detrimental to their own interests, in a manner akin to 1930s desires for totalitarian figures. Thatcherite authoritarianism thus appears as *Brazil's* "structured absence" replacing male authoritarian figures of Orwell's 1948, the year he wrote *1984*. *Brazil* is Britain's "Back to the Future" rendered in a much more historically oriented manner. Despite its unspecific location "somewhere in the 20th century," the *mise-en-scène* presents a world which has not developed beyond the austere world of the early 1950s except in urban squalor, out-moded technological bureaucracy, authoritarian Fascism such as the SAS, and government torture chambers. If Spielberg attempts to reconstitute the flawed nuclear family of the 80s, Gilliam's film illustrates the dominant hold of old institutional ideas in terms of a visual society of the spectacle that seeks to fantasize and deny the real conditions of existence. Its fictional triangular desire is part of common conceptions and ideological premises existing in eighties Britain.

Sam's masochistic mother fixation reveals the authoritarian danger that lurks behind the figure of the mother (whom some feminists idealize) just as much as the father. As Toril Moi points out, "sometimes a woman imitating male discourse *is* just a woman speaking like a man. Margaret Thatcher is a case in point. It is the political context of such mimicry that is surely always decisive."[42] Gilles Deleuze notes that the masochist has the power to persuade woman to take up the role of master and has the power to "fashion the woman into a despot."[43] If Sam resents his mother in *Brazil*'s realistic discourse, the excessive dream sequences reveal his slavish dependence on her. Although the early mother-child bond is a crucial one, and not to be denied for its positive associations, it can also have dangerous psychic authoritarian implications similar to the Law of the Father, if its power structures oppress the individual and hinder true development.[44]

Brazil thus uses the modes of spectacle and excess to present a displaced representation of *1984* Britain in which no possible positive solution appears possible at the present moment. It shows us that the figure of the mother and pre-Oedipal fantasies are as much threats to true liberation as patriarchal forces. If Winston Smith ends up loving Big Brother, Sam Lowry finishes his life as an impotent, bound figure fantasizing the mother in the society of his own masochistic spectacle. But is this the final end? Revelation of psychic mechanisms affecting British society have a positive function within the very fact of that representation. They reveal the excessive hyperreal nature of a society that can claim no realistic validity for the maintenance of its sign systems in a world where there is no present nor future but a continuing ever-present apocalypse on the personal and social levels. It is a society still dominated by the old Oedipal myths and hero master-narratives that are completely redundant. Pryce's Winston Smith suffers at the hands of no imposed Cold War enemy but the logical implications of his society's simulacrum state. *Brazil* presents a postmodernist apocalyptic/catastrophic end of British society. By doing this, revealing the false millennic end of the return of the agrarian landscape and the united heterosexual couple, it logically asks "what next?" There is no necessity for a pessimistic answer outside the film's construction as there is within. Speaking of Dostoyevsky's work, Girard comments that "To perceive the metaphysical structure of desire is to foresee its catastrophic conclusion. Apocalypse means development. The Dostoyevskian apocalypse is a development that ends in the destruction of what it has developed."[45] Certainly, this is not true of *Brazil*. A recuperation of a crisis situation is, indeed, possible. But *Brazil's* bleak scenario belies any such optimistic hope. In its fantastic representation of post-industrial decline and psychic masochistic malaise, we see an irreversible situation testifying to the end of individuality and the impossibility of collective opposition to the status quo. In its postmodernist formation, *Brazil* depicts a similar scenario to Derek Jarman's *The Last of England* (1986). Using anti-narrative techniques, Jarman presents an urban landscape ravaged by Thatcherism testifying to the final decline of the post-war consensus and the end of individual freedom. *Brazil* presents a catastrophic wasteland, a world of a signifying abyss that articulates nothing that may reverse its crisis scenario. The roots are too deep, historically, socially, and psychically. Catastrophe reigns supreme on all these levels.

Notes

1. For one recent evaluation of the historical situation see Kenneth O. Morgan, *The People's Peace: British History 1945-1989* (New York: Oxford University Press, 1990), p. 440. The following recent works are important in understanding trauma as a psychological condition particularly in relation to a historical situation. Gilbert J. Rose, *Trauma and Mastery in Life and Art* (New Haven: Yale University Press, 1987); Bessel V. van der Kolk, M.D., ed., *Psychological Trauma* (Washington, D.C.: American Psychiatric Press, Inc. 1987); and Leonard Shengold, *Soul Murder: The Effects of Childhood Abuse and Deprivation* (New Haven: Yale University Press, 1988). Despite the differences between Arthur Clennam and Sam Lowry in terms of childrearing both share similar male characteristics of passivity and masochism which can be traced to their early development. See Shengold's observations on "Dickens, Little Dorrit and Soul Murder," pp. 181-208. For representations of the crisis of male subjectivity and maternal dominance in contemporary British cinema see Thomas Elsaesser, "Games of Love and Death or an Englishman's Guide to the Galaxy," *Monthly Film Bulletin* 55.657 (October 1988): 288-294; and Mary Desjardins, "Free from the Apron Strings of the Maternal State: Representations of Mothers in Some Recent British Films," a paper presented at the Society for Cinema Studies conference, May 24, 1991.

2. Raymond Williams, *The Long Revolution* (New York: Columbia University Press, 1961); *The Country and the City* (London: Oxford University Press, 1973).

3. Morgan, p. 439.

4. See Janet Bergstrom, "Alternation, Segmentation, Hypnosis: Inter-

view with Raymond Bellour," *Camera Obscura* 3-4 (1979): 71-103.

5. Dana B. Polan, "Above All Else to Make You See: Cinema and the Ideology of Spectacle," in Jonathan Arac, ed., *Postmodernism and Politics* (Minneapolis: University of Minnesota Press, 1986), p. 56.

6. Girard, *Deceit, Desire and The Novel* (Baltimore: Johns Hopkins University Press, 1965).

7. Girard, p. 226.

8. Jean Baudrillard, *Simulations*. Paul Foss, Paul Patton, and Philip Beitchman, trans. (New York: Semiotext(e), 1983), p. 141.

9. Baudrillard, p. 142. See also Arthur Kroker and David Cook, *The Postmodern Scene: Excremental Culture and Hyper-Aesthetics* (New York: St. Martin's Press, 1986), pp. 170-189.

10. Jean-Francois Lyotard, *The Postmodern Condition* (Minneapolis: University of Minnesota Press, *1984*); Polan, p. 64.

11. Polan, p. 59.

12. Salman Rushdie, "Outside the Whale," *American Film* 10 (1985): 16, 70-72.

13. Guy Debord, *Society of the Spectacle* (Detroit: Black and Red, 1983), paragraph 10.

14. Debord, paragraph 1.

15. Debord, paragraph 18.

16. John M. Jakaitis, "Two Versions of An Unfinished War: *Dispatches* and *Going After Cacciato*," *Cultural Critique* 3 (Spring 1986): 207.

17. Debord, paragraph 36.

18. Rosemary Jackson, *Fantasy: the Literature of Subversion* (London: Methuen, 1981), p. 72. See Jakaitis, p. 209, in relation to soldiers mystifying the events of the Vietnam war that "as well as their attempts to force their acculturated values concerning everyday life on the inflexible lived experience of Vietnam, and their final escape into superstition and imagination, we see exposed the basis of the society of the spectacle. Beneath the representations, the simulacra, there is nothing. The reified commodity consumption which prevents lived experience also prevents awareness of the purposelessness, the emptiness of spectacular experience."

19. For the film's relationship to Orwell, see J. P. Chaillet, "Un americain tres britanique," *Cahiers du Cinema* 369 (March 1985): 59-60; John Coleman, "Cobblers," *New Statesman* 109 (February 22, 1985): 35; R. Corliss and D. Worrell, "Happy Ending for A Nightmare," *Time December* 30, 1985: 84; Salman Rushdie, "The Location of *Brazil*," *American Film* 10 (September 1985): 50-52; John Pym, *Monthly Film Bulletin* 52.615 (April 1985): 107; Thomas Doherty, "A dark, difficult *1984* floor-show," *Cinefantastique* 16 (1986): 46; and Lenny Rubenstein, "*Brazil*," *Cineaste* 14.4 (1986): 48-49.

20. For one pertinent example ignoring the social and geographical factors which resulted in Thatcher's 1987 election victory see Francis X. Clines, "British Voters Fashion A Virtual Coronet for Thatcher," *The New York Times* July 14, 1987: Section 4, p. 1. On the British parallels between Orwell's *1984* and Thatcher's version see Jenny Taylor, "Desire is Thought-

crime," in Paul Chilton and Crispin Aubrey, eds., *Nineteen Eighty-Four in 1984* (London: Comedia Publishing Group, 1983), pp. 29-32; and Antony Easthope, "Fact and Fantasy in *Nineteen Eighty-Four*," in Christopher Norris, ed., *Inside the Myth: Orwell: Views from the Left* (London: Lawrence and Wishart, 1984), pp. 263-265.

21. Jack Mathews, *The Battle of Brazil* (New York: Crown Publishers, Inc., 1987), p. 5.

22. For a comprehensive survey of the diverse aspects of British national cinema see Charles Barr, ed., *All Our Yesterdays: 90 Years of British Cinema* (London: British Film Institute, 1986).

23. See John Hill, *Sex, Class and Realism: British Cinema 1956-63* (London: British Film Institute, 1986); R. Barton Palmer, "What Was New in the British New Wave? Reviewing *Room at The Top*," *Journal of Popular Film and Television* 14.3 (Fall 1986): 125-135; and Alexander Walker, *National Heroes: British Cinema in the Seventies* (London: Harrap, 1985), p. 263.

24. For details of this battle see Mathews, 1-94.

25. Jean Baudrillard, "On Seduction," *Jean Baudrillard: Selected Writings*. Mark Poster, ed. (Stanford, CA: Stanford University Press, 1988), pp. 156-157.

26. Kristin Thompson, *Eisenstein's Ivan the Terrible: A Neoformalist Analysis* (Princeton, NJ: Princeton University Press, 1981), p. 111. My understanding of *Brazil's* excess elements differs considerably from Thompson's neo-formalist analysis (pp. 287-302), particularly in viewing them more as exaggerated metaphors of condensation and displacement in the Freudian sense which do have a relationship to the main narrative.

27. For Oedipal resonances in both *Time Bandits* and *Brazil* see Mathews, pp. 100 and 224. On the Oedipal complex in relation to Orwell's work see Richard Smyer, *Primal Dream and Primal Crime: Orwell's Development as a Psychological Novelist* (Columbia: University of Missouri Press, 1979); J. Brooks Bouson, "The 'Hidden Agenda' of Winston Smith: Pathological Narcissism and *1984*," *University of Hartford Studies in Literature* 18.1 (1986): 8-20 and Earl G. Ingersoll, "The Decentering of Tragic Narrative in George Orwell's *Nineteen Eighty Four*," *Studies in the Humanities* 16.2 (December 1989): 69-83.

28. "As Hubert Damisch has argued in his book, *Theorie du nuage* (Paris, 1972) clouds have been an essential ingredient in the whole apparatus of spectacle in European art. In offering to the spectator's gaze a set of forms which mask and fill in an otherwise empty and potentially infinite space (the sky) while simultaneously signifying the very emptiness and infinity that they mask, clouds have come to function, in a sense, to signify spectacle itself," Steve Neale, "*Triumph of the Will*—Notes on Documentary and Spectacle," *Screen* 20.1 (Spring 1979): 67.

29. For Blake's role as a critic of early technological civilization see Donald Ault, *Visionary Physics* (Chicago: University of Chicago Press, 1974) and Michael Farber, *The Social Vision of William Blake* (Princeton, NJ: Princeton University Press, 1985). For these, and other references to Orwell

criticism, I wish to express my gratitude to Denis Rohatyn.

30. See Mathews, p. 112. The scene uncannily evokes Michel Chion's description of the maternal voice existing within an umbilical net associated not only with early infantile existence but a moment prior to the creation of the world. Certainly, the dream idyll is destroyed when gigantic urban pillars erupt through the green landscape. See Michel Chion, *La voix au cinema* (Paris: Editions de L'Etoile, 1982), p. 57; Kaja Silverman, *The Acoustic Mirror: The Female Voice in Psychoanalysis and Cinema* (Bloomington: Indiana University Press, 1988), pp. 72-78.

31. Debord, paragraph 20.

32. See John Ellis, *Visible Fictions* (London: Routledge and Kegan Paul, 1982), p. 47.

33. See Kaja Silverman, "Masochism and Subjectivity," *Framework* 12 (1980): 2-9; and Gaylyn Studlar, "Masochism and the Perverse Pleasures of the Cinema," *Quarterly Review of Film Studies* 9.4 (January-February 1985): 267-82 and "Visual Pleasure and the Masochistic Aesthetic," *Journal of Film and Video* 37.2 (Spring 1985): 5-26.

34. Note also the predominant figural presence of umbilical ducts throughout the film. There is no reason to regard Gilliam's interpretation as the definitive one where he meant these objects to signify "both the *umbilical relationship* (italics mine) of the people to their centralized government and the loss of aesthetics in our cities,where lazy contractors routinely intrude on the architectural integrity of existing buildings by slapping grotesque amenities (plumbing and electrical) on the outside walls" (Mathews, pp. 99-100).

35. Neale, p. 85.

36. On the role of Orwell's pastoral imagery in relationship to the mother's body see Smyer, p. 145.

37. Girard, p. 282.

38. Girard, p. 283.

39. The funeral scene visually parallels Sam's earlier line to Jill before he erases her computer record out of existence—"I know a way to save you."

40. Girard, pp. 287-288. For a recognition of Brazil's incestuous associations see Stephen B. Safran, *"BRAZIL: A Cinematic Incest Fantasy,"* *The Psychoanalytic Review* 75.3 (Fall 1988): 473-480.

41. Smyer, p. 145.

42. *Sexual/Textual Politics: Feminist Literary Theory* (London: Methuen, 1985), p. 143.

43. Gilles Deleuze, *Masochism: An Interpretation of Coldness and Cruelty.* Jean McNeil, trans. (New York: George Braziller, 1971), p. 20.

44. For a criticism of the power dynamics behind the recent theoretical emphasis on masochism see Tania Modleski, "A Father is Being Beaten: Male Feminism and the War Film," *Discourse* 10.2 (Spring-Summer 1988): 74-77, especially n. 15.

45. Girard, p. 288.

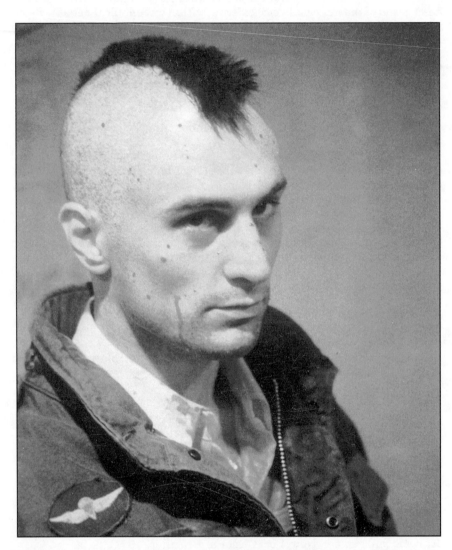

The returning warrior in postmodernity: Robert DeNiro as Travis Bickle in Martin Scorsese's *Taxi Driver* (1976) Warner Bros. Still courtesy of Jerry Ohlinger's Movie Materials.

Christopher Sharrett

The American Apocalypse: Scorsese's Taxi Driver

Apocalypticism is once again rampant in discourse. Since the Puritans,[1] the apocalyptic view of history and human destiny has been a controlling force in American art, and is manifest in postmodernism in such ideologically divergent forms of expression as TV evangelism and heavy metal/post-punk/hip-hop culture. Martin Scorsese's *Taxi Driver* (1976), a preeminent example of apocalyptic art of the 1970s, suggests very well the original Puritan belief in a divinely-ordained historical destiny which, when violated or ignored, will cause a cataclysmic retribution. *Taxi Driver* proposes that the divine contract has been undone and that concepts associated with Manifest Destiny are at an end. As the film deconstructs and debunks the conventions of various film genres, it provides not ideological criticism but the ahistorical and fatalistic vision of apocalypticism. This apocalypse is catastrophic and "non-revelatory" since alternative concepts of reality are beyond consideration. More significant, Scorsese's film expands on earlier notions of apocalypse by relying on elements of high culture, American millennialism, and contemporary notions of the subject to provide a framework that defines Armageddon as immanent to individual consciousness.[2]

In his discussion of the "mediation of desire," René Girard offers an insight useful to an understanding of the apocalypse-in-microcosm confronting Scorsese's protagonist, Travis Bickle.[3] Girard notes that certain aberrant forms of interchange, such as masochism and sadism, are based on a fixation within the subject on an unreachable, metaphysical idea that reflects a self-image and is actually distant from the ostensible object of desire. Masochism and sadism exist in a symbiotic relationship, since in both instances the subject recognizes as a model an image of power, oppression, and victimization that is a projection of guilt and inadequacy. The masochistic subject is never capable of autonomy; the acceptance of oppression becomes the acceptance of guilt but also the aspiration to a position of power. As Girard notes, the subject-object relationship is not direct, since the ideal mediating image remains suspended between the two as the real fixation of the subject's desire. Always unattainable, the image has a god-like quality but does not provide a "vanishing point" and allow an autonomous Self. Most essential to Girard's argument is his sense that sadism/masochism does not, in fact, represent aberrance but is basic to a social contract built on mimesis. In Western culture, value is determined by mimesis, by the fluctuating consensus whereby individuals value something because it is perceived as valuable by others. Mimesis creates desire, but it represents the beginning and the end of desire. Under this structure, value is in a most precarious position, subject to a volatile, Nietzschean will-to-meaning. The chief difficulty is the subject's perception of the imitated (desired) other as a rival; mimetic rivalry follows fast on the self's sense of the other as alluring. The rival becomes a mimetic (or "monstrous") double whose existence threatens both difference and the very concept of desire established by mimesis. As we shall see, the entire construct becomes extremely dangerous in the postmodern culture of simulation, with its nostalgia for "real" desire represented by the schizophrenic subject, a collage of media images divorced from history.

The subject's exaggerated mediator of desire results in a dualistic conception of Self as either god or devil, as the self-image fluctuates back and forth in the subject-object relationship without allowing a recognition of how the mediating image disturbs reasonable participation in the world. The apocalypse comes with a dissolution of the mediating image without the subject's reintegration into authentic experience or with the subject's belief that his/her sense of rivalry is fully reciprocated: in the master-slave mechanism of masochism (really simply mimesis), this would set up a hopeless climate of alienation where people are "recognized" by the subject insofar as they view the subject as contemptible, a condition Girard points to in Dostoyevsky's Underground Man (*Notes from Underground* is, of course, a central influence on *Taxi Driver*), Travis Bickle's descent in *Taxi Driver*, a descent incorporating important elements of the horror film and the western, follows Girard's thesis of the extreme mediating image that tends to dissolve itself and destroy the perceiving subject. The traditional American apocalypse is the result of projection, a transpsychical crisis reflecting the imminent vengeance of God as the American "mission" comes to an end and the divine contract fails. The typically American apocalypse of *Taxi Driver* may be associated with sacrificial violence, which for Girard is the lawful step in establishing difference, the recreation of the Other, and new totemic systems.[4] Sacrificial violence, absolutely central to the American civilizing experience, can become overwhelming unless it is quickly focused on a specific Other in discrete, "official" violence such as scapegoating. Travis Bickle's apocalypse is to a great extent about the failure of American sacrificial violence; neither Travis' position as alienated (modernist) Other nor his "last stand" free-floating act of propitiatory violence restores equilibrium to society.

Certainly a pathological case, Travis Bickle is also a rather ordinary reactionary personality for his internalization of the apocalyptic, refusing to examine events in a political/historical context, opting for a perception of all reality as angelic/demonic. From the early, hallucinogenic close-up of Travis' wary, judgmental eyes taking in the inferno of New York's Forty-Second Street (a shot recapitulated in Willard's bleary eyes superimposed on a vision of a burning jungle at the opening of *Apocalypse Now*, 1979), *Taxi Driver* projects a sense of the world propelled by the supernatural and the inevitable; when Wizard tries to console Travis he tells him, "You don't really have a choice anyway." As Travis' repetition-compulsion (the endless circling about in the cab, the consumption of pills and junk food, the watching of TV, the fixation on the self) leads lawfully to self-destruction, he sees this destruction as part of a preordained mission. Apocalypse becomes, above all, a means of providing drama and a sense of closure to the individual life (and the work of art)[5]—one aspect of apocalypse subverted by the film's conclusion.

Travis' pathology is coextensive with an atomization of society, a failure of shared myth. *Taxi Driver* is a sophisticated example of the new cinema of allusion[6] whose pessimism grows out of a sense of collective crisis rendered by the dismemberment of genres that is a key part of its project. *Taxi Driver* forms part of a new anti-genre and much of its horror emerges from a sense of loss and civilization's defeat. Paul Schrader's remark that this is "a film about [his] twenties"[7] speaks to the sentiments of nostalgia and revenge that drive the film, sentiments born out of the conflict of American expansionist values (nurtured by pop culture) with the collapse of the present society.

A case has already been made for *Taxi Driver* as a horror film,[8] a view easily substantiated by attention to the film's Powellian photography, its horrific bloodshed, the music of Bernard Herrmann, and the themes of descent and the psychopath-as-monster. Central to *Taxi Driver*'s apocalypse is its attempt to pile up, as if in panic, elements of many genres as the legitimacy of narrative fades away. The importance of *film noir* is evident in the morbid atmosphere of the film: the focus on misdirected or perverse sexuality, the chiaroscuro urban setting, psychopathology as a theme, and, again, the contribution of Herrmann's score. The western is important in the themes of revenge and rescue (comparisons have been made to *The Searchers*,[9] the dream of Utopia and a new frontier, the use of cowboy and Indian imagery, forms of gunplay that quote specific westerns, and the idea of the hero returning from war.

The contradiction of the narrative's apocalypse are based on the presences of Scorsese and fellow "movie brat," screenwriter Paul Schrader. As with the collaboration of Coppola and John Milius for *Apocalypse Now*, this collaboration is a problematic mixed bag of attitudes on the roles of violence and culture. The attention to so many elements of American popular art ultimately points to the desiccation of genres, despite the bravura gestures of the film's creators. The visionary element of European cinema quoted in *Taxi Driver* collides with bankrupt fixations of American myth; can Travis Bickle be both a Peckinpah character and Bresson's country priest? The film wants to accept purgative violence over a more dangerous introspection and solipsism, but then recognizes through its absurdist ending the failure of violence as social ritual. *Taxi Driver* nonetheless remains apocalyptic in its denial of historical causality.

The urban setting of the film works not solely as a citation of *film noir* but as a suggestion that such genres signify the frustrations of others (the western) and the culmination referred to earlier of the America civilizing process. The archetypal demonic city is cited by the use of Dostoyevsky and "high culture" to represent America as repository of extinct tradition and to attempt, in the manner of Coppola, to connect this culture to a mass audience in such a way that "high art" finally becomes accessible and an aid to the interpretation of the work at hand. In this sense Scorsese and Coppola share a populism diluted by an unremitting pessimism and a reactionary faith in tradition, even as tradition is shown as always-already compromised and mediated. Unlike Coppola, however, Scorsese has little sorrow for the failed "grand opera" of American utopian aspirations, best demonstrated by his anti-epic, *Goodfellas* (1990).

The character of Travis Bickle clearly refers to the narrator of Dostoyevsky's *Notes from Underground* and, tangentially, to a line of demented visionaries who can be seen as progeny of Saint John, the signal apocalyptist. Bickle, like Saint John and Dostoyevsky's narrator (and Willard in *Apocalypse Now*) has the appearance of moralist. As in Dostoyevsky, the text reveals ambivalence regarding the location of evil in subject or object; the idea of an omniscient Other, clearly linked in Bickle's case to images of patriarchy, aggravates this uncertainty and provokes crisis. Bickle is a hypochondriac ("I think I have stomach cancer") much like the Underground Man, who opens his narrative with a complaint about liver disease. But this hypochondria is the first signpost in the character's schizophrenia. While maintaining his moralism, Bickle is thoroughly ambivalent about every aspect of his argument as he continues his interior dialogue, which, as in *Notes*, is the substance of the work. Dostoyevsky's narrator decries his own malady and medical science, yet professes an admiration for doctors; Bickle, while he sees himself as "God's lonely man," shows contempt for a life of "morbid self attention."

George Steiner's commentary on *Notes from Underground* regards the word as a representative assault on capitalism from the right,[10] advancing the belief that evil and self-destruction are part of a concordance with God and are the inevitable tools of an apocalyptic destiny. Steiner shows Dostoyevsky's comradeship with Nietzsche, Stirner, and Sorel, who assert an absolute, unreasonable, and pessimistic individual liberty in place of any notion of social justice or economic progress. Scorsese's vision is not so retrograde, but the transposition of the Underground Man into an American context in compelling.

Travis Bickle is the returning warrior, but the battle he survives is even more vaguely defined than the one from which Ethan Edwards returns in *The Searchers*. Vietnam provides a backdrop for Bickle as the Civil War does for Edwards; both return as alienated men to a void, a void in the sense that the community cannot be located in any genuinely satisfying way (Ford's insistence on "the tragedy of the loner" merely highlights his insistence on individualism and his cynical dismissal of his idealized community). *Taxi Driver* confronts squarely questions raised in American art about the man of action versus contemplative man. Ethan Edwards attempts to force a role in the community by avoiding introspection; Bickle almost destroys himself and the community by contemplation that produces demons. In neither instance do the two films, in their respective periods, address the question of the viability of the community itself in any manner articulated along social or economic lines. The Indian-as-demon in *The Searchers* is a traditional element,[11] but Edwards' self-recognition has less to do with an understanding of regeneration through violence than with a self-abasing internalization of his own prejudice and irreconcilable separation from the community (there are obvious hints in *The Searchers* that Edwards' bigotry and alienation are a product of repression—Edwards' hidden love for Martha is, for Ford's conservatism, an assault on family/community). In Travis Bickle resides the frustrated frontiersman

whose demons are now generalized. His thinking refers to the Puritans
for its apocalyptic language. Travis dreams of the "real rain" that will
"wash all the trash and garbage off the streets." As Travis awaits
apocalypse, he begins to conceive of himself as a man of special destiny,
but even after the climactic moment he sees the destiny as wholly
arbitrary—we recognize in him the apocalyptic impulse centered on
provoking drama and crisis.

Bickle's turmoil is the culmination of Ethan Edwards' schizophrenia.
The frustration of both men is brought about by their tendency to think
in ultimate terms, their inability to connect any internal or external
evil to a specific historical situation. We discover the consequences of
this situation in Bickle's inability to form any consistency to his thinking,
his simultaneously idealized and catastrophic vision of the exterior world.
Bickle berates the "venal" people of New York street life, the "scum,
the pimps, buggers, and queers," but he is not only inexorably drawn
to violence and pornography, he is unable to distinguish between "filth"
and what he sees as a right and fitting ideal of beauty. A good instance
is when he takes Betsy to see the sex movie *Sometimes Sweet Susan*.
Betsy reacts violently, "This is like saying 'let's fuck.'" Travis says,
"I don't know much about movies. . . . Tell me what you want to see."
Travis accepts pornography and violence as a given of the natural world;
by asking Betsy what movies she likes. Travis is not so much trying
to find out if there is such a thing as an alternative vision, as he is,
indeed, trying to fuck Betsy (scopophilia now a path to empowerment).
The fascination with pornography is also Travis' half-apprehended
confrontation with the myth of romantic love. The fascination with
pornography is also a rather traditional device to introduce Travis'
misogyny and alienation; until the arrival of Iris, pornography represents
the "whore" side of popular culture's virgin/whore construction of the
female.

Travis is a moralist who watches only pornography; like the case
of Norman Bates in *Psycho* (1960), Travis' scopophilia signifies his
inversion and the incorporation of a dominant power the subject
consciously rejects. Travis is too demented to be a hypocrite; he genuinely
believes that this inversion is universal and can be changed only by
some external force. Travis asks the politician Palantine to "Flush the
whole thing down the fuckin' sewer." He believes (yet does not believe)
that Palantine must become responsible for a purgative activity that
is as supernatural as the great rain he envisions. That Travis respects
yet decides to kill Palantine can be seen as part of the same Oedipal
dilemma that causes Travis to write letters to his parents containing
flowery and misleading accounts of his life in New York. We are

constantly refocused on symptoms of Travis' psychopathology. His voyeuristic "gaze" at everything in his experience signifies his unsuccessful integration in the object-world. The fragmented taxi images early in the film are representative of Travis' disintegration. The association of the gaze with power and both homicidal and suicidal compulsions is clearly drawn when Travis watches a woman at her window while her crazed husband raves on about what a ".44 Magnum will do to a woman's pussy." An extension of the gaze's power, the .44 Magnum is the first gun Travis buys from Easy Andy.

The traditional pathology of repetition is the most transparent evidence of Travis' failure, and it is again a predicament portrayed as transpsychical, cumulative, and leading toward the apocalyptic crisis. Travis is stricken with a perpetual insomnia, and to make use of all those waking hours he drives his cab constantly. The insomnia is a clear emblem, along with his nostalgia, of Travis' repetition-compulsion and hysteria. "I go anywhere—the Bronx, Brooklyn, Harlem. Every night I clean the come off the back seat—sometimes I clean the blood off." Generative and sacrificial functions merge. In fact Travis goes nowhere: "One day blends into the next." The circularity of Travis' actions further

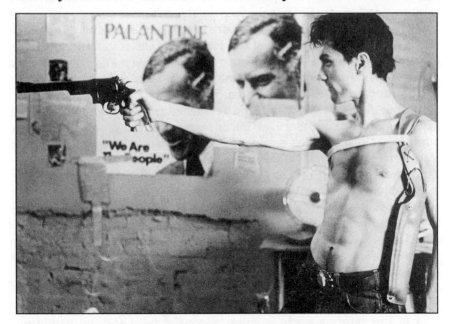

An extension of the gaze's power, the .44 Magnum is the weapon of choice for the hero as myth and media commodity. Robert DeNiro as Travis Bickle in *Taxi Driver*. Warner Bros. Still Courtesy of Jerry Ohlinger's Movie Materials.

provokes his crisis. As the circling continues, Travis' desires cause his thinking to fluctuate radically from self-deification to despair. The power of language to dispel the crisis becomes increasingly doubtful, a signal of Travis' general impotence. His conversation with Wizard is patently worthless, a fact made humorous by the Wizard's reputation as prophet and analyst, a watcher over the city. Wizard casually writes off Travis' anguish as a form of blues, but then admits he doesn't know that Travis is talking about. The most that Travis can articulate is his sense that: "Some bad things are going on in my head, you know—something—I want to do something—I got some bad things going on in my head." The "something" takes many minor forms: the admiration of the dream girl Betsy, the attempt to convert Iris, the vague interest in the Palantine campaign, the hatred of Sport and Tom. In each instance Travis misinterprets the value or meaning of the interaction, choosing instead to view each relationship in terms that will in some way respond to his self-image as god/demon. One irony here is his hatred for Betsy's co-worker, Tom, viewed by Travis as a rival (but rationalized to Betsy as some evil force) but who is one of the more impotent figures within Travis' circle: Tom jokingly tells Betsy "I'll be the male in this relationship" when Betsy asks him to chase Travis away.

On at least one level Scorsese seems to be repeating Steiner's criticism of the Dostoyevskian image of the Romantic individual and his sense of autonomy.[12] Travis is a figure out of the western and *film noir*: his illness and alienation are extensions of the sense of autonomy projected by the Romantic hero of American myth.

Travis' fluctuation between Old Testament moralism and self-abasing defeat is the consequence of his incorporation of a sense of heroic autonomy that contains an exaggerated system of power. In the role of reformer Travis assumes the position of God but also of simple aggressor; the failure of that extreme model propels him into masochism, but obviously the roles are interlinked in such a way as to ensure the self-perpetuation of the construct. What is being revealed is a utopianism that existed in Travis before the narrative began, and utopia, now heavily mediated, is at the heart of trauma. Certainly the entirety of Travis' thinking—from his dream of the great rain to the idealized vision of the family—depends on an apocalyptic impulse; the film suggests the millennialism dominant in American art to have a collective psycho-pathological foundation. Scorsese develops this by showing that Travis' view of the exterior world is simultaneously valid and hallucinatory. When Travis leaves the cafeteria with Wizard, a threatening black street gang passes by as if an apparition, as an "effect" and a projection of Travis' extreme state of mind. A similar scene occurs inside the cafeteria when a black cab driver comments on Travis' bankroll and points a make-believe pistol fashioned with thumb and forefinger. The camera tracks away with the same ethereal grace as when Travis spies the black gang a second later. Travis views the cab driver with the same anxiety and menace he aims at the gang. Yet what Travis consistently sees as a force of evil has also internalized the same vision that entraps him and ensures the circle of repetition. When Travis buys the .44 Magnum, Easy Andy reminds him he could as easily "sell it to a jungle bunny in Harlem for a thousand dollars." Andy sells everything from guns to drugs to Cadillacs, catering to the various manifestations of Travis in the city. In such instances the film translates the compulsion and frenzy of the city as a whole, with its conflicting mechanisms of desire, as the apocalypse in macrocosm.

The gun-buying scene is particularly important, as Travis sees it as a "moment of change" in a humdrum existence, a break in the cycle of repetition and inversion. This moment is for Travis another divinely-ordained circumstance moving him closer to a special destiny. This destiny "becomes clearer" in Travis' mind as he moves from his junk-food-and-pills existence to a Spartan period of physical training, self-

The last stand in postmodernity preserves both the "ludic" and the "sacrificial" in patriarchal culture. *Taxi Driver* (1976). Warner Bros. Still courtesy of Jerry Ohlinger's Movie Materials.

discipline, and resolve. This period, like what preceded it, is based on the same impulse toward self-destruction. In the purchase of the guns, we discover more evidence of Travis' incorporation of the dominant "venal" culture he claims to reject. The gun-buying scene has many intertextual aspects, presenting a kind of condensed repository of the popular culture that has been a contributing force in Travis delusions. Travis buys a Walther PPK (James Bond), a snub-nose Smith and Wesson .38 (Mike Hammer), a pocket-sized .25 automatic (also Bond ordnance) and the .44 Magnum (the most popular handgun in America following the success of *Dirty Harry* (1971). Travis mounts the .25 automatic on a retractable spring he wears up his sleeve, the trick of river boat gamblers and Robert Conrad in "The Wild, Wild West." He tapes a huge knife to his boot and pulls it free as he tumbles onto a cot, mimicking the death of Jim Bowie at the Alamo.

This "moment of change," in its extreme inversion, leads to the crisis Travis interprets as his transcendence to a new role: the man of action. But his buying of the guns reveals only the compulsive consumer, egged on by the sly manipulation of Easy Andy. This is also the moment where the film reveals Travis, the postmodern subject as image repository. The creation of the various stick-up rigs reflect his fetishization of these objects as his descent continues. Travis' solitary practicing with the guns (the famous "You talkin' to me?" sequence) is the grossest inversion of the Lacanian "mirror stage." DeNiro faces the camera for part of Travis' practice session; the camera lens has the function of Travis' mirror, with which there can be no reciprocation. At the same time the gesture necessarily equates the mirror with the lens and a connection with the audience. The lens becomes the instrument of crisis as trans-psychical and collective. At this moment the cinema seems actually a denial of the mirror stage's crossing into the (patriarchal) symbolic dimension. Travis' "free play," locked in the imaginary, preserves both the "ludic" *and* sacrificial, patriarchal culture.

That Travis' descent is now rapid is emphasized by a particularly telling scene. Travis watches a soap opera on TV while absent-mindedly holding the Magnum in one hand. Travis is not so much watching the TV as drifting in some vague deliberation, his left boot tipping the TV back and forth. It is as if Travis is almost consciously engaged in breaking the cycle of repetition and forcing some conscious reconciliation between activity and passive intake, but the banality of television and the empty super-revolver signify states of experience that have nothing to do with allowing the conscious mind attain self-recognition. When Travis tips over the TV, it for a moment seems an act of aggression against more of the "garbage" foisted on him, against repetition-compulsion that is reducing him (and the city) to base matter. The banality of television also refers to the banality of Betsy, her acceptance of the new, bankrupt language of politics ("We *are* selling mouthwash").Yet there is enough awareness remaining in Travis to have him view his destruction of his own property as a useless act (he murmurs "damn, damn it") ultimately aimed at himself; at the same time the game with the TV suggests a sense of caprice within Travis' suicidal tendency that marks advanced disintegration. This is American sacrificial excess as suicidal gesture.

This caprice is developed in Travis' final decision to act. He feels assured of the need for "true force," and that "All the king's horses and all the king's men could not put it together again." (Did Travis see the Robert Rossen film? What is his understanding of corruption?) The "it," clearly, refers both to society and to Travis himself. We are constantly reminded of Travis as a pastiche personality, a subject structured by American myth and pop culture. Travis' vision of a personal Armageddon is drawn along the lines of the "last stand" of Custer, of *The Magnificent Seven* (1960), *The Alamo* (1960), *The Wild Bunch* (1969), and *Walking Tall* (1973). The attempt on Palantine and the rescue of Iris lack any genuinely political dimension, since at this point Travis embodies the total atomization of the community, and his action is merely a desperate attempt at self-affirmation. Like his namesake who accepted martyrdom commanding the Alamo garrison, Travis sees his personal mission as above and beyond the interests of the collectivity; but the society must naturally benefit from any decision made since Travis, absolutely alienated, is always a representative man. The Mohawk haircut he adopts is the caricatured rendering of the psychotic Vietnam veteran, but as a reminder of the brutal effects of the military the shaven head refers to its psychoanalytic emblem in connoting the potential suicide. We cannot help but contemplate the emptying of signification in once potent symbols of culture; the vitality of the Native American has been drained in various ways, culminating in the co-optation of his symbols by punk culture, a radical force in fact representing the extreme disruption of a common code. With the Mohawk haircut Travis also actualizes the image of the Indian as demon/victim; Travis will either absorb the Indian's magic and revitalize the community or acquiesce to martyrdom, hoping, in the tradition of American melodrama, that death will provide an ennobling moment, a right place to go.

It is interesting that, in the wake of the attempted assassination of Ronald Reagan, *Taxi Driver* should be resurrected and used as propaganda. The mass media perpetuate Travis Bickle's thinking on a general scale, and in so doing reveal the tense dialectic in American society between apocalyptic and political world-views. Understanding the use of *Taxi Driver* in relation to the attempt on Reagan illuminates the perpetuation of this dialectic. BBC journalist Anthony Summers has termed the Zapruder film of the Kennedy assassination "apocalyptic" footage while proceeding to examine this assassination in a political context.[13] It seems natural to look at the assassinations of the 60s as acts of mythic dimension and of overwhelming consequence to American life, but it is possible for a mythic mechanism to remain intact while allowing for analysis that does not depend on loosely defined notions of "American character" and spiritual destiny. This is not the thinking operating in the media observations of the Reagan attempt *vis-à-vis* Scorsese's film. As in the 1960s, violence is again represented as something endemic to the American character, frequently manifest in the works of irresponsible or exploitative artists, whose works in turn go on further to provoke the " sick minds" of society. It is rare for this pervasive violence to be examined in a political or economic framework—violence is simply "there" in tautological existence, the only explanation for it being its long-developing history in American experience. The focus on the universality of violence creates an extreme situation; if evil is everywhere, how can it be defined? To mystify this subject is obviously to remove it from a political/historical dimension. The individual (and society) becomes a victim who, by incorporating the total system of violence of the amorphous oppressor, becomes also a demon; because of the individual's basic impotence in the face of the law and self-doubt, s/he can only live in suspicion or turn violence inward. As if to intuit this extreme potential situation in the collectivity, an occasional mythic apparatus can be constructed to displace violence, as in Watergate. While Nixon was utilized as the demon/scapegoat through whom violence was to be displaced, thus regenerating the organism ("Our long national nightmare is over"), the mythic function dissolved. The sacrifice of Nixon clearly failed as ritual, not only because it was incomplete, but because it was revealed as ritual per se and one that did not genuinely respond to a consensus. That consensus had long since fragmented with the polarization of society and the adversary relationship of the population to the sources of power that traditionally embody mythic beliefs. The sacrificial crisis of Watergate occurred as the true nature of the scandal as embodiment of the gangsterism, betrayal, and fragmentation at the upper reaches of power was revealed. As political and economic analyses of the dominant ideology were avoided, the population could only fall into the self-deprecating belief that the "disease" of violence had overtaken the sources of power as it had long since overtaken and polluted the rest of the body politic, resulting in the "moral schizophrenia" Tobe Hooper wanted to respond to in *The Texas Chainsaw Massacre* (1973).[14]

Travis' situation suggests very well this fragmentation and dysfunction of mythic narrative. Travis Bickle's assault on the brothel at the end of *Taxi Driver* is plausible in its characteristic arbitrariness. Travis' violence is born out of his fixation on the romance of the individual, which develops into a pathological situation as his isolated judgments lack any frame of reference in society. On the conscious level he is both God and self-abasing devil; he wants to rid the world of a nondescript and "venal" politician, or save the naive Iris from pimps and gangsters, but neither action is sensible in terms of the traditional hero's rescue of the community. Palantine is chosen because he is a demon who circulates in Betsy's world, from which Travis is excluded. Sport and his friends are demons who interfere with Travis' idealized vision of Iris. The choice to attack the brothel does not come about simply because the attempt on Palantine failed. The hatred of Sport and the disgust at corruption focused on Palantine are framed by a much larger anger. Travis' violence is the all-encompassing apocalyptic gesture that chooses both the self and the world, emphasized in Travis' attempted suicide after the bloodbath, which he goes about as deliberately as the other killings.

Scorsese and Schrader seem intent in this ending to expose an important element of the "last stands" of American action film by addressing some of its philosophical premises. There is little question that they have tapped the apocalyptic belief within this type of violence, which proposes the redeeming value of death, the preference for death over rational reform, and the belief in massive violence as a redemptive ritual of the community. But the belief in the ritual function of violence described by René Girard, Richard Slotkin, and others is criticized in *Taxi Driver*'s conclusion, which many critics have attacked as far more fantastic than the violence that precedes it. Travis is not valorized in death; rather, he survives to be rewarded by a community in a way that Shane and Ethan Edwards never really were. But Travis' rewards are slim and he does not fully integrate into the community; at the most he commands some temporary respect from the male group and some fleeting fascination from the girl who spurned him. More important, the admiration Travis now enjoys is born out of a superficial and misleading image of him perpetuated by the media (the news clippings on the wall) and by the political structure afraid to examine its own bankruptcy. Travis is thus fed into the media to become the type of apparition that constructed him. It is easier to make a media hero out of Travis than reveal his ties to an assassination attempt and reawaken concerns about violence, and, possibly, internal strife overall. This interpretation may be giving the film a bit much, since its apolitical view of assassination and its casual incorporation of the Arthur Bremer-"lone nut" construct ignores any critical interpretation of the criminal's relationship to dominant ideology, nor, as noted, does it treat assassination precisely as a political act. Yet the very apocalyptic current of this film, with its cynical ending and emphasis on the collapse of codes and pervasive alienation, may suggest a new and necessary cataclysm that must precede radical transformation.

While *Taxi Driver* criticizes the apocalyptic current in American art, it is itself apocalyptic in its view of the current atmosphere as irredeemable. On one level the film seems to show little belief neither in the redeeming quality of violence nor the apocalyptic "sense of an ending" that is relied upon to provide dramatic closure to a work. It is unimportant whether or not Travis' final drifting into the night suggests that the cycle of violence may begin again. It is apparent that general alienation is profound, pervasive, and resistant to any interpretation or cure. This thoroughly nihilistic position is enough for us to regard *Taxi Driver* as a work of postmodern horror about the apocalypse of American narrative. As the film embodies currents of several genres, it projects apocalypse as the destruction of art and all created reality (seen as tainted and corrupt), an idea of the end that is deliberately suicidal (and religious) in conception.

Notes

1. The scholarship examining this line of thought is, of course, voluminous. A useful recent collection of essays on apocalypticism in American culture is Lois Parkinson Zamora, ed. *The Apocalyptic Vision in America: Interdisciplinary Essays on Art and Culture* (Bowling Green, OH: Popular Press, 1982). Important to an understanding of apocalyptic consciousness and its roots in American thought is Perry Miller, *The New England Mind: From Colony to Province* (Cambridge: Harvard University Press, 1952).

2. The question of apocalypse's immanence to experience is discussed in Frank Kermode, *The Sense of an Ending: Studies in the Theory of Fiction* (New York: Oxford University Press, 1966).

3. René Girard, *Deceit, Desire, and the Novel: Self and Other in Literary Structures.* Yvonne Freccero, trans. (Baltimore: Johns Hopkins University Press, 1965). Especially useful to a study of *Taxi Driver* is Girard's chapter, "The Dostoyevskian Apocalypse," pp. 256-289.

4. René Girard, *Violence and the Sacred.* Patrick Gregory, trans. (Baltimore: Johns Hopkins University Press, 1977).

5. This is a central topic in Kermode.

6. The tendency of contemporary films allude to older films is examined in Noel Carroll, "The Future of Allusion: Hollywood in the Seventies (and

Beyond)," *October* 20 (date): 51.

7. See Richard Thompson, "Screenwriter: *Taxi Driver*'s Paul Schrader," *Film Comment*, March-April, 1976: 19.

8. Discussed in Robin Wood, "The Incoherent Text: Narrative in the 70s," *Movie* 27-28 (Winter 1980/Spring 1981): 26.

9. Wood, p. 30.

10. See George Steiner's introduction to Dostoyevsky's *Notes from the Underground* and *The Gambler* (New York: The Heritage Press, 1967).

11. The Indian-as-devil construct is a topic of discussion in Richard Slotkin, *Regeneration Through Violence: The Mythology of the American Frontier, 1160-1860* (Middletown, CT: Wesleyan University Press, 1973), pp. 18, 66, and elsewhere.

12. This is illuminated in Girard, pp. 257-289.

13. Anthony Summers, *Conspiracy* (New York: McGraw-Hill, 1980), p. 47. This book is fairly unique in its ability to recognize the "mythic" dimensions of the John Kennedy assassination while undertaking an examination of this moment precisely as a political assassination. The failure to attempt the same sort of exploration may be *Taxi Driver*'s principal defect, one rather foregrounded as the film was used as propaganda. The quite sensational attempts by the media to use *Taxi Driver* to explain the John Hinckley matter are important insofar as they reflect a long-term tendency of dominant ideology to sidetrack discussion of political acts, particularly those that reveal the clandestine police apparatus. Our chief concern here is the impact of reactionary politics on *Taxi Driver*. The sensationalism surrounding the Hinckley case seemed to have caused current audiences to view the film as an "explanation" of American violence, a tendency encouraged by many of the film's recent presentations (especially those on network and local television stations). It may be very difficult hereafter to view *Taxi Driver* as a work of art outside of this propaganda context, but this difficulty may itself be an important representation of the contradiction of the current society, emblems of the apocalypse the film addresses.

14. See Ellen Farley and William K. Knoedelseder, Jr., "The Real Texas Chainsaw Massacre," *Los Angeles Times* September 5, 1982: Section 4, p. 1. Over the past decade-and-a-half there has been an increased tendency to view the horror film as a crucial contemporary genre for its representation of mass psychosis and social dysfunction. The representative example is Robin Wood, et al., *The American Nightmare* (Toronto: Festival of Festivals Publications, 1979).

Apotheosis of the simulacra: Rutger Hauer's Blakean cyborg in *Blade Runner* (1982). Warner Bros. Still photograph courtesy of Jerry Ohlinger's Movie Materials.

Giuliana Bruno

Ramble City: Postmodernism and Blade Runner

"History is hysterical: it is constituted only if we consider it, only if we look at it—and in order to look at it we must be excluded from it. . . . That is what the time when my mother was alive before me is— History. No anamnesis could ever make me glimpse this time starting from myself—whereas, contemplating a photograph in which she is hugging me, a child, against her, I can waken in myself the rumpled softness of her crepe de chine and the perfume of her rice powder."[1] This is history for Roland Barthes and history for the replicants of *Blade Runner*. The replicants are perfect "skin jobs"; they look like humans, they talk like them, they even have feelings and emotions (in science fiction the ultimate sign of the human.) What they lack is a history. For that they have to be killed. Seeking a history, fighting for it, they search for their origins, for that time before themselves. Rachel succeeds. She has a document—as we know, the foundation of history. Her document is a photograph, a photograph of her mother, hugging her, a child against her, wakening in her the rumpled softness of, most probably, a hamburger. History is hysterical; it is constituted only if we look at it, excluded from it. That is, my mother before me—history. History/Mother/My mother. "My mother? I'll tell you about my mother. . . ."[2]

* * *

The debate on postmodernism has by now produced a vast literature. Roughly, we might distinguish three positions: one elaborated with reference to the human sciences and literature, by Jean-Francois Lyotard and Umberto Eco, among others; one concerning the visual arts, recently developed in particular in the U.S.; and one related to the discourse of and on architecture.[3] It is the latter which, for the most part, constitutes the theoretical groundwork for this paper, in which *Blade Runner* will be discussed as a metaphor of the postmodern condition. I wish to analyze, in particular, the representation of narrative space and temporality in *Blade Runner*. For this I will use two terms, pastiche and schizophrenia, in order to define and explore the two areas of investigation. The terms are borrowed and developed from Fredric Jameson's discussion of postmodernism. In his essay, "Postmodernism and Consumer Society"[4] and in the later expanded "Postmodernism, or the Cultural Logic of Late Capitalism,"[5] Jameson suggests that the postmodern condition is characterized by a schizophrenic temporality and a spatial pastiche. The notion of schizophrenia which Jameson employs is that elaborated by Jacques Lacan. According to Jameson's reading of Lacan, schizophrenia is basically a breakdown of the relationship between signifiers, linked to the failure of access to the Symbolic. With pastiche there is an effacement of key boundaries and separations, a process of erosion of distinctions. Pastiche is intended as an aesthetic of quotations pushed to the limit; it is an incorporation of forms, an imitation of dead styles deprived of any satirical impulse. Jameson's suggestion has proved a viable working reference and a guideline in analyzing the deployment of space and time in the film. Pastiche and schizophrenia will thus act, in the economy of my argument, as what Umberto Eco calls umbrella terms, operational linguistic covers of vast and even diverse areas of concern. My discussion of postmodernism and *Blade Runner* will involve a consideration of questions of identity and history, of the role of simulacra and simulation, and of the relationship between postmodernism, architecture, and postindustrialism.

1. Pastiche

It is useful to note that Jameson has derived his view of postmodernism from the field of architecture: "It is in the realm of architecture . . . that modifications in aesthetic productions are most dramatically visible, an that their theoretical problems have been most centrally raised and articulated; it was indeed from architectural debates that my own conception of postmodernism began to emerge."[6] It is in the architectural layout of *Blade Runner* that pastiche is most dramatically visible and where the connection of postmodernism to postindustrialism is evident.

The film does not take place in a spaceship or space station, but in a city, Los Angeles, in the year 2019, a step away from the development of contemporary society. The link between postmodernism and late capitalism is highlighted in the film's representation of postindustrial decay. The future does not realize an idealized, aseptic technological order, but is seen simply as the development of the present state of the city and of the social order of late capitalism. The city of *Blade Runner* is not the ultramodern, but the postmodern city. It is not an orderly layout of skyscrapers and ultra comfortable, hyper-mechanized interiors. Rather, it creates an aesthetic of decay, exposing the dark side of technology, the process of disintegration.

Next to the high-tech, its waste. It is into garbage that the characters constantly step, by garbage that Pris awaits J. F. Sebastian. A deserted neighborhood in decay is where Deckard goes to find the peace he needs in order to work. There he finds the usual gang of metropolitan punks exploring the ruins for unexpected marvels. In an abandoned, deteriorating building, J. F. Sebastian lives surrounded by nothing but his mechanical toys. It is a building of once great majesty, now an empty shell left to disintegrate. The rain completes the ambience. It falls persistently, veiling the landscape of the city, further obscuring the neo-baroque lighting. It is a corrosive rain which wears things away.

The postindustrial decay is an effect of the acceleration of the internal time of process proper to postindustrialism. The system works only if waste is produced. The continuous expulsion of waste is an indexical sign of the well-functioning apparatus: waste represents its production, movement, and development at increasing speed. Postindustrialism recycles; therefore it needs its waste.[7] A postmodern position exposes such logic, producing an aesthetic of recycling. The artistic form exhibits the return of the waste. Consumerism, waste, and recycling meet in fashion, the "wearable art" of late capitalism, a sign of postmodernism. Costumes in *Blade Runner* are designed according to this logic. The "look" of the replicants Pris and Zhora and of some of the women in the background in the bar and in the street scenes reinforces this aesthetic. Pris, the "basic pleasure model," is the model of postindustrial fashion, the height of exhibition and recycling.

The postmodern aesthetic of *Blade Runner* is thus the result of recycling, fusion of levels, discontinuous signifiers, explosion of boundaries, and erosion. The disconnected temporality of the replicants and the pastiche city are all an effect of a postmodern, postindustrial condition: wearing out, waste. There is even a character in the film who is nothing but a literalization of this condition. J. F. Sebastian is twenty-five years old, but his skin is wrinkled and decrepit. His internal process and time are accelerated, and he is wearing out. "Accelerated decrepitude" is how the replicant Pris describes his condition, noting that he and the replicants have something in common. What Pris does not say is that the city suffers from it as well. The psychopathology of J. F. Sebastian, the replicants, and the city is the psychopathology of the everyday postindustrial condition. The increased speed of development and process produces the diminishing of distances, of the space in between, of distinction. Time and tempo are reduced to climax, after which there is retirement. Things cease to function and life is over even if it has not ended. The postindustrial city is a city in ruins.

In *Blade Runner*, the visions of postindustrial decay are set in an inclusive, hybrid architectural design. The city is called Los Angeles, but it is an L.A. that looks very much like New York, Hong Kong, or Tokyo. We are not presented with a real geography, but an imaginary one: a synthesis of mental architectures, or *topoi*. Quoting from different real cities, postcards, advertising, movies, the text makes a point about the city of postindustrialism. It is a polyvalent, interchangeable structure, the product of geographical displacements and condensations. *Blade Runner*'s space of narration bears, superimposed, different and previous orders of time and space. It incorporates them, exhibiting their trans- formations and deterioration. It is a place of vast immigration, from countries of overpopulation and poverty. While immigrants crowd the city, the indigenous petite bourgeoisie moves to the suburbs or to the

We are not presented with a real geography, but an imaginary one: a synthesis of mental architectures, of *topoi*. Harrison Ford as Dekard in *Blade Runner* (1982). Warner Bros. Still courtesy of Jerry Ohlinger's Movie Materials.

"off-world" as the case may be. Abandoned buildings and neighborhoods in decay adjoin highly populated, crowded old areas, themselves set next to new, high-tech business districts. The film is populated by eclectic crowds of faceless people. Oriental merchants, punks, Hari Krishnas. Even the language is pastiche: "city speech" is a "mish-mash of Japanese, Spanish, German, what have you." The city is a large market; an intrigue of underground networks pervades all relations. The explosive Orient dominates, the Orient of yesterday incorporating the Orient of today. Overlooking the city is the "Japanese simulacrum," the huge advertisement which alternates a seductive Japanese face and a Coca Cola sign. In the postindustrial city the explosion of urbanization, melting the futuristic high-tech look into an intercultural scenario, recreates the third world inside the first. One travels almost without moving, for the Orient occupies the next block. The Los Angeles of *Blade Runner* is China(in)town.

The pertinence and uniqueness of architecture to specific places, cultures, and times has been lost in postmodernism. The metropolis of *Blade Runner* quotes not only from different spatial structures but from temporal ones as well. The syntactic rules are broken down in post-modernism and replaced by a parataxis, a regulated aesthetic of lists. The connections are not made at random, but ruled by a different logic. It is the logic of pastiche, which allows and promotes quotations of a synchronic and diachronic order. "The resultant hybrid balances and reconciles opposed meanings. . . . This inclusive architecture absorbs conflicting codes in an attempt to create (what Robert Venturi calls) 'the difficult whole'. . . . It can include ugliness, decay, banality, austerity. . . . In general terms, it can be described as racial eclecticism or adhocism. Various parts, styles, or sub-systems are used to create a new synthesis."[8] In *Blade Runner* recollections and quotations from the past are subcodes of new synthesis.[9] Roman and Greek columns provide a retro mise-en-scène for the city. Signs of classical Oriental mythology recur. Chinese dragons are revisited in neon lighting. A strong Egyptian element pervades the decor. The Tyrell corporation overlooks what resemble the Egyptian pyramids in a full sunset. The interior of the office is not high-tech, but rather a pop Egyptian extravaganza, to which the choreography of movement and make-up of Zhora adds exoticism. Elevators might have video screens, but they are made of stone. The walls of Deckard's apartment are reminiscent of an ancient Mayan palace. Pastiche, as an aesthetic of quotation, incorporates dead styles; it attempts a recollection of the past, of memory, and of history.

The result of this architectural pastiche is an excess of scenography. Every relation in the narrative space produces an exhibitionism rather than an aesthetics of the visual. The excess of violence is such an exhibitionism. The iconography of death as well is scenographic. The "scene" of death becomes a sort of "obscenity," the site of total, transparent visibility. The fight and death of Pris are rendered as a performance, Zhora dies breaking through a window in slow motion. The decor, the choreography of movement and editing, the neo-baroque cinematography emphasize visual virtuosity. It has been said that scenography is the domain of postmodern architecture. Paolo Portoghesi claims that "Postmodern in architecture can generally be read as the reemerging of the archetypes and the reintegration of the architectural conventions and thus as the premise of the creation of an architecture of communication, an architecture of the visual, for a culture of the visual."[10]

2. Schizophrenia

Pastiche and the exhibition of the visual celebrate the dominance of representation and the effacement of the referent in the era of postindustrialism. The postindustrial society is the "society of the spectacle," living in the ecstasy of communication." Addressing this aspect of postmodernism, Jean Baudrillard speaks of a twist in the relationship between the real and its reproduction. The process of reproducibility is pushed to the limit. As a result, "the real is not what can be reproduced, but that which is always already reproduced . . . the hyperreal . . . which is entirely in simulation."[11] The narrative space of *Blade Runner* participates in this logic: "All of Los Angeles . . . is of the order of hyperreal and simulation."[12] There, the machinery of imitations, reproductions, and seriality, in other words, "replicants," affirm the fiction of the real.

The narrative "invention" of the replicants is almost a literalization of Baudrillard's theory of postmodernism as the age of simulacra and simulation. Replicants are the perfect simulacra—a convergence of genetics and linguistics, the genetic miniaturization enacting the dimension of simulation. Baudrillard describes the simulacrum as "an operational double, a metastable, programmatic, perfect descriptive machine which provides all the signs of the real and short-circuits all its vicissitudes."[13] It could be difficult to find a better definition of the nature and function of the replicants and their capacity of simulation in the narrative motivation of *Blade Runner*. In L.A., year 2019, simulation is completely dominant as the effect of the existence and operations of the replicant/simulacrum. "The unreal is no longer that of dream or of fantasy or a beyond or a within, it is that of *hallucinatory resemblance of the real with itself.*"[14] The replicant performs such hallucinatory resemblance. "It" looks and acts like a he or a she. Perfect simulation is thus its goal, and Rachel manages to reach it. To simulate, in fact, is a more complex act than to imitate or feign. To simulate implies actually producing in oneself some of the characteristics of what one wants to simulate. It is a matter of internalizing the signs or the symptoms to the point where there is no difference between "false" and "true," "real," and "imaginary." With Rachel the system has reached perfection. She is the most perfect replicant because she does not know whether she is one or not. To say that she simulates her symptoms, her sexuality, her memory is to to say that she realizes, experiences them.

The fascination with the simulacrum has, of course, generated narratives before *Blade Runner*. We find in *Der Sandmann*, for example, one of the most influential fictional descriptions of simulacra. It is this tale, in fact, which inspired Freud's reflection on the uncanny. *Der Sandmann* concerns the android Olympia, who is such a perfect "skin job" that she is mistaken for a real girl, the daughter of the inventor. The protagonist of the tale, Nathaniel, falls in love with her, but reality triumphs; the android is unmasked and destroyed. In Hoffmann's time, replication is still a question of imitation, for the real still bears a meaning. The replicants of *Blade Runner* are, on the contrary, as the name itself indicates, serial terms. No original is thus invoked as a point of comparison, and no distinction between real and copy remains.

It is, indeed, in simulation that the power of the replicants resides. Since the simulacrum is the negation of both original and copy, it is ultimately the celebration of the false as power and the power of the false.[15] The replicants turn this power against their makers to assert the autonomy of the simulacrum.

But these replicants, "simulacra" of humans, in some ways superior to them, have a problem: a fragmented temporality. "Schizophrenic vertigo of these serial signs . . . immanent in their repetition—who could say what the reality is that these signs simulate?"[16] The replicant affirms a new form of temporality, that of schizophrenic vertigo. This is the temporality of postmodernism's new age of the machine. The industrial machine was one of production, the postindustrial machine, one of reproduction. A major shift occurs: the alienation of the subject is replaced by the fragmentation of the subject, its dispersal in representation. The "integrity" of the subject is more deeply put into question. Baudrillard describes the postindustrial age thus: "We are now in a new form of schizophrenia. No more hysteria, no more projective paranoia, but his state of terror proper to the schizophrenic. . . . The

schizophrenic can no longer produce the limits of its own being. . . .
He is only a pure screen."[17] A replicant.

Blade Runner presents a manifestation of the schizophrenic
condition—in the sense that Lacan gives this term. For Lacan, temporality, past, present, future, memory are of a linguistic order: that is to
say, the experience of temporality and its representation are an effect
of language. It is the very structure of language that allows us to know
temporality as we do and to represent it as a linear development from
past to present and future. The experience of historical continuity is
therefore dependent upon language acquisition, upon access to the realm
of speech. It is dependent upon the acceptance of the Name-of-the-Father,
paternal authority conceived as a linguistic function.

Schizophrenia, on the other hand, results from a failure to enter
the Symbolic order, it is thus essentially a breakdown of language, which
contributes to a breakdown of the temporal order. The schizophrenic
condition is characterized by the inability to experience the persistence
of the "I" over time. There is neither past nor future at the two poles
of that which thus becomes a perpetual present. Jameson writes, "The
schizophrenic does not have our experience of temporal continuity but
is condemned to live a perpetual present with which the various moments
of this or her past have little connection and for which there is no
conceivable future on the horizon."[18] Replicants are condemned to a
life composed only of a present tense; they have neither past nor memory.
There is for them no conceivable future. They are denied a personal
identity, since they cannot name their "I" as an existence over time.
Yet this life, lived only in the present, is for the replicants an extremely
intense experience, since it is not perceived as part of a larger set of
experiences. Replicants represent themselves as a candle that burns
faster but brighter and claim to have seen more things with their eyes
in that limited time than anybody else would even be able to imagine.
This kind of relationship to the present is typical of schizophrenia.
Jameson notes, in fact, that "as temporal continuity breaks down, the
experience of the present becomes powerfully, overwhelmingly vivid
and 'material.' The world comes before the schizophrenic with heightened
intensity."[19]

The schizophrenic temporality of the replicants is a resistance to
enter the social order, to function according to its modes.[20] As outsiders
to the order of language, replicants have to be eliminated. Theirs is a
dangerous malfunction, calling for a normalization, an affirmation of
the order of language and law. Their killing constitutes a state murder.
It is called "retirement," a word which connotes exclusion from the
productive and active social order.

If the replicants are to survive, the signifiers of their existence have to be put in order. Some semblance of a symbolic dimension has to be put together to release them from the trap of the present. Their assurance of a future relies on the possibility of acquiring a past. In their attempt at establishing a temporally persistent identity, the replicants search for their origins. They want to know who "conceived" them, and they investigate their identity and the link to their makers. The itinerary is that of an Oedipal journey. To survive for a time, the android has to accept the fact of sexual difference, the sexual identity which the entry into language requires.

Of all the replicants, only one, Rachel, succeeds in making the journey. She assumes a sexual identity, becomes a woman, and loves a man: Deckard, the blade runner. Rachel accepts the paternal figure and follows the path to a "normal" adult, female, sexuality: she identifies her sex by first acknowledging the power of the other, the father, a man. But the leader of the replicants, Roy Batty, refuses the symbolic castration which is necessary to enter the symbolic order; he refuses, that is, to be smaller, less powerful than the father. Roy commits the Oedipal crime. He kills his father, and the Oedipal topos of blindness recurs, reversed. Roy thus seals his (lack of) destiny, denying himself resolution and salvation.

In this tension between pre-Oedipal and Oedipal, Imaginary and Symbolic, the figure of the mother becomes a breaking point in the text. Replicants can be unmasked by a psychological text which reveals their emotional responses as dissimilar to those of humans.[21] Blade Runner begins with such a test as it is being administered to Leon, a replicant who is trying to hide his identity. Leon succeeds up to a certain point, but there arises a question which he cannot handle. Asked to name all the good things that come to his mind about his mother, Leon explodes, "My mother, I'll tell you about my mother," and kills the inquirer. The mother is necessary to the claiming of a history, to the affirmation of an identity over time. Unmasked by the same test, Rachel goes to her inquirer, Deckard, to convince him, or herself rather, that she is not a replicant. Her argument is a photograph, a photograph of a mother and daughter. "Look, this is me, with my mother." That photograph represents the trace of an origin and thus a personal identity, the proof of having existed and therefore of having the right to exist.

A theoretical link is established in Blade Runner between photography, mother, and history. It is a connection that we also find in Barthes' writings on photography. In Camera Lucida, reflections on photography are centered on the figure of the mother as she relates to the question of history. Photography and the mother are the missing link between past, present, and future. The terms of the configuration photography / mother / history are knotted together in dialectics of totality and division, presence and absence, continuity and discontinuity. "The name of Photography's noeme will therefore be 'that-has-been' or again the Intractable. In Latin, this would doubtless be said: *interfuit*: what I see has been there, and yet immediately separated: it has been absolutely, irrefutably present, and yet already deferred."[22] As a document of "that-has-been," photography constitutes a document of history, of its deferred existence. A history conceived as hysterical is established only in an act of exclusion, in a look that separates subject and object. History is that time when my mother was alive before me. It is the trace of the dream of unity, of its impossibility. The all-nourishing mother is there, yet as that which has been given up. The Imaginary exists as a loss.

Photographs are documents of existence in a history to be transformed into memories, monuments of the past. Such is the very challenge of history, as Michel Foucault has pointed out. "History is that which transforms documents into monuments."[23] The document is for Foucault a central question of history; for *Blade Runner* it is the essential element for the establishment of a temporality, of perceiving the past and future. Foucault defines history as "one way in which society recognized and develops a mass of documentation with which it is inextricably linked."[24] Photographs can be such documentation for the replicants. Not only does Rachel exhibit her document-photograph of that past moment with her mother, but she is fascinated by photographs generally. In a second visit to Deckard, she produces her memories in response to his photographs. She attempts to look like the woman in his old photograph, and plays the piano to recapture a memory, an atmosphere. Leon's preciously kept pictures serve no apparent purpose other than the documentation of the replicant's existence in history. Deckard understands this motivation when he finds the photos. "I don't know why replicants would collect photos. Maybe they were like Rachel, they needed memories."

The desire of photography in *Blade Runner* is essentially a phenomenological seduction: "In photography I can never deny that 'the thing has been there.' There is a superimposition here of reality and of the past."[25] Photography is perceived as the medium in which the signifier and the referent are collapsed onto each other. Photographs assert the referent , its reality, in that they assert its existence at that (past) moment which the person, the thing, was there in front of the camera. If a replicant is in a photograph, he or she is thus real.

The function of photography in film's temporal construction is further grasped in Barthes' observation that "the photograph's immobility is the result of perverse confusion between two concepts: the Real and the Live. By attesting that the object has been real, the photograph surreptitiously induces belief that it is alive.... Photography, moreover, began historically as an art of the person: of civil status of what we might call, in all senses of the term, the body's formality."[26] Replicants rely on photography for its perverse confusion, as it induces the surreptitious belief and hope of being alive.

Investigating the other side of the body's formality and the civil status of the replicants, blade runners also make use of photography. Once Deckard finds the photographs/documents in Leon's apartment, he proceeds by questioning them. History as a process of investigation is involved in a question of the document. "History now organizes the document, divides it up, distributes it, orders it, arranges it in levels, establishes series, distinguishes between what is relevant and what is not, discovers elements, defines unities, describes relations."[27] Foucault's description of the historical process exactly describes the way in which Deckard interrogates the documents/photographs producing history. Deckard puts a photograph in a video machine to analyze it. The photograph is decomposed and reconstructed visually through the creation of new relations, shifting the direction of the gaze, zooming in and out, selecting and rearranging elements, creating close-ups of what is relevant. The dissected and reorganized signifiers of photography result in a narrative. At work is the same process of investigation and detection that we find in *Blow-up*: the serialization of the still image, the photograph, produces a new meaning, a story, a filmic text. The revelation of the secret is an effect of the sequentialization, and thus narrativization of the still image. This is how and why lthe murder is discovered in *Blow-up* and the replicant Zhora is discovered in *Blade Runner*. Searching the document/photograph, Deckard unveils the investigative and narrative process of history. *Blow-up* stops at the level of the signifier of photography; *Blade Runner* wants to believe in its referent; Zhora has-been-there; therefore she is (to be captured) real and alive. Not far off is Barthes' comment: "I went to the photographer's show as to a police investigation."[28]

* * *

Blade Runner posits questions of identity, identification, and history in postmodernism. The text's insistence on photography, on the eye, is suggestive of the problematics of the "I" over time. Photography, "the impossible scene of the unique being," is the suppressed trace of history,

the lost dream of continuity. Photography is memory. The status of
memory has changed. In a postmodern age, memories are no longer
Proustian madeleines, but photographs. The past has become a collection
of photographic, filmic, or televisual images. We, like the replicants,
are put in the position of reclaiming a history by means of its reproduction. Photography is thus assigned the grand task of reasserting the
referent, of reappropriating the Real and historical continuity. The
historical referent is displaced by a photographic referent. In a world
of fragmented temporality the research of history finds its image, its
photographic simulacrum, while history itself remains out of reach.
Schizophrenia and the logic of the simulacrum have had an effect on
historical time. The meaning of history is changed, and changed too
is representation in which history, forever unattainable, merely exists.[29]

The loss of history enacts a desire for historicity, an (impossible)
return to it. Postmodernism, particularly in art and architecture, proclaims such a return to history as one of its goals. It is, however, the
instanciation of a new form of historicity. It is an eclectic one, a historical
pastiche. Pastiche is ultimately a redemption of history, which implies
the transformation and reinterpretation in tension between loss and
desire. It retraces history, deconstructing its order, uniqueness,
specificity, and diachrony. Again, as with the photographic reconstitution,
with the logic of pastiche, a simulacrum of history is established.

A tension is expressed in *Blade Runner* between the radical loss
of *durée* and the attempt of reappropriation. This very tension, which
seeks in the photographic signifier the fiction of history and which
rewrites history by means of architectural pastiched recycling, underlies
as well the psychoanalytic itinerary. An itinerary suspended between
schizophrenia, a fragmented temporality, and the acceptance of the
Name-of-the-Father, standing for temporal continuity and access to the
order of signifiers.

Notes

1. Roland Barthes, *Camera Lucida*. Richard Howard, trans. (New York:
Hill and Wang, 1981), p. 65.
2. Thus answers the replicant Leon when asked about his mother; he
then kills his questioner.
3. The literature is by now extensive. See, for example, Robert Venturi,
Denise Scott Brown, Steven Izenour, *Learning from Las Vegas* (Cambridge,
MA: MIT Press, 1977); Charles Jencks, *The Language of Postmodern
Architecture* (New York: Rizzoli, 1977): Paolo Portoghesi, *Postmodern·
l'architettura nella società postindustriale* (Milan: Electa, 1982).

4. Fredric Jameson, "Postmodernism and Consumer Society," *The Anti-Aesthetic.* Hal Foster, ed. (Port Townsend, WA: Bay Press, 1983), pp. 111-125.

5. Fredric Jameson, "Postmodernism, or the Cultural Logic of Late Capitalism," *New Left Review* 6 (July-August 1984): 53-92.

6. Jameson, "Cultural Logic," p. 54.

7. On the history of waste, see Dominique Laporte, *Histoire de la merde* (Paris: Christian Bourgeois, 1978). Laporte traces the history of waste as a cyclic process of repression and return.

8. Jencks, p. 90.

9. The city of *Blade Runner* includes a set called "New York street" built in 1929 and used in a number of Humphrey Bogart and James Cagney movies in addition to L.A. architectural landmarks such as the Bradbury building (1893) designed by George Wyman and the Ennis House (1924) designed by Frank Lloyd Wright.

10. Portoghesi, p. 11.

11. Jean Baudrillard, *Simulations.* Paul Foss, Paul Patton, and Philip Beitchman, trans. (New York: Semiotext(e), 1983), p. 146.

12. Baudrillard, p. 25.

13. Baudrillard, p. 4.

14. Baudrillard, p. 142. See also Guy Debord, *The Society of the Spectacle* (Detroit: Black and Red Press, 1983).

15. For this aspect of the simulacrum, see Gilles Deleuze, "Plato and the Simulacrum," Rosalind Krauss, trans. *October* 27 (Winter 1983): 45-56.

16. Baudrillard, p. 152.

17. Jean Baudrillard, "The Ecstasy of Communication," John Johnston, trans., in *The Anti-Aesthetic,* p. 132.

18. Jameson, "Consumer Society," p. 119.

19. Jameson, "Consumer Society," p. 120.

20. "schizophrenia emerges from the failure of the infant to accede fully into the realm of speech and language," "Consumer Society," p. 118.

21. A further observation on schizophrenia is made in regard to the test. In the novel from which *Blade Runner* was adapted, Philip K. Dick, *Do Androids Dream of Electric Sheep?* (New York: Ballentine Books, 1982), a moral question arises from the possibility that humans might be "retired" by mistake. It is proved, in fact, that a certain "type" of humans respond to the test the same as do replicants. This type is the schizophrenic. Thus replicants and schizophrenics are "scientifically" proved to be the same.

22. Barthes, p. 77.

23. Michel Foucault, *The Archeology of Knowledge.* A. M. Sheridan Smith, trans. (New York: Pantheon, 1982), p. 7.

24. Foucault, p. 7.

25. Barthes, p. 76.

26. Barthes, p. 79.

27. Foucault, p. 6.

28. Barthes, p. 85.

29. The debate on questions of memory and history in postmodernism is well represented in the special issue on "Modernity and Post-Modernity" of *New German Critique* 33 (Fall 1984).

Kitsch archetypes of the Warrior Woman in *The Road Warrior* (1983) and the parodical Messiah in *Mad Max: Beyond Thunderdrome* (1985). Warner Bros. Stills courtesy of Jerry Ohlinger's Movie Materials.

Mick Broderick

Heroic Apocalypse: Mad Max, Mythology and the Millennium

Those of us who did *Mad Max I* were the unwitting servants of
the collective unconscious, we definitely were, and for someone who
was fairly mechanistic in his approach to life, for whom everything
conformed to the laws of physics and chemistry, it is quite confronting for me to be suddenly made aware of the workings of mythology and I'm in wonder of it.[1]

—George Miller

Examined from a mythological perspective the *Mad Max* trilogy may
offer a number of readings, but the one under scrutiny here regards
it as a reconstitution of archetypal tales of social decline and rebirth.[2]
Predominantly, it appears a postmodern recasting of the Judeo-Christian
myth of a messianic hero-saviour who annihilates an oppressive tyranny,
liberating via atonement an elect few into a new dimension of communal
harmony. The progression of the texts from the first to third feature,
like that of its hero, is one of allusion, increasing sophistication and
deliberate mythopoeic construction.[3]

When defining the postmodern, Jean-Francois Lyotard argues that
it has an "incredulity toward metanarratives. . . . The narrative function
is losing its functors, its great hero, its great dangers, its great voyages,
its great goal." Although Lyotard does not use "master narrative"
explicitly, Fredric Jameson and others have appropriated the term from
this primary text. Indeed, in his "Foreword" to Lyotard's monograph,
Jameson argues "narrative also means something like *teleology*. The
great master-narratives here are those that suggest that something
beyond capitalism is possible, something radically different; and they
also 'legitimate' the praxis whereby political militants seek to bring
that radically different future social order into being."[4]

In an attempt to discern the political "agenda" of the trilogy, this essay examines the theoretical writings of "myth" scholar Joseph Campbell in order to ascertain whether these films constitute a postmodern rupturing of "master narrative" or merely reinforce the existing, predominant social myth of the hero.

1. Eschatology and the Apocalyptic Millennia

> As an undercurrent of Western imagination, apocalypticism is always with us. Consider its part in such sudden surges of intellectual and artistic life in our century as modernism, and, in particular, expressionism; communism and fascism, the most powerful apocalyptic political currents of our time; the unwelcome beginnings of the nuclear era and the cold war; then the countercultural explosion of the 1960s with its fear of technology, its yearning to recover the natural, and its millennarian dreams of a new Heaven and a new Earth.[5]
>
> —Saul Friedlander

The notion of "apocalypse" has been bastardized and appropriated across many fields in contemporary Western thought, especially in popular culture during the latter half of this century.[6] It is a term used indiscriminately to connote and conflate, amongst others, notions of "anarchy," "chaos," "entropy," "nihilism," "catastrophe," and "doomsday," yet by removal from its original mytho-religious association it assumes a randomly cliched definition. Lois Parkinson Zamora has stressed, "the current use of the word apocalypse as a synonym for "disaster" or "cataclysm" is only half correct: the myth comprehends both cataclysm *and* millennium, tribulation *and* triumph, chaos *and* order, and it is the creative tension, the dialectic between these opposites that explains, in part, the myth's enduring relevance," which also recognizes a profound relationship between between eschatological insight and private fantasies of vengeance.[7]

Many ancient world mythologies describe the cataclysmic obliteration of humankind, often by global conflagration, hence Joseph Campbell's belief that all creation myths are essentially tragic, in view of their ultimate description of and preparation for the eventual abolition/rebirth of the universe.[8]

According to Harald Reiche, archaic concepts of decline and end, "based on pagan notions of declining world ages and imminent catastrophe, underwent successive modifications and attenuations. . . . The new beginning following on the apocalyptic phase would be neither cyclic nor reciprocating, but millennial in format."[9] Unlike the mythological pessimism of the tragic Greek cosmos, the linear historical frame of Judeo-Christian apocalyptic thought evolved out of a cultural response to persecution by external oppressors such as the Roman Empire. The biblical tradition, therefore, viewed historical passage/progression as a time of hope and imminent amelioration through messianic intervention, rather than the (self-fulfilling?) Classical idea of eventual, predetermined decline.

In the first two centuries AD, Christian apocalypse was reappropriated from the Jewish tradition (which dated back to 586 BC) ironically just as the Judaic interest began to wane due to decreasing social alienation. This transfer emphasizes the dynamic of a religious imperative to accept (and explain) the brutalizing periods of history as crises which may herald the new age, and thereby invest such times with hope.[10]

Debra Bergoffen has argued that there are two distinct traditions within this eschatological schema—the "prophetic" and "apocalyptic."[11] The prophetic stream suggests that history is not deterministic and that God's redemption of the fallen world is achieved only through the direct intervention of a human saviour. Prophetic discourse speaks of a *possible* future, not a necessary one, which is intrinsically unpredictable because it depends on the choices people make in the present. The apocalyptic, however, is decidedly deterministic, predicting God's destruction of the world and the salvation of the just as historically immutable, and that human choices account for history being evil.[12] For believers, the messianic age is one in which (historical) time itself is obliterated, and a new period created.

In both Jewish and Christian theology the apocalypse was a means by which to spiritually and psychologically overcome the immediate calamity of social persecution, imbued with the scriptural revelation that an end to the eon of oppression was at hand via the millennial rule of the hero-saviour, and with it oblivion and eternal damnation of his foes.

The thousand-year reign of peace and prosperity prophesied to accompany the "second coming" of Christ caused great excitement throughout Christendom with the approach of the year 1000.[13] Similarly, the catastrophic toll of Europe's Black Death, and the threat to Christianity by Islam (with its own brand of eschatological doctrine) revived apocalyptic fervor throughout the Middle Ages.[14]

Umberto Eco draws an analogy with this sensibility by aligning seminomad medieval society's journeys through hostile terrains with a broader sense of insecurity, relevant to then and now: "Insecurity is a key word: This feeling must be inserted into the picture of chiliastic anxieties: The world is about to end, a final catastrophe will close the millennium. The famous terrors of the year 1000 are only legendary—this has now been demonstrated—but throughout the tenth century there was a sneaking fear of the end . . . (except that toward the end of the millennium the psychosis was already past). As for our own time, the recurrent themes of atomic and ecological catastrophe suffice to indicate the various apocalyptic currents."[15]

Taken out of its context, therefore, the apocalyptic vision of the end of history, which encompasses the destruction of the universe as it is known, becomes merely a pessimistic prediction of the material destruction of a civilization often already perceived in (moral/physical) decay.[16] Devoid of any direct mythological hermeneutic, contemporary secular fears of impending global disaster are based on techno-logical/ecological estimates and projections with metaphors dredged out of pre-existing popular culture in order to grant expression to the imagery of the unthinkable.[17]

As John Wiley Nelson says, "it is undeniably that the doomsday side of apocalyptic eschatology has captured our imagination and has manifested itself in our popular forms. Thus, in apocalyptic eschatology, evil seems everywhere victorious; that which is good and decent can no longer hold its own."[18]

Contemporary quasi-religious authors such as Hal Lindsay are exemplary as popular apocalypticists, predicting nuclear conflagration as the prophesied "battle of Armageddon."[19] Currently a heightened apocalyptic sensibility seems omnipresent, especially amongst the new right evangelism of neo-Christian Fundamentalists eagerly awaiting the second millennia's completion.[20] Many exploit current geopolitical events, such as the Gulf War, as evidence of the foretold battle of Armageddon.

2. The Contemporary Mood

The landscapes of disaster carry a powerful symbolic charge, representing not only the summation of former mistakes but also the prospects for rebuilding. . . . Above all, Armageddon simplifies: questions of morality and responsibility may legitimately be set aside in favor of basic matters like survival and the perpetuation of the species. Inner strengths are confirmed by external emergencies.[21]

—Philip Strick

Just as there is a strong prior tradition of apocalyptic rendition in other arts, the cinematic antecedents of millennial beliefs can be traced

right back to the origins of film, usually represented by violent cosmological interventions in such films as *The Comet* (1910) or *End of the
World* (1916) or drawing on projected technological means for mass
destruction as in *The Airship Destroyer* (1909).[22] Similarly, between the
World Wars, apocalyptic fantasies like *Metropolis* (1926), *Deluge* (1933),
and *Things To Come* (1936) provided vicarious thrills and reactivated
chiliastic fears.

However, the *Mad Max* trilogy would seem to owe more to post-
World War II imagery of both ecological and nuclear holocausts. Indeed,
the marauding bikers of *Mad Max* closely resemble the ruthless pack
from *No Blade of Grass* (1970), whereas the basic scenario of *The Road
Warrior* re-works aspects of the *Ultimate Warrior* (1975) while employing
the Cormanesque touches of *Death Race 2000* (1975).[23] *Beyond Thunderdome* is explicitly in the post-nuclear category, drawing from *Lord of
the Flies* (1963), *The Bed Sitting Room* (1968) and many other genres,
especially the Western, as an application of Will Wright's structuralist
hero hierarchy demonstrates (see "Mythological Progression" below).

Correspondingly, John Wiley Nelson regards the Western as "the
high mass of American popular cultural drama . . . [which] is in both
form and substance essentially eschatological," and also apocalyptic:
"good and evil are simplistically defined and radically distinguished;
evil is judged irredeemable and thus justifiably and violently destroyed;
the final battle in which good is victorious is chaotic and disruptive rather
than transitional."[24] The trilogy's generic link with the Western is also
explored in Philip Strick's excellent *Films and Filming* analysis, "Future
Movies: Reading the Signs," which argues that "The range-riders of
the nuclear plains are the bikers, and since the days of *Easy Rider* they
have increasingly poached on the territory of the cowboy hero." Strick
also describes neo-cold war films such as *Red Dawn* (in which the US
is invaded by Soviet troops after surgical nuclear strikes) as anecdotally
exploring heroism within a context of Hollywood mythology—the re-
staging of Westerns and War movies.[25]

Like all good exploitation movies, the *Mad Max* features must
inherently exploit either generic formulae or *a priori* audience
expectations for them to be commercially successful. In this respect they
have already aligned themselves with postmodern concepts of pastiche,
bricolage and parody.[26] Strick commends the power of Kennedy-Miller's
vision with, "The impact of any image can be measured by its imitations,
and the influence of *Mad Max* is visible in an assortment of rip-offs,"
evident in films like *Battletruck, Cafe Flesh, Survival Zone, Endgame,
The New Barbarians, Stryker, 2019: After the Fall of New York,
Exterminators of the Year 3000, Yor: Hunter from the Future, Metal*

Storm, Last Exterminators, City Limits, The Load Warrior, America 3000, In the Aftermath, Lunar Madness, Rats: Night of Terror, Eliminator 2000, Exterminator 2000, Hell Comes to Frogtown, Robot Holocaust, Cherry 2000, Creepzoids, Badlands 2005, Steel Dawn, World Gone Wild, Desert Warrior, and *Cyborg.*[27]

Apart from the countless imitators, the *Mad Max* sequels ostensibly explore their themes of "survivability" and the nuclear holocaust as a *fait accompli*, obviously a still potent and prevailing sensibility which frames so many of these rip-offs, coinciding with the 1980s wave of films concerning nuclear war (*The Day After, Testament, One Night Stand, The Dead Zone, Wargames, The Terminator, Dreamscape, Letters From A Dead Man, Miracle Mile,* etc).[28]

Apocalyptic mythology, usually embodied in a terminal nuclear metaphor, has seeped into the very *zeitgeist* of contemporary cinema, making some sort of reference or allusion virtually *de rigueur* (e.g. the "road-biker of the apocalypse" and *Dr. Strangelove* homage in *Raising Arizona* or the intertextual cameos by nuclear movie mutants in *Weird Science*). The influences can be traced from the modern horror film (especially George Romero's trilogy of irradiated "Living Dead"—itself spawning countless zombie imitations and the original film being remade twice within the last 18 months),[29] to the transcendental (parody?) fantasies of extraterrestrial or divine salvation ("cult" films: *UFOria, Repo Man, Static*; "mainstream": *Close Encounters, ET, Raiders of the Lost Ark,* and the entire *Superman* series), or via the recent "teen cycle" celebrating a neo-conservative ethic of "yuppie/ultra" materialism (*Weird Science, Back to the Future*), arguably as a denial of nuclear fatalism which is only occasionally recounted overtly (as in *The Unbelievable Truth* or in the abject nihilism of *River's Edge* with its portrayal of modern youth dispossessed of a future), and retrospective adolescent fears recounted for contemporary audiences (*Desert Bloom, Great Balls of Fire*).[30]

3. Mythological Progression

> The composite hero of the monomyth is a personage of exceptional gifts. Frequently he is honored by his society, frequently unrecognized or disdained. He and/or the world in which he finds himself suffers from a symbolic deficiency . . . in apocalyptic vision the physical and spiritual life of the whole earth can be represented as fallen, or on the point of falling, into ruin.[31]
>
> —Joseph Campbell

In Joseph Campbell's influential *The Hero with a Thousand Faces*, the monomyth is thus defined: "The standard path of the mythological adventure of the hero is a magnification of the formula represented in the rites of passage: *separation-initiation-return*" (p. 30).[32] Clearly, the *Mad Max* trilogy follows this path by foregrounding the evolution of Max as hero—from his rejection of the "outside world" due to personal tragedy in the first feature; his wanderings, trials and tests in the hostile wilderness of both sequels; through to his individual (if not yet communal) reconciliation with his "humane" self in *Beyond Thunderdome*. Campbell asserts the passage of the hero is fundamentally inward, "into depths where obscure resistances are overcome, and long lost, forgotten powers are revivified, to be made available for the transfiguration of the world" (p. 29).

Popular tales represent the heroic action as physical, whereas the "higher religions" show the deed to be moral, Campbell argues. The heroic exploits of Max adopt a discourse of both the material and the spiritual. It is precisely this rich embroidery of seemingly disparate mythological narratives that engenders the trilogy's cross-cultural appeal—an appeal obvious in the proximity of the *Mad Max* films to Western narratives, readily identified by comparison with Will Wright's structuralist study of Western heroic myth, *Sixguns and Society*,

Mad Moses and the postmodern monomyth: Mel Gibson in *Mad Max Beyond Thunderdrome* (1985). Warner Bros. Still courtesy of Jerry Ohlinger's Movie Materials.

especially his hierarchy of the "Vengeance Variation of the Classical Plot":

> The villains harm both the hero and society, but society can do nothing about it. The institutions of justice are inadequate to correct the wrong or punish the guilty. If retribution is to be exacted, the hero must do it himself, alone. In this sequence the hero, as individual, asserts his independence from the group. Since society is weak and unable to fulfil its obligations to its members, the individual must rely on himself if justice is to be done . . . In seeking revenge, the hero becomes very much like the men he is chasing. He becomes a skilled gunfighter, and he ignores or breaks the laws.[33]

In *The Road Warrior*, the past of the vengeful hero is established briefly in the opening sequence. As Wright points out, "Often, indeed, the initial sequences are not present in the film at all: the hero's past in society, the harm dome to him, and his reputation as a gunfighter are described in the dialogue rather than dramatized."[34] In both sequels Max is deliberately mythologized through oral history, as their epilogues reveal—descriptions which assume the rhetoric of prophetic discourse similar in tone to the revelatory biblical dreams and visions foretelling apocalypse.

Wright argues that while intent on vengeance, the hero is confronted by a member of society who points out his individualistic, antisocial behavior.[35] After this, the hero sooner or later abandons his hatred and his search for revenge, a feature aptly demonstrated by the calculated verbal abuse from Pappagallo, the leader of the petrol-drilling community in *The Road Warrior*, and the curt rejection of Max's patriarchal authority by desert nomad Savannah Nix in *Beyond Thunderdome*.

By his initial abandonment of society at the end of *Mad Max* and refusal of what Campbell describes as "the call" (Max rejects his Captain's desire to give society back its "heroes"), true to the monomyth, the first encounter of the hero-journey is with a "protective figure," such as *The Road Warrior's* Feral Kid and the "trickster" Gyro Captain, who "tests" Max's mind and body (reflexes).[36] In *Thunderdome*, the helpers are Pigkiller, who acts as a guide and "Ferryman" out of Bartertown's Underworld, and Savannah, the protector ("Virgin-Cosmic Mother") who leads Max out of the desert wilderness and saves him from certain death.[37] What such figures represent, according to Campbell, are the "benign, protecting power of destiny," all of which suggests the inevitability of a predetermined future.

This persistent reading, indeed celebration by Campbell, raises some uncomfortable questions about his advocacy of an unseen, relentless and preordained cosmic scheme which exerts force onto unwitting players. The absence of any real self-determining space afforded the hero in Campbell's theory can be read as highly reactionary.

Campbell's rhetoric relishing the hero's individuality and rejection of the social, and unquestioningly following one's destiny ("bliss") where might equates right, borders on the proto-fascist. Significantly, the popularity of Max and, in particular, the international success of *The Road Warrior*, suggests a nostalgic yearning for heroic narrative at a time when the central protagonist is most ideologically moribund.

Quite often in mythology the journey-quest of the hero may lead to social inertia rather than rebirth, with the hero failing to pass on his knowledge or skills to the community. Campbell argues "the norm of the monomyth, requires that the hero shall now begin the labor of bringing the runes of wisdom . . . back into the kingdom of humanity, where the boon may redound to the renewing of the community, the nation, the world. . . . But the responsibility has frequently been refused" (p. 193), evident in the revenge motive closing the first film, and Max's "contract" rejection of the besieged community in *The Road Warrior*, which portrays him simply retreating further into an alienated and self-destructive sense of autonomy.

In keeping with his messianic construction, however, Max's purgative role is best outlined in Campbell where "the mythological hero is the champion not of things become but of things becoming; the dragon to be slain by him is precisely the monster of the status quo: Holdfast, the keeper of the past. . . . The tyrant is proud, and therein lies his [*sic*] doom. He is proud because he thinks of his strength as his own; thus he is in the clown role, as a mistaker of shadow for substance; it is his destiny to be tricked" (p. 337). In this strategy, the reactionary (i.e. anti-millennial) hegemonies of *The Road Warrior* are Humungus and his marauders, representing the decaying remnants of an outmoded society, just as Bartertown later becomes the (il)logical extension of a post-nuclear capitalist microcosm attempting survival by synthesizing earlier Western modes. Symbolic of *Beyond Thunderdome's* entire aesthetic and narrative mode, Bartertown is essentially one enormous act of *bricolage*. Its postmodern frisson is also closely aligned with Lyotard, where "capitalism inherently possesses the power to derealize familiar objects, social roles, and institutions to such a degree that the so-called realistic representations can no longer evoke reality except as nostalgia or mockery, as an occasion for suffering rather than for satisfaction."[38]

Other "proud tyrants" are personified by Nightrider (who loses his life after failing at "Chicken of the Road"), Bubba who over-confidently drops his guard when he fells Max ("I know what I'm doing," he tells

Toecutter) in *Mad Max*, and Aunty Entity in *Thunderdome*, whose complacent dominion is usurped by an Underworld rebellion. As a trickster-hero, Max the pursued becomes pursuer (of Toecutter's gang), just as the Humungus is fooled into following the wrong group of vehicles and, miraculously, Max returns from Gulag to destroy Bartertown and liberate his allies.

Ultimately, the status of Max as a redemptive, mythological hero is confirmed by the act of his being the unwitting decoy of the Humungus in *Road Warrior*, and then *deliberate* decoy-sacrifice which enables the lost tribe to escape Aunty Entity in *Beyond Thunderdome*.[39] Both are catalytic interventions permitting the (material/spiritual) rebirth of two specific communal microcosms—one via the liberation of petroleum, the other, innocence, youth and fertility. Campbell asserts, "The effect of the successful adventure of the hero is the unlocking and release again of the flow of life into the body of the world" (p. 40).

Apart from abundant Christian parable, the trilogy clearly draws from the Classical deliverer-hero mythology of antiquity as well. Hence, in *Thunderdome*, Aunty Entity is akin to the inflated ego/"tyrant-monster" of Campbell's depiction of King Minos—mutual greed bringing downfall after both have been heroes to the societies they have helped rejuvenate.[40] In this sense Master-Blaster can be read as the symbiosis of Daedalus and the Minotaur, the creator of the underworld labyrinth and the monster who lives there. Max, correspondingly, is constructed as Theseus, the hero/slayer who enters the city from outside, whereas Savannah becomes Ariadne who assists Max in destroying the old regime, with Master/Daedalus providing the means (methane propelled rail truck) by which they escape the labyrinth. At this point *Beyond Thunderdome* conforms to Lyotard's notion of the prevailing Narrative of Legitimation of Knowledge in which "The subject of the [narrative] is humanity as the hero of liberty. All peoples have a right to science. If the social subject is not already the subject of scientific knowledge, it is because that has been forbidden by priests and tyrants. The right to science must be reconquered."[41]

After Max escapes from Bartertown, destroying it apocalyptically in the process, he is engaged in what Campbell describes as "the magic flight." Consider the following:

> If the hero in his triumph wins the blessing of the goddess or the god and is then explicitly commissioned to return to the world with some elixir for the restoration of society, the final stage of his adventure is supported by all the powers of his supernatural patron. On the other hand, if the trophy [Master and the freedom train] has been attained against the opposition of its guardian [Aunty]

... then the last stage of the mythological round becomes a lively, often comical pursuit [e.g. the antics of Ironbar and mimicry of the mute boy].[42] This flight may be complicated by marvels of magical obstruction [The "stick-up" by the Gyro Captain's son] and evasion [Max's decoy ride for the plane's departure]. (pp. 196-7)

This intercessory act by Max in *Thunderdome* heralds not only rebirth for the hero, but for the entire world—a return of the cosmogonic cycle— but as in Christian myth, the sacrifice of self means Max is unable to immediately partake of its fruits.[43] Hence, in opposition to the *ironic* hero deed in *The Road Warrior* of driving the tanker which permits escape and establishment of a future tribe ruled by the Feral Kid (related via an unexpected mythopoeic oral epilogue), his act of virtual apotheosis which closes the third film is reified for the audience by witnessing its result (i.e. Savannah's oral history, now a new world-mother, nursing an infant before the tribe populating the skeletal remains of Sydney).

4. Predeterminism and Judeo-Christian Myth

If you look at it a little more you will see that the hero of mythology is often, though not always, the reluctant servant of the greater purpose.[44]

—George Miller

The alignment of the trilogy's narrative strategy of predetermination (overtly to the point of having characters "revealing" the mythic scenario in their closing narrations) is fundamental to the ideology of apocalyptic intervention by the messianic deliverer-hero.

In *Mad Max*, Nightrider dementedly challenges "the bronze" to send in their best, crying "I am the chosen one; the mighty hand of vengeance sent down to strike at the un(road)worthy," and, naturally, the apoca- lyptic monster as challenging anti-christ must be slain (after others have failed) by Max the deliverer-hero, to usurp the authority of the "false prophet"/poseur. Max confronts the Nightrider literally head-on, defeating him at "Chicken of the Road," causing him to crash into a wall of petrol drums, exploding significantly in a fiery apocalyptic mushroom cloud. Not only is "Chicken" the favored game most often employed by nuclear strategists to describe the arms race in relation to deterrence, but it expressly underlies a suicidal nihilism exhibited by "atomic age" adolescents dating back to *Rebel Without a Cause* and *The Young Savages*. It also serves to neatly illustrate (via presumably unconscious, yet intrinsic metaphor) the precise, temporal logic of Judeo-

Christian philosophy: the headlong race down a finite linear path which accelerates until its anticipated teleological event—collision with the eschatological moment, which ushers in the apocalypse.

Mirroring the terminal nihilism of Nightrider, Toecutter's gang are constructed as destructive forces opposing social rebirth both metaphorically and materially. One of the film's womb motifs is represented in the customizing of motor vehicles, such as the one covered internally with lamb's wool, which the bikers penetrate with phallic tools before violating the couple.[45] The rapes are only suggested, yet the accompanying fade to a close-up of a black crow evokes a medieval allusion (e.g. the paintings of Breughel and Bosch) of sinister foreboding (just as ravens consolidated the revelatory apocalyptic theme in Hitchcock's *The Birds*). Significantly, the biblical tenor is also emphasised by the police radio description of the attack as "incident at wee Jerusalem."

Even during the revenge phase after Max calculatingly dispatches other gang members, there is an undercurrent of payback's relentless, cosmic logic. He leaves two family snap-shots on Toecutter's bike (similar to the Air-Cav death cards deposited on the NVA corpses in *Apocalypse Now* to "let Charlie know who did this"), identifying and announcing himself in a challenge which simultaneously ominates the remaining members' doom.

In both *The Road Warrior* and *Beyond Thunderdome* the complexity of narrative reliance upon a motif of predeterminism becomes more apparent. For example, on his return to the Gyro Captain's copter in the former film, Max discovers a marauder dead from snake bite. Having himself escaped precisely this fate/"trial" earlier, he goes through the dead man's pockets, finds a die and casts it away. For Max, the gamble of life is immutably prearranged—he merely operates within the confines of its inscrutable contingency. Even if unrecognized by its central protagonist/pawn, the cosmos awaits (and occasionally prompts) his preordained return to conscious acts of altruism, which recommences his journey to apotheosis.

Later, when someone protests about Max's departure from the compound, Pappagallo replies that, "he fulfilled his contract; he's an honorable man," demonstrating the community's foundation in a Protestant work ethic. Pappagallo's sense of fatalistic resignation is subtly contrasted to Max's assertive confidence. During this scene Pappagallo distractedly toys with a small hour glass and contemplates his hazardous future (symbolizing the irrevocable progression of the cosmological order), knowing that he will have to drive the decoy rig. When Max offers his services instead, realizing that to remain at the compound would be fatal, he proclaims ironically, "I'm the best chance you've got." Pappagallo, however, understands all too well that Max is the *only* chance he's got.[46]

For its foes, *The Road Warrior* draws heavily from both historical, cultural and biblical mythology, especially those forces viewed to obstruct Judeo-Christian socio-religious amelioration. For instance, the Humungus is introduced by a comic MC (similar to the ringmaster-compere of *Thunderdome*) as "the Lord of the Wasteland, the Ayatollah of Rock and Roller." The description emphasizes the cultural amorality and "otherness" of the marauders, since the Ayatollah epithet equates Islam as the terrible historical and contemporary foe of Western Judeo-Christian (significantly, petro-chemically dependant) capitalism.[47] Also the spartan attire of Humungus evokes a gladiatorial association reminiscent of the Roman Empire's persecution of the Judeo-Christian tradition (the Romanesque motif is rendered further in the post-punk neo-centurion garb of the warrior-class guarding Bartertown). Similarly, the rendering of sexuality outside of traditional, monogamous Christian mores is acquainted with defilement and perversion.[48]

As Max drives the rig through the Humungus camp, the mute mohawk Wes and others are shown grooming themselves, applying war paint before battle, like indigenous tribes or American Red Indians. There is no immediately visible technological or social means of support within their camp, and like the *Lord of the Flies* pig's head, several ram skulls are totemically mounted atop sticks, suggesting a pagan primitivism. Similarly, during that evening a number of overlapping vignettes depict the Humungus violently inciting his men with war dances, taunting their captive prisoners who are spread-eagle on giant wooden crosses (suggesting martyred Jews and Christians).[49]

Just as the ambiguous finale to *Mad Max* leaves Johnny Boy with only minutes to hack off his foot before Max's incendiary device ignites, some marauders enter the abandoned oil compound which has been wired (like Max's car) with a delayed booby trap, effectively annihilating the remnants of the old world through a "scorched earth policy." The explosive pyrotechnics are viewed from an olympian vantage, revealing an enormous, apocalyptic mushroom cloud which covers the desert, metaphorically prefiguring the global nuclear conflagration that occurs prior to *Beyond Thunderdome*.[50]

By the third feature, the admixture of biblical themes and predeterminism is well advanced. Inside the mud-wall fortifications, Bartertown takes on the appearance of a curious amalgam of Roger Vadim's decadent city in *Barbarella* populated by Felliniesque characters, adopting Old Testament imagery of Sodom, Gomorrah and Jericho (Max later warns the children not to venture there, describing the town as a "sleaze-pit"). When Aunty asks Max who he is, he replies: "I was a cop, a driver." Bemused, she retorts: "Well, how the world turns. One day cock of the walk, next a feather-duster. . . . Do you know who I was? *Nobody*. Except on the 'day after.' I was still alive. This nobody had a chance to be somebody. *So much for history*" (my emphasis). Interestingly, it is Aunty who employs the rhetoric of the apocalypticist, acting as false prophet, and it is ultimately the task of Max to destroy her credibility and replenish the Earth with a new vitality. Therefore, earlier, when she offers him some of her fruit (symbolizing Eve as "temptress," the agent of man's biblical fall) he perceives the gift for the deceit it is, matching his foe's treachery by drawing a concealed knife to ward off his attackers.[51]

Similarly, on leaving Underworld after discovering Blaster's acoustic Achilles heel, Pigkiller asks him: "Who are you? Who are you working for?", to which Max replies: "Nobody."[52] But as one of Bartertown's oppressed populace Pigkiller recognizes the face of cosmic destiny, even if Max does not. "Ah, I can feel the dice are rolling," he enthuses, embracing an anticipation of predetermined messianic salvation,

Shane in the Nuclear Wasteland; now it's Max and the Feral Kid in *The Road Warrior* (1982). Warner Bros. Still courtesy Museum of Modern Art.

heralding Max as the Saviour. Later, after Max refuses to kill Blaster and is prevented from leaving Thunderdome's ring, in an interesting reversal of the "free Barabbas/crucify him" New Testament chants, Pigkiller and the Gyro Captain incite the crowd to *support* Max by turning Aunty's Law against her, shouting: "Two men enter, one man leaves," engendering a popular sense of indignity and revolt at the Law not being justly administered.

Ironically, it is apparent that randomness is the logic of the Law which binds Bartertown together. When Max questions the nature of Thunderdome and its weapons, he is told: "Anything is possible. Chance will decide." Similarly, the shaman/compere explains the aleatoric concept of the Wheel: "All our lives hang by a thread. Now we got a man waiting for sentence, but ain't it the truth: you take your chances with the Law. Justice is only a roll of the dice, a flip of the coin, a turn of the Wheel."[53] Yet even as Max is forced to try his hand at chance it becomes the literal vehicle to ensure his hero-journey of liberation. Max spins "Gulag," which leads to his banishment and exile from Bartertown. Wearing a bizarre carnival mask, sitting bound and backward atop a horse (resembling Jodorowsky in the surreal, apocalyptic Western *El Topo*, 1971), he is sent out into the desert to die, but as a mythological hero, he is helped through this trial by supernatural aids in the guise of his monkey and "earth mother/protector" Savannah.[54]

It is during the mythopoeic origin story related at the lost tribe's camp that Max faces a messianic hero tale seemingly tailor-made for him. Before a large, primitive wall mural, Savannah recounts the departure of the elders: "*and then out of the nothing they looked back, and Captain Walker hollered 'Wait! One of us will come.'* And somebody did come." They then display an effigy of Max as Captain Walker, freshly painted onto the cave tableau, arms outstretched resembling a crucified Christ. This scene consolidates the truly millennial thrust of *Thunderdome's* narrative, for it positions Max as *returning* to free the elect (duplicating the Christian belief in the "second coming," as Max is destined to be both reborn to society at large and within himself).

Although Max initially rejects such suggestions, he eventually becomes the willing (if begrudging) protector of the children. In one sequence, Max is shown carrying an exhausted child on his shoulders, whose teddy-bear is attached to a stick crucifix above him, which connotes a humanitarian "change of heart" in Max and situates him symbolically as a journeyman/protector-hero (reminiscent of St. Christopher carrying the infant as a symbol of rebirth and renewed hope of civilization into the world). The motif also places Max antithetical to both Master-Blaster (Blaster, himself a child, literally supports the decadence of the old world, personified in Master's technological complicity with Aunty), and the sadism of Ironbar who has an Asian death mask atop his shoulders.[55]

Max rekindles his "hero-heart" by the rescue of Savannah in the desert, without thought of profit in his action. Through this action he has now become the vessel of divine protection and guidance for the lost tribe to rebuild humanity. Yet it is the final sequence of "flight" which unifies the trilogy's evolution in an apocalyptic strategy. As Max and the children liberate Pigkiller and Master from the Underworld, reversing their earlier exchange, Max asks Pigkiller enthusiastically, "What's the plan?" to which he replies anarchically that there is none, symbolically demonstrating the crucial aspect of apocalyptic eschaton— the radical rupturing of the old, linear cosmological order. As their methane propelled truck leaves the subterranean labyrinth it demolishes the fuel production, destroying both Underworld and creating a chaotic conflagration above in Bartertown, evoking a suitable flavor of apocalyptic wrath similar to the demise of decadent Old Testament cities.[56]

Inside the speeding truck while Master is packing all of his treasures from the pre-holocaust days, one of the tribal kids removes an alarm clock which under inquisitive shaking rings loudly. Another child abruptly smashes it, again emphasizing the violent transition to apocalyptic eschaton—the death of time. To strengthen the metaphor, the children are shown the application for their "sonic" (a old warped vinyl record) placed on Master's gramophone. It proves to be a bi-lingual teaching disk, asking the listener to repeat after it, "Good Morning. Where are you going? I am going home." Confused, the children comply, unaware that they are being taught anew, this time from the beginning.

The disruption of the "magic flight" by the Gyro Captain's son inadvertently leads the group to escape in a hidden plane. To enable their successful flight/rebirth Max selflessly leaves the plane and rides ahead, clearing a runway space sufficient for the others to exit. Finally, Max arrives at the point where he has consciously and willingly accepted his predestined role of sacrificial saviour; one which he deliberately rejected in *Mad Max*, and which *The Road Warrior* unwittingly served to rehearse/prepare him for.

Although Max is left at the end of *Thunderdome* with "his consciousness having succumbed, the unconscious nevertheless supplies its own balances, and he is born back into the world from which he came. Instead of holding to and saving his ego, as in the pattern of the magic flight, he loses it, and yet, through grace, it is returned" (*Hero with a Thousand Faces*, p. 216). The further role and adventure of the monomythic hero, Campbell maintains, is to bring that world-shattering knowledge to the rest of civilization. His journey therefore is incomplete and perhaps this is why Aunty ambivalently grants him freedom at the end of *Thunderdome* for she recognizes, as the cosmogonic cycle and the monomyth relate, like Classical heroes (e.g. king Minos or Oedipus) "The hero of yesterday becomes the tyrant of tomorrow, unless he crucifies himself today" (*Hero with a Thousand Faces*, p. 353).

As has been demonstrated, the *Mad Max* trilogy closely conforms to, if not reduplicates, the monomythic cycle outlined by Joseph Campbell. It would be foolish, however, to reduce its signifying status to the level of myth alone, as it would be to ignore the movies' enormous aesthetic-stylistic potency. From *Mad Max* to *Beyond Thunderdome* we can readily observe a consistency in their developing narrative ideology, one which overtly conforms to pre-existing apocalyptic metatexts of social legitimation, yet may simultaneously deflate this via an ironic artistic strategy of *bricolage*.[57] Whether or not the latter form will effectively deconstruct the former, or aid and abet its project is not quite clear, but certainly George Miller's trilogy has provided a fertile cultural arena for applying a litmus test to evolving paradigms of postmodernity.

Notes

1. Miller quoted in Sue Mathews, *35mm Dreams* (Melbourne: Penguin, 1984), p. 34.

2. For illuminating critiques, see Jon Stratton, "What Made Mad Max Popular? *Art and Text* 9: 37-56, Ross Gibson, "Yondering," *Art & Text* 19: 24-33 and Christopher Sharrett, "The Hero as Pastiche: Myth, Male Fantasy, and Simulacra in *Mad Max* and *The Road Warrior*," *Journal of Popular Film and Television* 13.2 (1985): 80-91.

3. Miller has admitted being greatly influenced by the writings of Joseph Campbell; see his interview by Mathews, p. 233.

4. See Jean-Francois Lyotard, *The Postmodern Condition: A Report on Knowledge* (Manchester, UK: Manchester University Press, 1986), p. xxiv. For Jameson, p. xix.

5. Saul Friedlander, *Visions of Apocalypse: End or Rebirth* (New York: Holmes and Meier, 1985), pp. 3-4. Norman Cohn also argues Nazi and Communist ideologies represent apocalyptic visions of final salvation, either by the death of capitalism replaced by the classless society, or fantasies of the Thousand-Year Reich; see *The Pursuit of the Millennium* (Fairlawn, NJ: Essential Books, 1957), pp. xv and 307.

6. Apocalypse literally means "pertaining to revelation or disclosure," hence the final book of the Bible is Revelation.

7. L. P. Zamora, *The Apocalyptic Vision in America* (Bowling Green, OH: Bowling Green University Press, 1982), p. 4.

8. Several examples are cited in Joseph Campbell, *The Hero with a*

Thousand Faces (Princeton. NJ: Princeton University Press, 1973), pp 261-265 and 374-378. See also Mike Perlman, "When Heaven and Earth Collapse: Myths of the End of the World," in Robert Bosnak et al., *Facing Apocalypse* (Dallas, TX: Spring Publications, 1987), pp. 171-195, and Miracea Eliade, *From Primitives to Zen* (London: Collins, 1977), chs. 2 and 4.

9. Harald A. T. Reiche, "The Archaic Heritage: Myths of Decline and End in Antiquity," in *Visions of Apocalypse, op. cit.*, pp. 21-43.

10. "Like the Jews, the Christians suffered oppression and responded to it by affirming ever more vigorously, to the world and to themselves, their faith in the imminence of the messianic age in which their wrongs would be righted and their enemies cast down. Not surprisingly, the way in which they imagined the great transformation also owed much to the Jewish apocalypses, some of which had indeed a wider circulation amongst Christians than amongst Jews." Cohn, *op. cit.*, p. 7.

11. Debra Bergoffen, "The Apocalyptic Meaning of History" in *The Apocalyptic Vision in America, op. cit.*, pp. 11-35.

12. Using this schema the narratives of, for example, *The Dead Zone* and *The Terminator* can be read as prophetic and apocalyptic respectively. Both employ messianic heroes—a psychic in the former and a post-holocaust soldier in the latter—who "reveal" future nuclear wars to the audience whilst in dream states.

13. This was due greatly to the pronouncement of official church doctrine. Writing early in the fifth century, St. Augustine propounded in his *The City of God* "that the Book of Revelation was to be understood as a spiritual allegory; as for the Millennium, that had begun with the birth of Christianity and was fully realized in the Church." Cohn, *op. cit.*, p. 14.

14. For Islamic examples see Norman O. Brown, "The Apocalypse of Islam," *Social Text* 83-84 (Winter date): 155-171; for others, see Norman Cohn, *op. cit.* and Amos Funkenstein, "A Schedule for the End of the World" in *Visions of Apocalypse, op. cit.*, pp. 52 and 57.

15. Umberto Eco, "The Return of the Middle Ages," *Travels in Hyperreality* (London: Picador, 1986), p. 79.

16. Fredric Jameson and Jean Baudrillard are fine examples of contemporary post-structuralist theorists who often employ apocalyptic discourse and metaphor in their writings.

17. For an insightful analysis, see John Wiley Nelson, "The Apocalyptic Vision in American Popular Culture" in *The Apocalyptic Vision in America, op. cit.*, pp. 154-182.

18. Nelson, p. 160.

19. See Hal Lindsay, *The Late Great Planet Earth*.

20. See Frank Kermode, "Apocalypse and the Modern," *Visions of Apocalypse, op. cit.*, p. 87. Ironically, conservative Christian sentiments may actually inform the very persona of Mad Max, as one Australian media commentator's acerbic wit demonstrated: "in our recent Federal Elections, Mel Gibson support[ed] a Christian Fundamentalist, Law and Order candidate to the far right of Premier Joh. Mel, the star of such monstrous pieces of mayhem as the *Mad Max* movies and, now, *Lethal Weapon*, mounted

a soapbox to protest the unhealthy tendencies in modern society, thumping the tub over the need to return to the old-fashioned values of the Christian family. Again and again, the intellect of an actor is inversely proportional to the size of their talent." Phillip Adams in *Weekend Australian Magazine*, August 8-9, 1987: 2.

21. Philip Strick, *Science Fiction Movies* (London: Gallery Press, 1979), p. 83.

22. *Visions of Apocalypse, op. cit.*, chs. 5 and 10.

23. For an insightful discussion of the post-apocalyptic status of the first two *Mad Max* films, see the interview with director George Miller in Danny Peary, ed., *Screen Flights, Screen Fantasies* (Garden City, NY: Dolphin Books, 1984), p. 281.

24. Nelson, pp. 165-66. This area of analysis has been largely ignored yet examples are abundant. For instance, consider the "Four Horsemen" metaphors in the climactic battles of both *Gunfight at the O.K. Corral* and the technological/generic apocalypse of *The Wild Bunch*, or the anti-hero as anti-Christ in *High Plains Drifter*.

25. Philip Strick, "Range Riders of the Nuclear Plains," *Films and Filming*, May 1985: 9.

26. Christopher Sharrett's substantial article "The Hero as Pastiche," *op. cit.*, explores many of the postmodern themes outlined above.

27. Whilst not an exhaustive list, this should at least indicate the international generic impact of the *Mad Max* series during the Eighties. Even 1980s television developed series clearly influenced by the *Mad Max* post-holocaust mise-en-scène, evident in *The Highwayman* and *Max Headroom*, let alone the scores of apocalyptic milieux present in music video.

28. Even in an era of Glasnost in which both Superpowers celebrate the end of the cold war, to date in the 90s the post-nuclear holocaust landscape remains a ubiquitous location. For a more comprehensive view, see my revised and expanded *Nuclear Movies* (Jefferson, NC: Mcfarland & Co., 1991).

29. The resurgence of the "living dead" zombie genre in the 70s and 80s draws upon biblical prophecies of resurrected dead in apocalyptic battles, often explicitly linked to radiation, mutation and nuclear war. In a recent article Jane Caputi cites the correlation between Robert Jay Lifton's psychological insights into the atomic age, evident in "psychic numbing," principally via Romero's *Night of the Living Dead*. Caputi's analysis is fine as far as it goes, but she fails to consider the enormous sub-genre of films which have overtly as well as metaphorically aligned apocalyptic fears of nuclear technologies with zombism. Contemporary filmmakers were undoubtedly exposed to these over the past five decades, dating back from pre-Hiroshima films like *Batman* (1943), to *Zombies of the Stratosphere* (1952), *Creature with the Atom Brain*, (1955), *Plan 9 From Outer Space* (1956) and *I Eat Your Skin* (1964) to name a few. Cf.: "Films of the Nuclear Age," *Journal of Popular Film and Television*, Winter 1988: 100-107.

30. See Robin Wood's excellent work examining the overt apocalyptic tenor of the horror genre in his book *Hollywood: From Vietnam to Reagan*.

Also Sarah R. Kozloff, "Superman as Saviour: Christian Allegory in the Superman Movies," *Journal of Popular Film and Television* 9.2 (1981): 78-82; Andrew Britton, "Blissing Out: The Politics of Reaganite Entertainment," *Movie* 31-32 (1985): 1-42; and Hugh Ruppersburg, "The Alien Messiah in Recent Science Fiction Films," *Journal of Popular Film and Television*, Winter 1987: 159-166. On adolescent responses to an expected nuclear war, see S. K. Escalona, "Growing Up with the Threat of Nuclear War," *American Journal of Orthopsychiatry*, October 1982: 600-607; M. Schwebel, "Effects of the Nuclear War Threat on Children and Teenagers," *American Journal of Orthopsychiatry*, October 1982: 608-618; and Richard L. Zeigenhaft, "Students Surveyed About Nuclear War," *Bulletin of the Atomic Scientists*, February 1985: 26-27.

31. Joseph Campbell, *The Hero With a Thousand Faces*, p. 36. All further numbered quotes are from this edition.

32. The George Lucas *Star Wars* trilogy was reportedly influenced by Campbell's writings on hero myth.

33. Will Wright, *Sixguns and Society* (Berkeley: University of California Press, 1977), pp. 155-156.

34. Wright, p. 157.

35. Wright, p. 158.

36. The snake wielding Gyro Captain's role becomes more problematic in *Beyond Thunderdome*, from "trickster" to "journeyman to the afterworld" of post-nuked Sydney. Campbell indicates, "Protective and dangerous, motherly and fatherly at the same time, this supernatural principal of guardianship and direction unites in itself all the ambiguities of the unconscious—thus signifying the support of our conscious personality by that other, larger system, but also the inscrutability of the guide that we are following, to the peril of all our rational ends" (p. 73).

37. Savannah Nix also represents the archetypal paragon of woman, an idealized recollection of his murdered wife Jessie (and in opposition to Aunty Entity's personification of the "temptress"), "she is the world creatrix, ever mother, ever virgin" (p. 114). "For she is the incarnation of the promise of perfection; the soul's assurance that, at the conclusion of its exile in a world of inadequacies, the bliss that was once known will be known again: the comforting, the nourishing, the 'good mother'—young and beautiful— who was known to us, and even tasted, in the remotest past" (p. 111). Just as significantly, she also signifies both the legendary "lost tribe" of Israel, prophesied to join with the messiah in his final apocalyptic struggle, as well as the nomadic troupes of believers awaiting the return of their saviour, akin to the chiliastic pilgrims of medieval Europe.

38. Lyotard, p. 74. See also "Style as Bricolage" in Dick Hebdige, *Subculture: The Meaning of Style* (London: Methuen, 1984), pp. 102-106.

39. For Miller, "that is when Max begins to be, in the classic sense, heroic." Interviewed by Mathews, p. 251.

40. It is the ego challenge to Aunty's rule, i.e. the methane embargo imposed by Master-Blaster, that aggravates her. Master cuts the power to Bartertown until she reluctantly proclaims over loudspeakers to all that

"Master-Blaster runs Bartertown." Master is an ambiguous figure, like Daedalus, who according to Campbell "in the service of the sinful king [Aunty Entity], was the brain behind the horror of the labyrinth, [but] quite as readily can serve the purposes of freedom" (p. 24). See also G. S. Kirk, *The Nature of Greek Myths* (Middlesex: Penguin, 1979), pp. 152-156, and Robert Graves, *The Greek Myths*, Vol. 1 (Middlesex: Penguin, 1985), pp. 292-370.

41. Lyotard, p. 31.

42. For an example of Aunty's chase, refer to the "Taliesin" myth in Campbell, p. 198. Obviously, the magical flight structure is equally important in the two earlier films.

43. Campbell, p. 259.

44. Quoted in Mathews, p. 245.

45. The suggested homosexual rape of the man and (mock?) gay antics of the bikers is a precursor to the legion of Mad Max rip-offs temporally located in the future after a nuclear war which exploit this trope. In films such as *Exterminators of the Year 3,000*, the narrative's homophobic ideology is more clearly drawn, with marauding gangs deliberately out to destroy heterosexual survivors as a means of bringing about the demise of the species. See my "Surviving Armageddon: Beyond the Imagination of Disaster," Working Paper, Center on Violence and Human Survival, John Jay College of Criminal Justice, New York, 1991.

46. Of course Pappagallo is constructed within the narrative as one potential alterego for Max, projecting a community-before-self ideal, starkly contrasting Max's nonchalant but mercenary bravado. Ironically, however, it is *Pappagallo* who dies in the attempt to save the fleeing community, and we later discover that the previously mute feral kid, strongly allied to Max throughout, inherits tribal leadership of that surviving clan.

47. At the time of writing, the Gulf War entered its fifth week. In the lead up to hostilities a plethora of anti-Islamic and apocalyptic sentiments have gained broad media coverage throughout the West, with Fundamentalists declaiming the events as the precursor to the battle of Armageddon. For an historical reading of Christian/Islamic antagonisms within an apocalyptic frame, see Norman Cohn on the Medieval holy wars and crusades in *Pursuit of the Millennium*.

48. Sharrett suggests the depiction of homosexuality is a decadent menace within the trilogy is highly problematic, at once reactionary yet within its postmodern frame: "Miller suggests an apocalypticism both to the feminist movement, punk/new wave/gay culture, as well as to dominant ideology," *op. cit.*, p. 90. The director himself has stated, "We repeatedly asked ourselves what price sexuality would pay in this kind of medieval world. It certainly wouldn't function as it does in our contemporary society. People wouldn't have time for recreational sex. There's no time for a woman to have a baby, to nurse infants, etc. It's very unlikely that a pregnant woman or a woman with a child could survive. This could be one of the things that resulted in homosexual relationships in both stories. One of the other things, however, was that we changed a lot of the sexes of charac-

ters without changing their roles. . . . So the women and men and their sexual roles are not as defined in this primitive world as they are in our society. Men and women are simply interchangeable" in Peary, p. 283.

49. Earlier, escapees from Pappagallo's band are slain or tortured by multiple arrow wounds from surrounding marauders, recalling the iconic effigies of St. Stephen, the first Christian martyr.

50. The desert (wilderness) has been the most frequent milieu of post-nuclear survival tales in both literature and cinema. The original Trinity A-bomb was detonated in the New Mexico desert and tests still continue into the 1990s at the Nevada range, and its strong biblical associations have no doubt continued to provide popular cultural associations. In relation to *Beyond Thunderdome*, Max is offered some "H_2O" by a street vendor on his way into Bartertown, but his Geiger-counter goes off the scale, to which the man says rhetorically, "What's a little fallout? Have a nice day." This statement immediately introduces us to a milieu of post-nuclear catastrophe, possibly implying American irresponsibility echoed in ironic rhetoric (US bases/targets on *Australian* soil, but it's business as usual, so "have a nice day").

51. Clearly laden with a sexual subtext, Max's phallic prowess easily defeats Aunty's matriarchal cunning.

52. Like so many mythological heroes, Max enters his site of contestation unknown. The character with no name also became synonymous with apocalyptic (anti)heroes of the Western, especially in the Clint Eastwood and Terrence Hill personae of Spaghetti Western fame.

53. The Wheel reduplicates the "Wheel of Fortune" from the TV game series, complete with simulacra hostess/models.

54. The mask motif is apparent throughout the entire trilogy, e.g. the rubber monster face in *Mad Max*, the leather coverings of Humungus and his marauders in *The Road Warrior*, Blaster's helmet and Ironbar's Asian mascot.

55. The construction of Master-Blaster may also be read as a post-Marxist critique of a set of class relations under late capitalism whereby the mindless and directionless brawn of labor is driven by disaffected technocrats in the service of a redundant aristocracy.

56. See, for instance, the mushroom cloud destruction of Sodom and Gomorrah in John Huston's *The Bible* (1966).

57. Indeed, perhaps the earlier critical attention to the trilogy's iconography serves to disguise and submerge these "master-narratives," in an effect resembling Jameson's act of the "political unconscious," cf. Jameson, *The Political Unconscious: Narrative as a Socially Symbolic Act* (Ithaca, NY: Cornell University Press, 1981).

Notes on Contributors

Mick Broderick works for the Australian Film Commission. He has taught in both the Cinema Studies and Peace Studies programs at La Trobe University, Bundoora, Australia. He is the author of *Nuclear Movies: A Filmography*, and is completing a history of nuclear imagery in the mass media entitled *The Apocalyptic Muse.*

Giuiliana Bruno teaches film studies at Harvard University. She has published in *October, Cinema Journal, Camera Obscura,* and elsewhere. She has recently completed a book on Pasolini.

Scott Bukatman teaches film studies at New York University. His book, *Terminal Identity: The Virtual Subject in Postmodern Science Fiction,* will be published in 1993 by Duke University Press.

Frank Burke is Associate Professor of Film Studies at Queen's University. He has published in *Canadian Journal of Political and Social Theory, Film Quarterly, Film Criticism, Romance Language Annual,* and elsewhere. He is the author of a two-volume study of Federico Fellini.

James Combs is on extended leave from Valparaiso University. His many books include *Dimensions of Political Drama, Subliminal Politics: Myths and Myth-Makers in America,* and *A Primer of Politics.* He is currently working on a study of political propaganda in cinema.

Michael Dorland teaches cinema and communication studies at Concordia University. He has written for *CineAction* and *Canadian Journal of Political and Social Theory.* He is a contributor to the *Panic Encyclopedia.*

A. Keith Goshorn did his Ph.D. work at the Institute for Liberal Arts at Emory University. He is the author of "Baudrillard's Radical Enigma" in *Jean Baudrillard: The Disappearance of Art and Politics.* He has been a long-term observer youth and music sub-cultures. He is currently preparing an essay on Irish Film.

Arthur Kroker is Professor of Political Science and Humanities at Concordia University. His books include *The Possessed Individual, Technology and the Canadian Mind: Innis/McLuhan/Grant* and (with David Cook) *The Postmodern Scene: Excremental Culture and Hyper-Aesthetics.* With Marilouise Kroker, he has edited adn introduced *Body Invaders: Panic Sex in America* and *The Hysterical Male: New Feminist Theory.*

Jon Lewis is Associate Professor of English at Oregon State University. He has published in *Quarterly Review of Film Studies, Journal of Popular Culture, Afterimage, Persistence of Vision, Minnesota Review,* and elsewhere. His new book is titled, *The Road to Romance and Ruin: Teen Films and Youth Culture.*

Catherine Russell teaches film studies at Concordia University. Her work has appeared in *Cinema Journal, CineAction,* and the *Canadian Journal of Film.* She is currently writing about ethnography, aesthetics, and avant-garde film and video.

Philip Turetzky is Assistant Professor of Philosophy at Ripon College. His work has appeared in *Philosophy Today, Philosophy and Rhetoric, Colorado Review,* and elsewhere.

Christopher Sharrett is Associate Professor of Communication at Seton Hall University. His work has appeared in *Persistence of Vision, Journal of Popular Film and Television, Canadian Journal of Political and Social Theory, Literature/Film Quarterly,* and elsewhere. He is currently writing a book on sacrifice, excess, and postmodernism.

Tony Williams is Associate Professor of Cinema Studies at Southern Illinois University—Carbondale. His work has appeared in the *Journal of Popular Film and Television, CineAction,* and elsewhere. He is co-author of a book on the Italian Western and has contributed to various anthologies, including *The American Nightmare,* a critical anthology on the horror film. He has just published *Jack London: The Movies* (1992).

Index

Acknowledgments

A number of people have been important to this project's completion, most of whom will go unmentioned as memory fails. Paul M. Buonaguro has been helpful through his friendship and our many conversations on popular culture over twenty-five years. Prof. Ramiro S. Fernandez of Wake Forest University has been a great source of insight on American apocalypticism as well as a good friend. Prof. Sidney Gottlieb of Sacred Heart University has been helpful with this project at various stages of development, and helpful to its editor in time of need. Robert Merrill of Maisonneuve Press could not be a more supportive publisher. A special thanks to each contributor for working with me through the long editorial process.

"Ramble City: Postmodernism and *Blade Runner*" has been reprinted from *October*, 41 (1987) by permission of MIT Press.

"Panic Cinema: Sex in the Ages of the Hyperreal" originally appeared in *CineAction!*, 10 (1989). Reprinted by permission of the authors.

An earlier version of "The American Apocalypse: Scorsese's *Taxi Driver* appeared in *Persistence of Vision*, 1 (1984). Reprinted in *Crisis Cinema* with the author's permission.

PostModernPositions

A book series in critical cultural studies